TAXATION IN DEVELOPING COUNTRIES

———

INITIATIVE FOR POLICY DIALOGUE AT COLUMBIA

INITIATIVE FOR POLICY
DIALOGUE AT COLUMBIA

JOSEPH E. STIGLITZ AND JOSÉ ANTONIO OCAMPO,
SERIES CO-EDITORS

Macartan Humphreys, Jeffrey D. Sachs,
and Joseph E. Stiglitz, eds.
Escaping the Resource Curse

Ann Florini, ed.
The Right to Know: Transparency for an Open World

Gérard Roland, ed.
Privatization: Successes and Failures

José Antonio Ocampo, Codrina Rada, and Lance Taylor
Growth and Policy in Developing Countries: A Structuralist Approach

TAXATION
in
DEVELOPING
COUNTRIES

SIX CASE STUDIES AND POLICY IMPLICATIONS

EDITED BY

Roger H. Gordon

COLUMBIA UNIVERSITY PRESS

NEW YORK

Columbia University Press
Publishers Since 1893
New York   Chichester, West Sussex

Copyright © 2010 Columbia University Press
All rights reserved

Library of Congress Cataloging-in-Publication Data

Taxation in developing countries : six case studies and policy
implications / edited by Roger H. Gordon.
p. cm. — (Initiative for policy dialogue at Columbia)
Includes bibliographical references and index.
ISBN 978-0-231-14862-7 (cloth : alk. paper) —
ISBN 978-0-231-52007-2 (ebook)
1. Taxation—Developing countries—Case studies.
2. Taxation—Developing countries.   I. Gorden, Roger H.
(Roger Hall), 1949–   II. Title.   III. Series.

HJ2351.7.T393 2010

336.2009172'4—dc22
2009048024

Columbia University Press books are printed
on permanent and durable acid-free paper.
This book is printed on paper with
recycled content.

Printed in the United States of America
c 10 9 8 7 6 5 4 3 2 1

INITIATIVE FOR POLICY
DIALOGUE AT COLUMBIA

JOSÉ ANTONIO OCAMPO AND JOSEPH E. STIGLITZ,
SERIES EDITORS

The Initiative for Policy Dialogue (IPD) at Columbia University brings together academics, policy makers, and practitioners from developed and developing countries to address the most pressing issues in economic policy today. IPD is an important part of Columbia's broad program on development and globalization. The Initiative for Policy Dialogue at Columbia: Challenges in Development and Globalization presents the latest academic thinking on a wide range of development topics and lays out alternative policy options and trade-offs. Written in a language accessible to policy makers and students alike, this series is unique in that it both shapes the academic research agenda and furthers the economic policy debate, facilitating a more democratic discussion of development policies.

Observed tax structures among developing countries are sharply different from both those observed among developed countries and those recommended by conventional models of optimal tax policy. Excise taxes have played an important role among developing countries, with tax rates differing substantially by industry. Yet the optimal taxation literature argues for uniform tax rates. The corporate income tax plays a large role, presumably creating large distortions to investment decisions within these countries, contrary to the conventional wisdom that a country should take full advantage of gains from trade in the world capital market. Tariffs are also commonly high, raising similar questions.

The objective of this book is to examine the economic pressures that have generated such tax structures. The book contains detailed studies of six developing countries: Argentina, Brazil, India, Kenya, Korea, and Russia. These six countries constitute a diverse group of developing countries, coming from all parts of the globe, both large and small, and including some of the poorest and some of the richest among developing countries. Yet they share many key attributes of their tax systems. Their tax structures have been changing over time, and the chapters lay out the pressures generating such changes.

The book includes two additional chapters that reflect on the nature of the economic pressures leading to observed choices for the tax structure. One chapter argues that a uniform VAT fails to take into account the implicit differential tax rates faced in the formal versus informal sectors. The other additional chapter argues that the problems of enforcing taxes, leading to a large informal economy, may be the key explanation for the seemingly anomalous choices for the tax structure, with structures evolving toward those forecast by the theory as informal activity becomes less attractive.

The intended readership is anyone interested in tax reform among developing countries. The analysis is nontechnical, focusing instead on the many conflicting economic pressures faced by the tax authorities in these six countries.

For more information about IPD and its upcoming books, visit www .policydialogue.org.

CONTENTS

ACKNOWLEDGMENTS

The book is the outcome of the research of a task force on Taxation of the Initiative for Policy Dialogue (IPD) at Columbia University, directed by Roger H. Gordon and Joseph E. Stiglitz. IPD is a global network of over 250 economists, researchers, and practitioners committed to furthering understanding of the development process.

In addition to the contributing authors, we gratefully acknowledge the dedication of IDP staff members Lauren Anderson, Sarah Green, Shana Hofstetter, Ariel Schwartz, Farah Siddique, and Sylvia Wu, who helped coordinate the research and ultimate production of this book. Our thanks also to IPD intern Emily-Anne Patt.

We thank Bridget Flannery-McCoy, Ron Harris, Marina Petrova, and Myles Thompson at Columbia University Press for bringing this book into publication.

Finally, we are most grateful to The John T. and Catherine D. Mac-Arthur Foundation for funding the meeting of the IPD Task Force on Taxation, out of which this book was conceived.

AFIP	The Federal Agency for Public Income
BP	Balance of payments
CAG	Comptroller and Auditor General of India
CBDT	Central Board of Direct Taxes
CED	Customs and Excise Department
CenVAT	Central VAT
CIDA	Canadian International Development Agency
CIDE	Fuel Tax
CIS	Commonwealth of Independent States
CIT	Corporate Income Tax
COFINS	Turnover Tax (later a VAT) to Finance Social Security
CPMF	Provisional Contribution on Financial Transactions
CSLL	Federal social contribution on net profits
CST	Central Sales Tax
DGA	General Customs Bureau
DGI	General Tax Bureau
DTAA	Double Taxation Avoidance Agreement
DTD	Domestic Tax Department
EET	Exempt-Exempt-Tax
FGTS	Workers' Retirement Contribution
FINSOCIAL	Contribution to Social Investment Fund
GDP	Gross domestic product
GST	Goods and Services Tax
ICEGATE	Customs e-commerce gateway
ICES	Customs Electronic Data Interchange System
ICMS	Tax on the Circulation of Goods and Services
IMFL	Indian Made Foreign Liquor

IOF	Tax on Loans, Purchase of Foreign Exchange, and Insurance Premiums
IPI	Tax on industrialized products
IPTU	Urban property tax
IPVA	Tax on ownership of vehicles
ISS	Municipal tax on certain services
ITCD	Inheritance and donation tax
KRA	Kenya Revenue Authority
KSh	Kenyan Shilling
KTF	Kelkar task force
LTO	Large Taxpayer Office
MANVAT	Manufacturing stage value-added tax
MAT	Minimum alternate tax
NSDL	National Securities Depository Ltd.
OECD	Organisation for Economic Co-operation and Development
OLTAS	Online Tax Accounting System
PAN	Permanent account numbers
PAYE	Pay As You Earn
PIS	Turnover Tax (later a VAT) to Finance Social Security
R&D	Research and Development
SEZs	Special economic zones
STT	Tax on Sale of Financial Securities
TDS	Tax deduction at source
TIN	Tax Information Network
TMP	Tax Modernization Programme
TRC	Tax Reform Committee
UTS	Unified Tax System
VAT	Value-added tax

TAXATION IN DEVELOPING COUNTRIES

Introduction

Overview of Tax Policy in Developing Countries

Roger H. Gordon

This volume provides a detailed assessment of the current tax structure in six developing countries: Argentina, Brazil, India, Kenya, Korea, and Russia. Each of the six case studies lays out the current statutory provisions, how they have evolved over time, the resulting changes in tax revenue, and the key fiscal pressures faced currently looking forward.[1] The volume also includes two overview chapters that reassess the conventional wisdom about the appropriate design of tax policy in developing countries.

As is seen from Table I.1, these six countries include both some of the poorest and some of the richest developing countries. As of 2004, per capita gross domestic product (GDP) in Korea and Russia was well over $10,000, in Argentina and Brazil it was a bit under $4,000, while India's per capita income was only $695 and Kenya's $469.

Populations also differ dramatically. India's population is over a billion, Brazil is the next largest with a population of 182 million, while Korea, Argentina, and Kenya are all roughly a quarter as large as Brazil. The countries cover all parts of the globe. The three largest of these countries have a federal system of government, while in the remaining three countries the national government plays a dominant role.

The tax systems in these countries, though largely typical of those in other developing countries, are strikingly at odds with what the public finance literature recommends as the optimal design of a country's tax structure. To begin with, the public finance literature at least since Mirrlees (1971) focuses heavily on the optimal rate structure under the personal income tax as a means of best trading off equity and efficiency considerations in the collection of tax revenue. Reflecting this focus in the academic literature, the personal income tax is typically the main source of

Table 1.1   Summary Statistics on the Six Countries

Variable	Argentina	Brazil	India	Kenya	Korea	Russia
Per capita GDP	3,983	3,654	695	468.6	14,161	13,205
Population (millions)	38	181.6	1089	33.8	48.1	142.5
Consumption/GDP	73.9 %	58.5 %	64.0 %	74.8 %	51.5 %	66.0 %
Labor income/GDP	NA	49.1 %	70.7 %	NA	44.2 %	NA
Nonfinancial corporate income/GDP	NA	35.5 %	9.1 %	NA	15.8 %	NA
% of GDP from agriculture, forestry, and fishing	9.6 %	6.9 %	18.8 %	23.8 %	3.4 %	5.1 %
% of GDP from mining, manufacturing, construction, and utilities	42.2 %	30.1 %	27.6 %	16.7 %	36.2 %	18.2 %
Tax revenue/GDP	25.6 %	32.8 %	16.4 %	17.0 %	24.6 %	16.6 %
Personal income tax/tax revenue	16.8 %	10.0 %	10.0 %	18.0 %	13.9 %	5.1 %
Corporate income tax/tax revenue	13.8 %	6.1 %	16.7 %	11.0 %	14.3 %	8.2 %
Indirect taxes/tax revenue	44.1 %	24.8 %	49.8 %	44.0 %	33.7 %	26.0 %
VAT/tax revenue	26.3 %	21.7 %	20.1 %	25.0 %	18.0 %	24.2 %
Debt/GDP	144.1 %	47.0 %	90.8 %	43.0 %	26.1 %	8.5 %
Tariffs/tax revenue	11.6 %	1.4 %	11.7 %	11.0 %	3.7 %	36.9 %
Imports/GDP	18.3 %	NA	17.4 %	33.9 %	39.6 %	21.1 %
Shadow economy (% of GDP)	28.9 %	42.3 %	25.6 %	36.0 %	28.8 %	48.7 %

All data are for 2004. Monetary figures are expressed in U.S. dollars. The data for the size of the shadow economy come from Schneider (2005). All the other data were provided by the authors.

tax revenue among developed economies.[2] As seen in Table I.1, however, the personal income tax plays little role in any of these six countries. The presumption must be that the countries are not in a position to monitor enough of the income accruing to each individual to make an income tax a feasible option.

These countries collect a quarter to a fifth of their tax revenue with a value-added tax (VAT), a tax also used heavily by developed countries. Since the VAT is a proportional tax without any exemptions for the poor, developed countries tend to supplement this tax with more generous social safety-net programs. Developing countries, including the six highlighted here, do not in the main have equivalent safety-net programs, thereby imposing a larger tax burden on the poor than is the case with an income tax.

The optimal taxation literature also recommends equal tax rates on all forms of consumption, as seen, for example, in Atkinson and Stiglitz (1976).[3] Over time, developing countries have been replacing excise taxes, through which rates often vary dramatically by good, with a VAT having one rate or at least only a few rates. The effective rates, though, are low due to a combination of exempt (or zero-rated) goods and evasion. As can be calculated from the figures in Table I.1,[4] for example, the effective VAT rate (VAT revenue as a fraction of consumption) varies from 4 percent in Russia to 12 percent in Brazil.

The optimal tax literature shows that a small open economy should take full advantage of any gains from trade, and not distort trade patterns. As Table I.1 shows, tariffs are a significant source of revenue in all the six countries except Brazil and Korea. However, these tariffs may be serving to offset differential tax rates across domestic industries, with higher tariff rates in industries where domestic firms face higher domestic tax rates. To this extent, these tariffs may lessen rather than exacerbate trade distortions.

The chapters on optimal taxation also conclude that a country that is small relative to the world capital market should not distort international flows of capital. Yet we see in these countries that the corporate income tax is an important source of tax revenue, collecting on average even more than do personal income taxes.[5]

Another striking characteristic of the tax structures in these six countries is the low tax revenue relative to GDP. Here, Brazil is an outlier, with government revenue equal to 35 percent of GDP, a figure approaching those seen among some richer countries. The next highest among this group of countries is Korea with revenue equal to 25 percent of GDP, while India collects only 16.4 percent of GDP in tax revenue. Although the revenue figures for Brazil (and to some extent Argentina) have been growing over time, in most of these countries tax revenue has not changed much as a fraction of GDP during the past 20 years.

These low tax revenue figures do not seem to reflect countries choosing relatively low tax rates.[6] For example, top personal tax rates are now around 30 percent in these countries, VAT rates range from 10 percent in Korea to around 27 percent in Brazil, while corporate tax rates among these countries range from 25 percent in Brazil to 35 percent in Argentina.[7]

The key difference in the fiscal situation faced in these and other developing economies, compared with the situation among developed economies, is much greater difficulties in tax administration and enforce-ment. Part of the problem is that many firms can evade tax entirely, oper-ating in the informal economy. Table I.1 reports estimates presented by Schneider (2005) on the size of the shadow economy in these six econo-mies, as a fraction of GDP.[8] The estimated size of the informal economy ranges from a quarter to a half of GDP.

Even firms that are part of the formal economy can easily understate their tax base. The chapters in this volume provide many examples of such techniques. Among them is that sales can occur in cash, leaving no paper trail. Under the VAT system, firms can claim that goods were exported (in order to qualify for a zero tax rate) even if the goods never left the country or were quickly smuggled back into the country for resale. Firms can also exaggerate expenses using fake invoices. Firms can use transfer prices to shift profits or value-added into a firm, which then disappears without paying the associated taxes, or at least shift profits into a firm subject to a lower tax rate. As a result, effective tax rates can be much be-low the statutory tax rates[9] and can vary dramatically by industry[10] and by size of firm.

Government attempts to aid certain sectors have in practice opened up further evasion opportunities. The Russian government, given its lack of direct assistance to the disabled, tried to provide indirect aid by granting a tax exemption to firms in which the disabled constituted at least 50 per-cent of the workforce. This encouraged some of the most profitable capital-intensive firms to put just enough disabled on the books to qualify for this tax exemption. Both India and Russia grant tax preferences to firms lo-cated in particular regions. In response, firms can set up a subsidiary in such regions and use transfer pricing to report most of its profits (or value-added) there.[11]

It is perhaps surprising that none of the chapters in the present volume mentions capital flight. Perhaps as a reflection of this threat, many of these countries have very low effective tax rates on income from financial assets.

With evasion being such a dominant issue, countries face additional pressures to lower tax rates in order to draw firms into the formal econ-omy and to reduce the incentives on those already in the formal economy to underreport their income or value-added. For example, several of these countries use presumptive taxes for smaller firms, with the effective tax rate much lower than for larger firms. With lower tax rates reducing eva-sion as well as increasing overall economic activity, it is much more likely that countries have the opportunity to reduce tax rates and yet gain revenue on net. For example, India has reduced its personal and corporate income tax rates dramatically in recent years, yet its income tax revenue has doubled as a fraction of GDP. Similarly, Korea reduced its effective corporate tax rate from 53 to 27 percent, while corporate tax receipts doubled as a fraction of GDP.

These governments have also pursued a variety of other means to deal with enforcement problems. To limit the revenue loss from firms underreporting sales under the VAT, for example, several chapters emphasize that governments are not willing to provide cash rebates to firms reporting negative value-added and instead require firms to carry forward these credits to use against future tax liabilities. Yet firms that export a sizeable fraction of their output, as well as firms that have large new investments, would legitimately have negative value-added. The restriction preventing rebates then leads to an effective tax rate for these firms exceeding the statutory tax rate. According to the chapter on Kenya (Chapter 6), when firms sell to the government the government directly withholds the VAT due on these sales, and yet is very slow (at best) to rebate the VAT already paid by these firms on inputs they purchased, yielding an effective tax rate much above the statutory tax rate.

To reduce the attractiveness of using cash as a means of tax evasion, several of these countries (Argentina, Brazil, India, and Korea) impose a tax on bank debits.[12] In part, information on these withdrawals also provides information that is helpful in locating evading firms. In addition, Korea has created a subsidy to use credit cards, presumably hoping to shift transactions to a form that can be monitored and taxed more easily.

Another approach for lowering tax evasion, emphasized by the chapter on India, is government control over key firms. The chapter reports that 38 percent of the income tax revenue and 42 percent of VAT payments come from public enterprises. Similarly, in Korea a large fraction of revenue originates from a few large firms, which have incentives to cooperate with the government in exchange for easy access to credit and implicit loan guarantees.

Effective tax rates can also vary from statutory tax rates due to unchecked enforcement powers of the tax authorities. When tax officials are given incentives simply to collect more revenue, it is not surprising that they do so even beyond what the statutes would allow. When officials have such unchecked powers, of course, corruption is inevitable. Several of these countries have set up independent tax authorities in order to free the tax authorities from political influence and from civil service restrictions. Another approach is to give taxpayers better access to the courts to appeal unreasonable assessments.

In sum, given the conflicting pressures from evasion and overaggressive enforcement, the tax law in practice can have little relationship to the statutory provisions. Kenya, for example, reports tax revenue equal to 20 percent of GDP even while Eissa and Jack (Chapter 6 in this volume) estimate that only 30 percent of GDP is part of the formal economy subject to tax. While this suggests that the effective average tax rate on the formal sector is around two-thirds, the top statutory income tax rates are only 30 percent and the top VAT rate is only 16 percent. The chapters on Argentina and Brazil also suggest that effective tax rates can be extremely high.[13]

This large variation in effective versus statutory tax rates of course raises serious questions about the effect of tax reforms on the economy. Of central importance to economic activity are effective tax rates. How these rates vary as statutory tax rates change may not be at all clear, raising serious challenges in forecasting the effects of possible tax reforms on economic activity or on government tax revenue.

One other issue pertinent especially to the larger of these countries is fiscal federalism. Regional and local governments in these countries commonly have responsibility for a substantial fraction of overall government expenditures. In response, countries give regional/local governments control over particular taxes, often the VAT. However, given the administrative difficulties of monitoring interregional trade, a VAT is an awkward tax for a regional government.

As a result, these national governments normally help to finance regional and local governments through mechanisms such as direct grants. More common among these countries, however, is a formula that allocates some fraction of the tax revenues collected by the national government to the region where the taxes were collected. India faces particular complications in this respect because its constitution allocates control of the income tax on the nonagricultural sector, the VAT on manufacturing, and taxes on services to the national government, while taxes on other sectors are allocated to regional and local governments. Exempting agriculture from national income taxes in practice creates ample opportunities for tax evasion. Trying to create a well-functioning VAT with common rates at one stage of production and differential rates at other stages, with workable cross-state crediting arrangements, has also proven to be a serious problem.

Together the chapters in this volume suggest that improving tax administration is the key problem these countries will face in the future. Effective tax rates vary dramatically across firms and individuals in the economy, owing both to aggressive enforcement where enforcement is easy and extensive evasion where it is not. The result is very high tax rates on a narrow tax base and low overall tax revenue. As a result, taxes can be highly distorting, even while they collect relatively little revenue.

How best to improve tax administration is a difficult problem, and one the present volume only touches on. One approach mentioned is to improve the incentives faced by tax officials, so that their objective will be to enforce the law rather than simply to collect revenue. Another approach is to improve the oversight over these officials, perhaps through the courts. This work also emphasizes the importance of improving the quality of information available to tax officials. This can be done by sharing information among different tax departments (e.g., those overseeing the income tax, the VAT, and customs duties) or among tax departments in different regions. It can also be done by collecting new information, for example, on bank transactions or securities transactions and by trying to tax activities that are more readily observable, for example, property sales rather than property values. Given the main problems described in the present volume, future tax reform efforts will inevitably need to focus on these areas.

Given the results of these six case studies, the volume also includes two additional chapters reflecting on the pressures faced by tax authorities in developing countries. The first, by Stiglitz, reexamines the merits of relying on a value-added tax as a major source of revenue among developing countries. While a VAT may be a relatively nondistorting tax in richer countries, the six case studies provide ample evidence that a VAT can be highly distorting in poorer countries. The large informal sectors in these countries evade the tax entirely, while the formal sector can evade a substantial fraction of the tax, for example, through fake invoicing or income shifting to informal firms or other formal firms that face much lower tax rates. Even with this extensive evasion in the formal sector, a VAT nonetheless discourages formal activity and likely economic development in general.

The question this work then asks is how best to reduce these economic costs. One recommendation is to tax imports at a rate above the VAT rate. This surtax would still be rebated for imports purchased by formal firms but would raise the effective tax rate on the informal sector. By reducing the differential tax rates across sectors, economic efficiency should increase.

The second additional chapter, by Gordon (Chapter 2), focuses on the low reported tax revenue in developing countries, examining in particular the experiences in China and India. In both countries, tax revenue during the initial years of their economic reforms came from a narrow tax base facing high tax rates. In the case of China, nonstate firms paid little in tax revenue, at least to the national government. In the case of India, national revenue came heavily from the manufacturing sector. Even though services generated half of GDP, they were untaxed.

When a country faces such a narrow tax base, with effective rates varying dramatically by sector, a variety of restrictions on economic activity may make sense, as described at more length in Gordon and Li (2009). Tariffs may serve to offset differential tax rates by sector, whether from excise taxes or income taxes. Statutory rates may appropriately vary by sector, with lower rates in sectors where it is easier to shift into the informal economy. Restrictions on activity in the informal sector can help reduce the degree to which taxes unduly shift activity from formal to informal sectors.

Inflation may serve to inhibit activity in the cash economy. In Brazil, for example, substantial inflation in earlier years led not only to an expansion of the size of the formal sector but also to a major expansion in the role of the financial sector. The resulting improvements in productivity in the financial sector, which presumably were the result of learning by doing, kept the financial sector large even after the inflation rate fell.

The resulting policies favoring the formal sector, and in particular those industries facing the highest tax rates, may reduce the immediate efficiency costs due to differential tax rates by sector. However, the resulting difficulties faced by firms in the informal sector can easily reduce rates of entry, innovation, and growth. Chapter 2 then examines the fiscal implications of the economic reforms undertaken in both China and India, in each case dramatically reducing the restrictions faced by the informal sector and smaller firms in the formal sector.

The result in each country was a rapid rate of entry and (more so in China than in India) a sharp drop in tax revenue owing to the fall in profits in the formal sector resulting from the increased competition. Without the prior restrictions, the differential tax rates on the formal vs. the informal sector become far more distorting. In spite of the fall in revenue, tax rates were cut in order to avoid further undercutting the formal sector.

The fall in tax revenue presented each government with difficult choices: either government expenditures must fall or government debt must increase. The fall in expenditures can undercut development due to the resulting poor education and inadequate infrastructure. The fall also risks increasing political opposition to the reforms, since many individuals lose more from the drop in services than they gain from the new economic opportunities. Debt, in contrast, allows services to continue but creates the risk of a financial crisis if the government does not have the revenue in the future to repay the debt. China chose to cut services and to finance remaining services through user fees. India initially borrowed heavily in order to maintain services, but recently has shifted to cutting services. To what degree this fall in services will undercut growth is yet to be seen.

A third alternative is to leave in place some provisions protecting the formal sector. Both China and India, for example, maintained a sizeable state-owned sector. Both countries also relied on local governments to better monitor and tax smaller firms that could not effectively be monitored by the national government. Such provisions, though contrary to the conventional wisdom, may be important in reducing the risks faced when undertaking economic reforms.

With the immediate loss in current tax revenue from economic reforms, and the combined political and financial risks resulting from the loss in tax revenue, economic reforms can seem daunting for any government that does not have a long time horizon. Problems with tax administration in developing countries not only create difficulties in raising current revenue, as documented at length in the six chapters in this volume, but also create substantial hurdles when considering the adoption of policies that encourage a more rapid rate of economic growth.

NOTES

1. The Russian study more narrowly focuses on the evolution of the value-added tax during the past 15 years, given its complicated history.

2. In the United States, as of 2004, for example, the personal income tax together with the payroll tax accounted for 80 percent of federal tax revenues.

3. The key assumption is that consumption patterns do not vary by ability levels, even if they do vary by labor income.

4. Note that VAT/Consumption = (VAT/Tax Revenue) * (Tax Revenue/GDP)/ (Consumption/GDP).

5. Among developed economies as a whole, corporate tax revenue on average is under half of personal tax revenue and under a quarter of personal tax revenue in the United States.

6. Even when tax rates are low, as they commonly are among these countries for smaller firms, this choice seems to be in response to the threat that firms will shift into the informal sector if rates are any higher rather than because the desired size of government expenditures is low.

7. These rates are broadly comparable, for example, to those in the United States, given that U.S. state income and retail sales tax rates together are roughly comparable to the VAT rates in these countries.

8. The comparable figure among OECD countries, again according to Schneider (2005), is 16.3 percent.

9. The chapter on South Korea reports estimates that the effective VAT rate is only about 65 percent of the statutory rate. The chapter on Argentina reports comparable figures averaging around 30 percent.

10. The chapter on India includes a table comparing the effective corporate tax rates among major corporate groups, and finds rates ranging almost uniformly between 0 percent and 40 percent.

11. This apparently was the technique that the Russian firm Yukos used in order to reduce its tax obligations.

12. However, bank accounts may shift in response to more informal cooperative banks that are not in practice subject to these taxes.

13. The Brazilian chapter uses the term *asphyxiating.*

REFERENCES

Atkinson, A. B., and Stiglitz, J. E. (1976). "The Design of Tax Structure: Direct vs. Indirect Taxation." *Journal of Public Economics,* 6, pp. 55–75.

Gordon, R. H., and Li, W. (2009). "Tax Structures in Developing Countries: Many Puzzles and a Possible Explanation." *Journal of Public Economics,* 93, pp. 855–66.

Mirrlees, J. A. (1971). "An Exploration in the Theory of Optimal Income Taxation." *Review of Economic Studies,* 38, pp. 175–208.

Schneider, F. (2005). "Shadow Economies of 145 Countries All over the World: Estimation Results over the Period 1999 to 2003." Mimeo.

CHAPTER 1

Development-Oriented Tax Policy

Joseph E. Stiglitz

INTRODUCTION

No public policy issue is more important than the *structure* and level of taxes. Governments have fallen because of tax reform. Proposals to extend the value-added tax (VAT) or increase its rates have caused political agitation in many countries, including Ecuador and Mexico. In many less-developed countries, a shortage of funds impedes development efforts, yet attempts to increase tax revenues not only meet enormous political resistance but are often futile. Simplistic recommendations to increase the power of the tax police often backfire, generating substantially more revenue for the tax collectors but very little extra for the public fisc.

Part of the problem lies in the fact that those providing advice on taxation to developing countries are insensitive to the differences in economic and political structures both among developing countries and between these countries and more developed ones, to the administrative difficulties faced by developing countries, or to their differing objectives. To take but one example: standard textbook expositions of the objectives of tax policy *for developed countries*, for instance, emphasize efficiency, and more recent expositions discuss problems of tax avoidance and evasion but seldom note corruption. But corruption has increasingly come to be recognized as one of the major challenges facing developing countries. Designing institutions and policies, *including tax structures*, that reduce the scope for corruption—what we call *corruption-resistant tax structures*—thus should be a central concern in tax design. While outside advisers often lecture moralistically on the need to improve tax administration and reduce corruption, they seldom address corruption as part of tax *design*. This illustrates how differences in the structure of the economy (where that term embraces institutional capacities—the ability to control corruption) and objectives (reducing corruption) dictate a difference in tax policy.

One important reason that differences in economic structures are important is that they affect compliance costs and the set of feasible taxes. Any particular tax can only be assessed relative to the set of feasible taxes and in the context of the *totality of taxes* imposed. Thus, although both developing and developed countries may view redistribution as an objective of tax policy, fewer instruments for redistribution may be available to developing countries. For instance, a well-known result holds that with an optimal income tax, there is (in a central case) no need to rely on commodity taxation for redistribution.[1] For countries that can impose a progressive income tax, the design of commodity taxation need not, accordingly, pay much attention to distribution concerns; for developing countries, which often have difficulty in enforcing effective progressive income taxes, distributive concerns may be paramount.

Objectives also differ. It is quite possible that tax policy should be used to promote development, or at least be designed not to impede it. And differences in economic structure interact with differences in objectives.

The Value Added Tax (VAT) illustrates many of these issues. One of the theses of this chapter is that, regardless of the virtues of a VAT for developed countries, such a tax may be inappropriate for many developing ones. This is partly because it may undermine development (a difference in objectives) and partly because differences in economic structures make it less successful in achieving commonly shared distributive and efficiency objectives: (1) a VAT may have an adverse distributive impact; (2) it may be less conducive to economic efficiency than other taxes. In developed countries, one of the reasons that a VAT is "efficient" is that it is comprehensive. It can be part of an overall progressive tax system because it can be combined with a progressive income tax as part of an "optimal" tax structure, achieving distributive goals at low compliance costs. By contrast, in most developing countries, the VAT is typically collected from just a fraction (often less than 50 percent) of the economy. This means that it interferes with *productive efficiency*, encouraging movement of production into the informal economy. It is effectively a tax on the organized sector of the economy—a distortionary tax on development. And because most developing countries find it difficult to implement a comprehensive progressive income tax, not only is it potentially highly distortionary, but the VAT can also result in a regressive (or at least not highly progressive) overall tax structure.

Even the VAT's alleged administrative advantages (low compliance costs) may not be true for developing countries. One of the virtues of the

VAT in more-developed countries is its self-enforcing nature. Taxes paid at a lower level are refundable at the next level. Consequently, it would seem, the downstream firm has an incentive to report purchases, which are, of course, others' sales. If both the upstream and downstream firms' incomes are not easily observable (they are based on cash payments), however, the VAT may be difficult to collect at any stage of production. The so-called self-enforcing property of the VAT can easily unravel—and it often does in developing countries where farmers and small producers sell directly to consumers.

Similarly, if just some of the downstream firm's sales are hard-to-detect cash transactions, then it can claim a rebate on the VAT paid by the upstream firm without fully reporting revenues received—with the result that they record negative value added. If firms reporting negative value added receive rebates, the net revenue collected by government may be seriously undermined. However, if the government does not grant rebates to firms reporting negative value added, it may discourage legitimate negative value-added activities, such as start-ups.

Both developed and less-developed countries typically provide rebates on exports under the VAT. This is supposed to ensure that the tax is on domestic consumption, not on domestic production. But one developing country after another has had problems in its rebate system. Sometimes rebates are paid only after a long lag. For firms facing a shortage of capital, this can be crippling. Even worse, the rebates have become a source of corruption, as fake documents have been used to secure large payments to corporations. (Kenya provided the most infamous example.[2])

As we have noted, a key issue in evaluating alternative taxes is the set of feasible taxes. Advocates of the VAT often argue that it is better than the existing tax structures (e.g., that the VAT may be an improvement over a corruptly enforced set of tariffs). The question, though, is, "What is the relevant set of alternatives?" Could a VAT be improved upon by the imposition of a tax on luxury imports at a higher rate? (Because there may be no domestic production of the luxury good, such a tax is equivalent to an excise consumption tax.) In many developing countries, a tax on oligopoly profits would be better in terms of both efficiency and equity than an increase in the VAT tax.

In many developing countries, a VAT may be a *part* of a well-designed tax structure. In a sense, this chapter is a critique of the excess zeal of VAT advocates, who sometimes suggest that there should be *just* a uniform tax on all goods. This chapter argues that that is seldom the case.

There should, in general, be differential taxation. It may also be wise to impose differential taxes on imports, including to promote development. It may be desirable to impose differential taxes on luxuries or oligopolies for a number of reasons, including that of promoting equity.

In the next two subsections, we take a closer look at two of the key differences between the structures of developed and developing countries: the fact that market failures are more pervasive in developing countries and information imperfections more widespread.

SECOND-BEST CONSIDERATIONS AND CORRECTIVE TAXATION

Taxation is quintessentially a problem of second best. With full information, there would be optimal lump-sum (nondistortive) taxation. Even distributive objectives could be achieved, because tax authorities could identify those with the capacity to earn higher income and impose higher lump-sum taxes on them.

But modern tax theory is based on the recognition that tax authorities never have the requisite information. They base taxes on observables (such as income). As a result, taxation is distortionary. All taxation is thus an exercise in the economics of the second best. One of Frank Ramsey's (1927) great contributions was to show what this implies for the design of tax structures. His analysis demonstrated the falsity of the simplistic argument that an income tax (which taxes interest income and thus affects intertemporal trade-offs) is worse than a consumption tax (which only affects the consumption/leisure choice) because it involves an extra distortion. The conclusion may be right, but it must be based on a much more subtle and complete analysis. The modern theory of taxation is remarkable because, despite the complexity of second-best economics, it has been able to derive a number of precise results.

Much of modern tax theory, while recognizing the distortionary nature of taxation, has assumed that in the absence of taxation, markets would be perfectly efficient. But another important strand of research over the past quarter century has analyzed a large number of market imperfections, including those derived from imperfect and asymmetric information. Tax distortions may interact with market distortions in various ways. In particular, taxes may be used to *correct* market distortions: One distortion may, at least partly, undo the effects of the other.

Modern tax theory thus emphasizes the role of corrective taxation—taxes designed to correct market failures, such as those associated with externalities. If market failures are more pervasive in developing countries, it means that there may be more scope for corrective taxation.

Discussions of corrective taxation have, for the most part, been relegated to environmental issues. Yet in developing countries, market failures (including imperfections of information and incomplete markets, associated with pervasive unemployment and capital market imperfections) provide a much wider scope for corrective taxation. Recent work on imperfections of information and incompleteness of markets has emphasized how a variety of actions/choices give rise to externality-like effects.[3] Many of the endogenous growth models[4] recognize the existence of returns to scale and externalities.

Remarkably, however, discussions of tax policy have often ignored the role that corrective taxes might play, generating revenues as they *improve* economic efficiency.[5] A case in point is short-term capital flows, which are a major source of instability in developing countries. Chilean-style taxes on capital inflows can thus play an important role in stabilizing the economy, thereby promoting economic growth while raising revenue.[6]

Similarly, many developing countries have pervasive unemployment. Efficiency wage models provide a convincing explanation of this unemployment.[7] But market equilibrium in efficiency wage models is generally not Pareto efficient, which provides scope for corrective taxation that would simultaneously raise revenue and increase market efficiency.

INFORMATION, THE SET OF ADMISSIBLE TAX STRUCTURES, AND CORRUPTION

Imperfections of information are at the core of many of the market failures prevalent in developing countries (including the efficiency wage models just discussed). But an understanding of the imperfections of *information* is central to an analysis of admissible tax structures: One can only tax what one can observe.[8] Optimal lump-sum redistributive taxes are impossible because the government cannot directly observe individuals' abilities. It can only observe proxies, such as income, and using proxies causes distortions. In the informal sector, the government typically cannot observe market transactions.

New technologies and organizational structures have changed the calculus of observability. Large organizations need to record many transactions. (People are "replaceable parts.") As a result, they leave an observable trail for tax authorities. Modern computers have made information control easier and, at the same time, have eased the burden of the tax collector. It is difficult for firms to maintain two sets of books (and, outside of certain limited areas, illegal), so that information provided to investors (intended to increase share market value) must jibe with information provided to the tax collector (designed to minimize tax burden), which in turn must agree with the *true* information required for managing the organization.[9] The use of credit cards has provided an audit trail that makes collecting taxes from retailers far easier, and bank accounts have become so pervasive that a person who relies only or largely on cash becomes immediately suspect.

Yet these changes have largely bypassed developing countries. Financial depth is limited, and credit card usage is unusual. It is not just that many individuals might hide some income from the tax collector; they often do not even know their own income. They may know their savings—how much they have left over at the end of the year—but have no records showing how much of the revenues are spent on consumption and how much are used to purchase inputs into production. For an American or European firm, the lack of such information would be a great handicap; for the typical African, barely literate farmer, keeping such records would constitute an enormous burden.

In earlier stages of their development, the United States and Europe relied a great deal on tariffs, because imports often must go through a limited number of ports. (The cost of not going through such ports, of smuggling, can often be quite high.) That made them easy to monitor, which in turn made them easier to tax. Of course, industrial tariffs quintessentially represented a development-oriented tax structure, as explicitly recognized in the heated debates surrounding those tariffs in nineteenth-century America.[10]

By the same token, until quite recently, even in advanced industrial countries such as the United States, tax avoidance[11] among the self-employed was rampant. (Even today, aggregate reported incomes of partnerships in some recent years in the United States are negative, though that has more to do with taking advantage of certain tax loopholes than with nonreporting.) In developing countries, small businesses are the dominant form of economic organization. Why should we expect that they have greater success in tax collection from small businesses than the United States or other advanced industrial countries?

Thus, information is at the root not only of admissible tax structures but of problems of enforcement, including issues of corruption. If there were perfect information, corruption would not be a problem. It would be known who was bribing the tax official, and presumably it would be easy to control. Corruption is a problem because it is so hard to observe. Understanding the limitations on available information is central to the design of corruption-resistant tax structures.

Many developing countries face a fine balance because the value of encoded information of the kind that can be used by tax authorities may be less, sometimes far less, for them than that for advanced industrial nations. Basing such taxes on this information (e.g., information contained in bank accounts) is more likely to destroy the information (the tax authorities get no more revenue and economic efficiency is impeded). It is noteworthy that the Chinese and Korean governments deliberately decided to foreswear the use of such information, by allowing no-name bank accounts. This allowed proportional taxation of savings but made it impossible for the government to use banking information for more general tax purposes (e.g., for the imposition of progressive taxation).

NEOCLASSICAL ECONOMICS AND THE DESIGN OF TAX STRUCTURES

Although this chapter focuses on developing countries, much of the analysis is also applicable to developed countries. Modern tax theory (particularly optimal tax theory) has developed within the framework of standard neoclassical models, in which market failures play no role. Increasingly, we have come to realize that such models cannot explain key market phenomena. Interactions between market failures and tax distortions can be of first-order importance in both developed and developing countries.

VARIATIONS AMONG COUNTRIES

We should also underline the importance of differences *among* developing countries. This chapter argues that economic and political structures that affect, for instance, the set of admissible taxes and the extent of market failures are of first-order importance in designing taxation. But even among developed (or developing) countries there can be large differences in economic structures, with different countries facing different constraints, which implies that a tax structure that might be desirable for one could be undesirable for another. (In this paper, we have nothing to say about *political constraints* and the broad set of political economy issues that affect the set of ideas that might constrain the set of taxes under consideration. This is partly because it is hard to know the nature of these constraints: What might have seemed "impossible" at one moment suddenly becomes possible in the next.)

A few developing countries have implemented an effective progressive income tax. Hence the redistributive argument against the VAT is irrelevant for them. In addition, a few countries may have other instruments to offset the adverse development impacts of the VAT; consequently, such a critique of the VAT would also be inapplicable to them.

GENERAL EQUILIBRIUM INCIDENCE ANALYSIS

Central to our analysis of the desirability of different tax structures is *a general equilibrium analysis:* an analysis of the impact of the imposition of one set of taxes (e.g. VAT) versus another set of taxes on the behavior of the entire economy, today and in the future, with particular attention to incidence—who actually bears the burden of taxation. General equilibrium incidence analysis of the kind attempted here is always complicated, but especially so when one departs from the simplistic competitive equilibrium with perfect information models that have been the basis of most analyses of tax policy. Even the distributive effects of a VAT are not always obvious. If a VAT were uniformly and comprehensively enforced, it would be equivalent to a wage tax (the reason it is loudly criticized by many developed countries). In developing countries, it is typically not imposed on the rural sector, in which the poorest people reside. This unintended exception may make the tax on net progressive, or at least not as regressive as critics suggest.

AN ASSESSMENT OF THE VAT FOR DEVELOPING COUNTRIES: A CASE STUDY IN THE PRINCIPLES OF TAXATION FOR DEVELOPING COUNTRIES

This section provides the analytic framework for our critique of the VAT. We focus on the VAT because it is the tax structure that has been consistently pushed on developing countries by the IMF and others. But our interest is more by way of illustration: showing how sensitivity to the differences in objectives and economic structure should inform tax policies for developing countries. We thus present simple analytics showing how in models designed to capture key aspects of the economic structure of developing countries, the VAT is distortionary, may impede development and growth, and may result in increased unemployment *compared with other tax-feasible tax structures.*

THE VAT AS DISTORTIONARY TAXATION

As noted earlier, advocates of the VAT argue for both its efficiency and its ease of administration. It is efficient because it is comprehensive. They contend that these advantages more than offset a major disadvantage, its lack of progressivity. The question is, "Is it really efficient in developing countries?"

Economists have long recognized that any market taxation encourages nonmarket production, which can constitute a significant distortion. For instance, a family's decision to buy a dishwasher (entailing a market transaction) can be affected by the tax rate. Labor inside the family (washing dishes) is not taxed; labor in the market (working to buy a dishwasher) is taxed. The high elasticity of labor supply associated with secondary workers may reflect the fact that, to some extent, the secondary worker is simply buying goods that are a substitute for the services the secondary worker would otherwise provide at home. As a result of the high elasticity, taxes on wages of secondary workers are highly distortionary.

Similar issues arise in developing countries. However, it is not only labor within the household that escapes taxation. Work in the informal sector, which typically cannot be easily monitored, or monitored at all, also slips through the net of taxation. Accordingly, a VAT shifts resources away from the formal sector into the informal sector, leading to an inefficient allocation of resources.

The question naturally arises, "Is there an alternative tax structure that is less distortionary than the VAT?" The answer is yes. Emran and Stiglitz (2002, 2004, 2005) provide a more complete analysis than is possible here. The following discussion provides a heuristic.

Assume there is an imported intermediate input used in both the formal and the informal sectors. Although we cannot monitor the output of the informal sector and therefore cannot tax it directly, we may be able to tax it indirectly by taxing the usage of the imported intermediate good. A standard result of optimal tax theory—when all outputs can be taxed—is that one should not tax intermediate inputs, including imported inputs.[12] But as Dasgupta and Stiglitz (1971, 1972, 1974) showed, in the more reasonable case where not all outputs can be taxed, it may be desirable to tax intermediate inputs. Assume, at the extreme case, that a unit of output requires a unit of this imported intermediate input. In this case, a tax on the intermediate input is equivalent to a tax on the output—in both the formal and the informal sectors. The tax is completely nondistortionary. Converting this tax on imports into a value-added tax introduces a distortion: The formal sector faces a tax on its total value added, whereas the informal sector faces a tax only on its intermediate input (assuming it does not get a rebate on its input).[13]

More generally, of course, taxing the intermediate input does introduce a distortion—there is a substitution away from using this intermediate input (and toward other inputs—in the simplest case, labor). But introducing a surtax on imports of the intermediate input (with a corresponding reduction in the VAT) into a situation where only the formal sector pays the VAT always increases output, because the surtax reduces the effective differential tax rates between the formal and the informal sectors. In short, *it is never optimal to rely solely on a value-added tax.* (See Appendix A.)

This is one example in which tax policy for developing countries differs from that in developed countries. Another example is provided by Ramsey's classic result (1927) in optimal tax theory, which suggests that taxes should be levied at a rate inversely proportional to the elasticity of demand. Atkinson and Stiglitz (1976) showed that Ramsey's result depended on the absence of an optimal redistributive income tax, and Stiglitz (2009) showed that even with a simple linear income tax, the benefits of Ramsey taxation were very limited. The conclusion was that Ramsey's analysis was of limited relevance to developed countries. In developing countries, on the other hand, where income taxation is very limited, Ramsey's analysis is relevant. In particular, the Ramsey-like analysis argues that the government should, rather than imposing uniform tax rates, impose lower taxes on those formal industries that can most easily shift into the informal sector. (More generally, Atkinson and Stiglitz [1972] show how efficiency and distributive concerns can be balanced within an optimal tax structure in the absence of a redistributive income tax.) Again, this goes against the spirit of the VAT, which suggests that one should not have differential taxation on different commodities.

The essential point of the Atkinson-Stiglitz (1976) analysis is that each tax needs to be viewed as part of the overall tax structure, particularly in light of other taxes that can be (or are) imposed. This, in turn, depends on what is observable. For instance, it is difficult to observe hours worked, which limits the use of an optimal wage tax—which might be better, in some respects, than an optimal income tax. It is difficult to observe any individual's consumption of particular commodities, and this limits governments' ability to use commodity-specific nonlinear consumption taxes. (Electricity is an exception, and nonlinear charges are typically imposed there.)

Much of the advocacy of the VAT is based on the simplistic pre-Ramsey reasoning to which we alluded in the introduction that assumes that uniform taxes are less distortionary than differentiated taxes because there are fewer distortions. This view turned out to be approximately correct for advanced industrial countries, for reasons that have little to do with the analyses employed by the advocates of VAT, but for developing countries it is clearly wrong.

HOW THE VAT MAY IMPEDE GROWTH

The previous section showed how the VAT lowers national income. It may also lower growth, which is of particular concern to developing countries. To see this, assume that the rate of productivity growth is higher in the formal sector. The simple case occurs when there is no productivity growth in the rural (informal) sector. Assume $Q_u = F(\lambda L_u)$, where Q_u is output in the formal sector, L_u is labor input, and λ is the productivity measure. Then the rate of growth of national output can be written $g_Q = g_\lambda\ sm$, where s is share of formal sector in national output, g_λ is the rate of growth of λ, and $m \equiv F' \lambda L_u /F$ (the share of labor in the formal sector. It is immediately clear that the larger m, the higher the rate of growth of national output, provided that as labor shifts into the formal sector, the share of labor does not decrease too much. The effect is even stronger if we introduce learning by doing. With learning by doing, $g_\lambda = \xi(L_u)$, $\xi' > 0$, so that the larger the size of the formal sector, the faster the rate of growth of productivity.[14]

HOW THE VAT MAY RESULT
IN INCREASED UNEMPLOYMENT[15]

Typically, the incidence of alternative taxes is analyzed within simple, competitive equilibrium models of the economy. While it is widely recognized that market economies differ in important ways from the competitive ideal, there is no widely accepted alternative model. Moreover, incidence analysis in models of economies with oligopolies, incomplete markets, monopolistic competition, and imperfect information is sufficiently complicated that the economics profession has shown a strong preference for being precisely and simply wrong rather than imprecisely and complexly correct. But developing countries are typically developing not just because they have few resources. Their markets, information, and institutions are often much less perfect. Such imperfections cannot be ignored.

Many developing countries have high levels of urban unemployment, which is associated with high urban wages (as a result, for example, of "efficiency wages") that induce migration from the rural sector.[16] A VAT imposed only on the urban sector (or collected more extensively in the urban sector than in the rural) is effectively a tax on urban wages.

In a standard migration equilibrium model with efficiency wages, labor productivity is higher in the urban than in the rural sector. Hence a VAT (effectively imposed only on the urban sector) lowers overall output by inducing labor to move to the low-productivity sector. If the rural sector has diminishing returns, a VAT leads to lower wages in the rural sector. Firms in the urban sector will then not have to pay workers as much to induce them to work hard, but the differential between the urban and rural wages will still increase. The equilibrium will entail not only lower urban wages but also higher unemployment. Thus, once again, the VAT has both adverse efficiency and distributional consequences. Appendix B provides a formal model showing this and demonstrates the existence of alternative tax frameworks without these adverse effects.

CONCLUDING REMARKS ON THE VAT

The usual argument for the VAT is that it is efficient, though not progressive. Governments should resort to other instruments for dealing with distribution. *But for developing countries, the VAT is not an efficient tax; it* can, furthermore, lower growth and increase unemployment. Given the absence of other progressive taxes, however, the lack of progressivity of the VAT is of particular concern.

Our analysis shows not only that a VAT is not optimal but also that a country should tax imported goods differentially. If imported goods are disproportionately consumed by the well off, such differentiation introduces an element of progressivity.[17]

Even with World Trade Organization (WTO) restrictions on discrimination against imported goods, it may be possible to differentiate tax rates between *final* goods produced at home and imported final goods because they may differ in certain characteristics (e.g., imported goods may, on average, be of higher quality [price]). The country can impose a higher excise tax on luxury biscuits or luxury automobiles than on ordinary biscuits or ordinary automobiles; this discrimination may, at the same time, have favorable distributional consequences.

THE DESIGN OF CORRUPTION-RESISTANT TAX STRUCTURES

Recent policy discussions have focused on corruption in general and on tax systems in particular. Interestingly, traditional tax policy discussions have paid little attention to corruption.

Corruption takes many forms, including underreporting incomes by rich taxpayers, sometimes with the connivance of government officials, and insisting on bribes not to overreport incomes of "honest" taxpayers. Corruption can be viewed as a problem in observability. That is, if the income could be costlessly and objectively observed, then it would presumably be easy to devise administrative structures to ensure that every taxpayer paid exactly the amount that he should.

Some tax structures provide less opportunity for corruption than others. Some bases of taxation are easier to observe and verify. Consider, for instance, the window tax imposed in medieval England. The tax was very distortionary—it led to dark homes. It did have one advantage, however. It was easy to count the number of windows, and consequently it would have been easy to check on the collection efforts of any tax official: A random check could quickly ascertain whether he had by and large counted the number of windows correctly. If a tax official tried to charge a taxpayer for having too many windows, the aggrieved taxpayer could appeal to a court, which could then verify the number of windows.

In today's world, other bases of taxation exist that can similarly be easily verified (e.g., the number and size of cars or the square meters of a house). It may be easier to design institutional arrangements for the collection of such taxes without corruption.

These "reforms" stand in marked contrast to many of the standard approaches to curbing corruption, which have often failed. For instance, one response to the failure of taxpayers to pay what they should has been to give the government strengthened powers of enforcement. Such policies enable corrupt tax police to extract more money from the private sector, thereby inhibiting development, often without generating much revenue for government.

Modeling corruption-resistant tax structures is beyond the scope of this chapter, but it focuses not simply on the issue of *observability* but also on that of *verification*. Tax collectors must not just "know" the income of the taxpayer, but be able to prove it in a judicial proceeding. By the same token, those trying to circumscribe corruption among government officials must not just "know" that some government official has acted corruptly, but be able to establish it in court. One must be able to distinguish between honest errors in judgment and outright corruption. There must be some confidence in the integrity of the judicial proceeding. But no judicial proceeding is without error. Penalties must exist, but they must be designed with the recognition that errors in judgment may occur.

GLOBAL GENERAL EQUILIBRIUM EFFECTS

If the VAT is imposed in all developing countries, it increases output of goods produced in the informal sector, with global general equilibrium effects. (The price of the *commodities* produced in the informal sector falls.) To the extent that differences exist between these goods and those produced in the formal sector, global effects on prices can occur. Many of the goods produced in the informal sector are inputs into production processes in the advanced industrial countries, whereas many of the goods produced in the formal sector are substitutes for goods produced in developed countries. To the extent that this is true, on a global scale, the VAT shifts the distribution of income/welfare to benefit developed countries at the expense of developing countries.

Each country, as it chooses its own tax structure, typically ignores these global general equilibrium effects. (It might be desirable for developing countries to attempt to coordinate tax structures, to shape "global general equilibrium effects" in ways that advantage—or at least do not disadvantage—themselves. Such a level of coordination does not yet exist.) But when international institutions like the IMF and the World Bank provide advice to developing countries, they should not.

CONCLUDING COMMENTS

This chapter (and this book) focuses on the many ways in which tax policy in developing countries ought to be different from that in developed countries. Policy objectives, economic structures, and administrative capacities differ. This book highlights these differences.

We have focused here on the VAT, in part because it illustrates so well the difference between the design of tax policies in developed and less-developed countries. For developed countries, it is efficient but regressive (or at least not progressive). But, in theory at least, progressive income taxes make up for the VAT's lack of progressivity. Typically, developing countries have no effective income tax to make up for the VAT's lack of progressivity. The VAT is also inefficient, however, and may impede development. When it is imposed in *all* developing countries, it may have further adverse effects through impacts on terms of trade.

One of the key issues on which tax policy for developing countries should focus is promoting development, which entails shifting resources into sectors with faster economic growth and more spillovers. Every successful country has imposed industrial policies. Under WTO rules, it may be more difficult for countries to use tariffs. This may imply that tax policies will become increasingly important in designing industrial policies and promoting development.

Some suggest that a lack of political will explains the slowness of developing countries to make the tax reforms advised by the International Monetary Fund (IMF). Politics do matter, but the developing countries may sense that the VAT is neither fair nor efficient and does not promote their development. They may also recognize that other, more important tax reforms—such as taxing the rents of oligopolies and monopolies—might increase both equity and efficiency. In most cases, politics helps explain the failure to tax these sectors. (The vested interests use their resources to influence the political process.) It might be well if the international community in general and the IMF in particular devoted more of their efforts to these tax reforms.

It is not the intention of this book to provide all the answers, or even to provide a simple template. Indeed, one of the central themes of this book is that because countries differ in structure and objectives, the tax policy that is appropriate to one developing country may differ markedly from what would be best in another. Rather, our intent is to open up the debate on tax policy, which has too often been excessively circumscribed, with developing countries being encouraged to follow a simplistic formula (adopt a VAT) and to enhance understanding of how developing countries have been striving to raise taxes in a fair and efficient way.

APPENDIX A
PROOF OF THE INEFFICIENCY OF THE VAT

We present a simple, heuristic argument showing why it is generally desirable to impose a differential tax on an imported good, used in both sectors, enabling one to lower the VAT tax rate *applied nonuniformly because of the unobservability of output in the informal sector.* The higher-input tax serves as an indirect tax on the output of the informal sector, which otherwise would have escaped taxation.

For simplicity, we assume constant returns in the formal sector and decreasing returns (but homotheticity) in the informal sector:

$$Q_u = F(X_u, L_u)$$

$$Q_r = G(X_r, L_r),$$

where Q_i is the output in the ith sector, X_i is the input of the imported good, and L is input of labor. The dual of the formal sector production function (giving the competitive equilibrium price of the output as a function of the wage and the price of the input) is written

$$P_Q = \Phi(w, p_X),$$

where P_Q is the (producer) price of output, p_X is the price of the input, and w is the wage.

The international prices of traded input and output are both assumed to be unity (these are just normalization), which implies that before taxes, the function

$$1 = \Phi(w, 1)$$

determines the real domestic wage in the formal sector. If the VAT is imposed to be non-trade-distorting (i.e., there are full rebates of the tax for exported goods), then the preceding equation still holds.

On the other hand, the price facing domestic consumers with a VAT is

$$q = 1 + t,$$

where t is the VAT. By assumption, the VAT is not collected on the output of the rural sector, but is imposed on the imported intermediate good that is used in its production. Thus producers in the rural sector maximize

$$qG - wL - x(1 + t)$$

so that

$$G_X = 1$$

$$G_L = w/(1 + t).$$

The VAT thus shifts production toward the informal sector and distorts the input mix in the rural sector toward labor. It is clearly distortionary.

We now ask, "What happens if we add a surtax on imported intermediate goods (fully rebated in the formal sector, on payment of the VAT) at the rate τ, which allows a reduction in the VAT rate (keeping government revenue constant)?"[18] The revenue raised by the VAT is equal to the value of the output of the formal sector that is not exported. We assume trade balance, so that exports equal imports. Hence the VAT revenue is $t(F - X) + tX_r$. The net revenue raised by the import duty surtax is τX_r. Hence total revenue is

$$R = t(F - X) + (\tau + t)X_r,$$

and at $\tau = 0$,

$$d\tau/dt = -\{[F-X] (1 - t\eta_C) + X_r(1 - t\eta_\gamma)\} / [X_r - t\,\eta_{rX}]$$

where η_C is the (absolute value of the) elasticity of formal sector net output that is not exported with respect to the tax rate, η_γ is the elasticity of imports used in the informal sector with respect to the VAT tax rate, and η_{rX} is the (absolute) value of the elasticity. As the VAT increases, more output shifts to the untaxed sector, so that normally we would expect VAT revenue to be reduced.[19]

We can assess social welfare by an indirect social welfare function

$$V = V(q, \pi(q,(1 + t + \tau))),$$

where π is the rent in the rural sector. An increase in the surtax on imports allows a reduction in the VAT, which lowers q, which increases welfare. On the other hand, it will normally lower rents in the rural sector. *If we put little weight on the welfare of landlords (rents), then it is clear that it is desirable to have a tax on imported inputs.* Even if we put full weight on the income of landlords, however, normally a tax on imported inputs is desirable, because the gain in welfare to consumers from the lowering of the VAT outweighs the loss in landlord rents, which can be ascertained by taking the total derivative of V with respect to t.

APPENDIX B
IMPACT OF THE VAT ON UNEMPLOYMENT
IN AN EFFICIENCY WAGE MODEL

In this appendix we analyze the impact of a VAT on unemployment, using a variant of the Shapiro-Stiglitz efficiency wage model and the Harris-Todaro-Stiglitz migration equilibrium model. It is easy to derive (using the equilibrium migration constraint and the no-shirking constraint) that there is a simple relationship between the equilibrium urban wage w^u (which in turn is equal to the no-shirking wage at the equilibrium level of urban unemployment), w^s in the urban sector, urban employment, L^u, and the unemployment rate, u: [20]

$$w^s = w^r(L^u/(1 - u))g(h(w^s)).$$

Moreover, since in equilibrium $u = h(w^s)$, we have what might be called a *generalized no-shirking constraint,* which we simplify as

$$w^s = \psi(L^u).$$

On the other hand, the labor demand equation gives

$$L^u = z(w^u).$$

In equilibrium $w^u = w^s$, so the equilibrium (before tax) is given by

$$w^* = \psi\,(z(w^*)).$$

The effect of a VAT (imposed only on the formal sector) is to shift down the urban demand curve for labor.

Figure 1.B.1 shows the standard equilibrium in the urban labor market with a demand curve for labor and the no-shirking constraint. In panel A, the rural wage is fixed, and the no-shirking wage can, accordingly, be drawn as a horizontal line. The VAT has the effect of shifting the demand curve for labor down, lowering urban employment but leaving the wage unchanged. That means, of course, that the unemployment rate is also unchanged. The tax simply shifts labor from the formal sector to the informal sector. National output

$$Q = F(L^u) + w^r(N - L^u/(1 - u^*))$$

is lowered as L^u is lowered, since (under the hypothesis that the urban rural migration equilibrium condition takes the form $w^r/w^u = 1 - u$)

$$dQ/dL^u = [F' - w^r/(1 - u^*)] = tF',$$

where t is the VAT rate.[21] Thus, even though each individual's labor supply is inelastic, so that in a standard model, the VAT, which is equivalent to a tax on labor, would have no adverse effect on output, here it clearly does.

In the case in which the rural wage is not fixed, the value added not only lowers the urban wage, but, as it drives workers into the rural sector, lowers the rural wage, so much so that the equilibrium unemployment

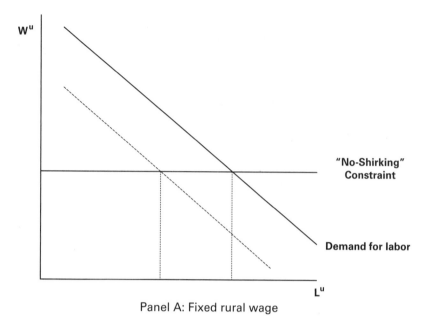

W^u

"No-Shirking"
Constraint

Demand for labor

L^u

Panel A: Fixed rural wage

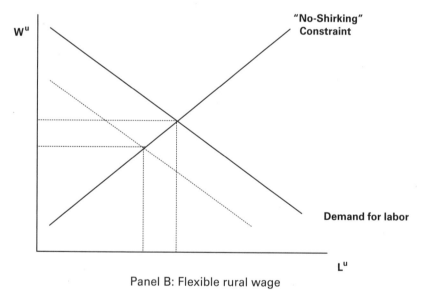

"No-Shirking"
Constraint

W^u

Demand for labor

L^u

Panel B: Flexible rural wage

Figure I.B.I Standard Equilibrium in the Urban Labor Market.

rate actually rises. Let $G(L^r)$ represent rural output, where N^r is rural employment, then

$$Q = F + G$$

and

$$dQ/dt = (\partial Q/\partial L^u)(dL^u/dt)_{u=u^*} - w^r\, L^u/(1-u)^2\, du/dt,$$

which is even more negative, since not only does labor move from the more productive to the less productive sector, but more labor moves into unemployment (zero productivity).

<h2 style="text-align:center">ALTERNATIVE TAXES</h2>

There may be alternative tax structures with less adverse effects on output and welfare. One obvious candidate is a tax on land, which leaves unaffected all the relations described in this model.

Similarly, a tax on imported consumption goods (which are not at the same time produced within the country) consumed by the rentier classes again leaves all the relationships unchanged and thus is nondistortionary.

Taxes on goods consumed by rentiers but produced within the country, or consumed by workers, have more complicated effects. A tax on imports of a good consumed by rentiers but produced within the country drives up the price of the domestically produced goods, shifting, in effect, the demand curve for labor. This has exactly the opposite effect of a VAT, increasing national output and lowering unemployment.

By contrast, a *uniform* tax, both on the production and import of the good, leaves the demand curve for urban labor unaffected and thus has no labor reallocation effect, except to the extent that the higher price of the good shifts demand toward or away from goods produced in the urban sector. If nontraded domestically produced goods in the urban sector are complements of the taxed imported good, then the demand curve for urban labor shifts down, with adverse effects on rural wages, workers' welfare, and unemployment.

<h2 style="text-align:center">NOTES</h2>

Financial support from the MacArthur Foundation, the Mott Foundation, the Hewlett Foundation, and the Ford Foundation is gratefully acknowledged. Much of the work reported in this paper is joint with M. Shahe Emram of George Washington University. The author is also indebted to Dan Choate and Jonathan Dingel for research assistance, and to Roger Gordon for helpful comments.

1. See, e.g., Atkinson and Stiglitz (1976), Mirrlees (1975), or Stiglitz (1998).

2. Kenya has since required large refund claims to be certified by a certified public accountant. This has reduced refund claims by 40%, suggesting that many prior refund claims were indeed fraudulent. See Harrison and Krelove (2005).

3. Indeed, Greenwald and Stiglitz (1986, 1988) show that whenever information is imperfect and markets are incomplete, actions of competitive agents give rise to externality-like effects.

4. See, e.g., Lucas (1988), and Romer (1986).

5. See, e.g., Stiglitz (1998).

6. See, e.g., Stiglitz et al. (2006).

7. Efficiency wage theories are based on the presumption that productivity increases with wages, so that it may benefit a firm to pay a wage above the minimum level required to recruit workers (the "market" wage). It is worth noting that while modern efficiency wage theory focuses on problems of adverse selection and moral hazard based on imperfections of information, see Shapiro and Stiglitz (1984), the theory was originally developed by Leibenstein (1957) and Stiglitz (1974, 1976, 1982) for developing countries.

8. These ideas are developed further in the general theory of Pareto-efficient taxation. See Stiglitz (1987) and Brito et al. (1990).

9. See, e.g., Stiglitz and Wolfson (1988).

10. A few emerging markets have succeeded in implementing broad-based tax systems, but even today, most of the least-developed countries find it difficult to do so. The waning enthusiasm for import substitution strategies of development has undermined in some quarters the developmental argument for tariffs. Our later discussions question this growing orthodoxy.

11. Or evasion—the boundaries in this arena are tenuous.

12. Diamond and Mirrlees (1971).

13. See Emran and Stiglitz (2002, 2004), and Munk (2005).

14. See, e.g., Greenwald and Stiglitz (2006), where it is explained why one might expect the pace of productivity growth to be higher in the formal sector than in the informal sector. Of course, if there are high costs to entering the formal sector, those with entrepreneurial skills (and learning abilities) might be concentrated in the informal sector, in which case the adverse consequences that we have identified might not arise.

15. See also Stiglitz (1999).

16. See, e.g., Stiglitz (1969), Todaro (1968, 1969), Harris and Todaro (1970), Sah and Stiglitz (1992), Anam and Chiang (2007), Yabuuchi (2007), and Yang (2006).

17. In a sense, this analysis can be viewed as a special case of Dasgupta and Stiglitz (1971), which showed that the Diamond-Mirrlees result (1971) that there should not be differential taxes was not true if there are restrictions on taxes that can be imposed. (Here the restriction is on taxes in the informal sector.)

18. The new equations describing production in the rural sector are

$$G_X = (1 + t + \tau)/(1 + t)$$

$$G_L = w/(1 + t).$$

We solve this pair of equations for X_r and labor input into the rural sector (and hence output in the rural sector) as a function of t and τ.

19. Obviously, this could be reversed if informal sector production is sufficiently more import intensive than formal sector production, but normally, we would expect the opposite, reinforcing the general conclusion that the shift toward informal sector production reduces VAT revenue.

20. It is easiest to construct the no-shirking constraint in the case of a fixed rural wage, but one can also construct the curve with a wage in the rural sector that depends on the number of rural workers.

As in Shapiro-Stiglitz (1984), the no-shirking wage is a function of the unemployment rate (given an unemployment benefit, which for most developing countries can be assumed to be zero).

$$w^s = f(u), f' < 0,$$

or inverting,

$$u = h(w^s).$$

In equilibrium, the "no-shirking" wage is the urban wage (at the equilibrium level of unemployment), i.e., $w^s = w^u$ The equilibrium unemployment rate in turn is a function of the urban and rural wages:

$$w^u/w^r = g(u)$$

or

$$w^u = w^r(L) \, g(u),$$

where L is the number of urban job seekers. (If the total population is N, then the number of rural workers is $N-L$). We focus, in particular, on the Harris-Todaro model, where

$$w^r/w^u = 1 - u.$$

By definition

$$L^u / L = 1 - u,$$

where L^u is urban employment, or substituting once again, we obtain the generalized no-shirking constraint, where L^u is urban employment,

$$w^s = w^r(L^u/(1 - u)) \, g(h(w^s)).$$

21. In equilibrium, the urban wage is equal to the marginal product of labor, after tax, i.e., $w^u = (1 - t)F'$.

REFERENCES

Anam, M., and Chiang, S. H. (2007). "Rural-Urban Migration of Family Labor: A Portfolio Model." *Journal of International Trade and Economic Development*, 16(3), pp. 325–35.

Atkinson, A. B., and Stiglitz, J. E. (1972). "The Structure of Indirect Taxation and Economic Efficiency." *Journal of Public Economics*, 1, pp. 97–119.

———. (1976). "The Design of Tax Structure: Direct Versus Indirect Taxation." *Journal of Public Economics*, 6, pp. 55–75.

Brito, D. L., Hamilton, J. H., Slutsky, S. M., and Stiglitz, J. E. (1990). "Pareto Efficient Tax Structures." *Oxford Economic Papers*, 42, pp. 61–77.

Dasgupta, P., and Stiglitz, J. E. (1971). "Differential Taxation, Public Goods, and Economic Efficiency." *Review of Economic Studies*, 38, pp. 151–74.

———. (1972). "On Optimal Taxation and Public Production." *Review of Economic Studies*, 39(1), pp. 87–103.

———. (1974). "Benefit-Cost Analysis and Trade Policies." *Journal of Political Economy*, 82(1), pp. 1–33.

Diamond, P. A., and Mirrlees, J. A. (1971). "Optimal Taxation and Public Production I: Production Efficiency." *American Economic Review*, 61(1), pp. 8–27.

Emran, M. S., and Stiglitz, J. E. (2002). "Consumer and Producer Price-Neutral Tax Reform with an Informal Economy." Working Paper.

———. (2004). "Price-neutral Tax Reform with an Informal Economy." Working Paper. George Washington University.

———. (2005). "On Selective Indirect Tax Reform in Developing Countries." *Journal of Public Economics*, 89(4), pp. 599–623.

Greenwald, B., and Stiglitz, J. E. (1986). "Externalities in Economies with Imperfect Information and Incomplete Markets." *Quarterly Journal of Economics*, 101(2), pp. 229–64.

———. (1988). "Pareto Inefficiency of Market Economies: Search and Efficiency Wage Models." *American Economic Review*, 78(2), pp. 351–55.

———. (2006). "Helping Infant Economies Grow: Foundations of Trade Policies for Developing Countries." *American Economic Review: AEA Papers and Proceedings*, 96(2), pp. 141–46.

Harris, J. R., and Todaro, M. P. (1970). "Migration, Unemployment and Development: A Two-Sector Analysis." *American Economic Review*, 60(1), pp. 126–42.

Harrison, G., and Krelove, R. (2005, November). "VAT Refunds: A Review of Country Experience," IMF Working Paper WP/05/218.

Leibenstein, H. (1957). "The Theory of Underemployment in Backward Economies," *The Journal of Political Economy*, 65(2), pp. 91–103.

Lucas, R. E. (1988). "On the Mechanics of Economic Development." *Journal of Monetary Economics*, 22, pp. 3–42.

Mirrlees, J. A. (1975). "Optimal Commodity Taxation in a Two-Class Economy." *Journal of Public Economics*, 4(1), pp. 27–33.

Munk, K. J. (2005). "Tax-tariff Reform with Costs of Tax Administration." Working Paper No. 2005-21. Department of Economics, University of Aarhus.

Ramsey, F. P. (1927). "A Contribution to the Theory of Taxation." *Economic Journal*, 37(1), pp. 47–61.

Romer, P. M. (1986). "Increasing Returns and Long-Run Growth." *Journal of Political Economy*, 94(5), pp. 1002–37.

Sah, R. K., and Stiglitz, J. E. (1992). *Peasants versus City-Dwellers: Taxation and the Burden of Economic Development.* Oxford: Clarendon Press.

Shapiro, C., and Stiglitz, J. E. (1984). "Equilibrium Unemployment as a Worker Discipline Device." *American Economic Review*, 74(3), pp. 433–44.

Stiglitz, J. E. (1969). "Rural-Urban Migration, Surplus Labor and the Relationship Between Urban and Rural Wages." *East African Economic Review*, 1–2, pp. 1–27.

———. (1974). "Alternative Theories of Wage Determination and Unemployment in L.D.C.s: The Labor Turnover Model." *Quarterly Journal of Economics*, 88(2), pp. 194–227.

———. (1976). "The Efficiency Wage Hypothesis, Surplus Labor and the Distribution of Income in L.D.C.'s." *Oxford Economic Papers*, 28(2), pp. 185–207.

———. (1982). "Alternative Theories of Wage Determination and Unemployment: The Efficiency Wage Model." In: *The Theory and Experience of Economic Development: Essays in Honor of Sir Arthur W. Lewis*, M. Gersovitz, et al., eds. London: George Allen & Unwin.

———. (1987). "Pareto Efficient and Optimal Taxation and the New New Welfare Economics." In: *Handbook on Public Economics*, A. J. Auerbach and M. Feldstein, eds. North Holland: Elsevier Science Publishers.

———. (1998, January). "Pareto Efficient Taxation and Expenditure Policies, with Applications to the Taxation of Capital, Public Investment, and Externalities." Presented at a conference in honor of Agnar Sandmo.

———. (1999). "Taxation, Public Policy and The Dynamics of Unemployment." *International Tax and Public Finance*, 6, pp. 239–62. (Paper presented to the Institute of International Finance, Cordoba, Argentina, August 24, 1998.)

———. (2009). "Simple Formulae for Optimal Income Taxation and the Measurement of Inequality." In: *Arguments for a Better World: Essays in Honor of Amartya Sen, Volume I, Ethics, Welfare, and Measurement*, K. Basu and R. Kanbur, eds. Oxford: Oxford University Press, pp. 535–66.

Stiglitz, J. E., Ocampo, J. A., Spiegel, S., Ffrench-Davis, R., and Nayyar, D. (2006). *Stability with Growth: Macroeconomics, Liberalization, and Development.* The Initiative for Policy Dialogue Series. Oxford: Oxford University Press.

Stiglitz, J. E., and Wolfson, M. (1988). "Taxation, Information, and Economic Organization." *Journal of the American Taxation Association*, 9(2), pp. 7–18. Paper presented for delivery to the American Accounting Association, August 1987.

Todaro, M. P. (1968). "The Urban Employment Problem in Less Developed Countries: An Analysis of Demand and Supply." *Yale Economic Essays*, 8(2), pp. 331–402.

———. (1969). "A Model of Labor Migration and Urban Unemployment in Less Developed Countries." *American Economic Review*, 59(1), pp. 138–48.

Yabuuchi, S. (2007). "Unemployment and International Factor Movement in the Presence of Skilled and Unskilled Labor." *Review of Development Economics*, 11(3), pp. 437–49.

Yang, D. (2006). "Why do Migrants Return to Poor Countries? Evidence from Philippine Migrants' Responses to Exchange Rate Shocks." *Review of Economics and Statistics*, 88(4), pp. 715–35.

CHAPTER 2

Taxes and Development: Experiences of India vs. China, and Lessons for Other Developing Countries

Roger H. Gordon

The rapid and sustained economic growth experienced by India and China, the two most populous countries in the world, during the last 15 to 25 years is probably the most momentous change in the world economy in our lifetimes. Both countries were among the poorest in the world before the start of their economic reforms. The rapid changes since the beginning of these reforms have been breathtaking.

What policy changes helped initiate the sharp improvement in these two countries' economic performance? What further policy changes have been needed to sustain it? To what degree are there common lessons to be learned from their reforms that may benefit other countries?

In this chapter, the focus is on reforms in China's and India's tax structure. To what degree did tax reforms help generate the observed economic growth? Did the growth force changes in the tax structure? How similar have the experiences of these two countries been?

As described in the first chapter, the two countries had very similar economic positions at the beginning of their economic reforms. While there may be some disagreement about the initial date of these reforms, we compare China in 1979 with India in 1991. In those years not only per capita GDP but also the industrial structure of the economy and the initial role of government in the economy were very similar.

The tax policies that were in place during the early years of the reforms were also comparable, with heavy reliance on excise taxes, corporate income taxes, and tariffs, and sharp variation in effective tax rates by sector. These policies are very typical of those seen in the poorest countries throughout the world and presumably reflect shared problems in monitoring taxable activity, so that taxes are collected primarily from those few sectors that can be monitored effectively. Because China and India had the same tax structure as exists in other poor countries, taxes cannot in themselves explain why the two countries grew so rapidly during the reform period.

The growth process itself generated serious pressures on these initial tax structures, since with the reforms firms could respond much more aggressively to existing tax distortions. In contrast, most poor countries maintain many controls limiting the degree to which resources can leave the highly taxed sectors. Yet the reform process in India and China removed most of these controls, leading to a rapid reallocation, and a resulting rapid loss of the tax base.

In addition, because of the initial economic growth, the government was able to develop mechanisms for monitoring taxable activity more effectively, making it feasible to consider a broader range of tax structures. After 15 years of the reform process, both countries undertook major tax reforms. These reforms were remarkably similar, replacing excise taxes with a value-added tax, reducing corporate tax rates substantially, and sharply cutting tariff rates.

These tax reforms helped reduce the tax distortions not only for firms but also for the government itself. Unless the tax structure imposes equal tax rates regardless of the allocation of resources, the government has an incentive to choose policies that shift resources toward more heavily taxed sectors. Any such policies not only can generate more revenue but also in the process can improve economic efficiency by decreasing the misallocations induced by differential tax rates. In contrast, a neutral tax structure gives the government fiscal incentives to choose policies that increase the size of the economy as a whole. Given China's experience, it is projected that India will also increasingly shift to policies that support market allocations, which in the process will raise its growth rate yet further.

Both countries continue to struggle with similar fiscal problems, with low overall tax revenue and poor-quality local public services. India in particular faces serious pressures in the immediate future owing to poor infrastructure (water, electricity, transportation, telecommunications, port facilities, etc.) and substandard education and health services. These problems threaten to undermine its future economic growth rate, yet the government lacks the budget to do much to address these problems. The strategies China adopted to try to alleviate these problems—relying on private sources or user fees to finance improvements—might be helpful in guiding future discussions in India.

These similarities in tax structure are remarkable, particularly given the dramatically different political structures in the two countries. Whereas India has had democratic governments since its independence, a free press, an independent judiciary, and many other British-modeled political institutions that should support a market economy, China has one-party rule, with at best only limited independent roles for the press and the courts. As a result, political pressures and the political decision-making process should be very different in the two countries, and the reform process should plausibly have taken very different directions. That many key decisions were so similar suggests that the shared economic pressures overwhelmed the implications of the countries' different political decision-making processes.

The first section of this chapter lays out the initial conditions at the beginning of each country's reform process. The following sections describe the initial reforms, the initial tax structure, and their implications for government policy more generally; subsequent tax reforms, responding to the pressures created by market reallocations; the implications of these tax reforms for other government policies; fiscal pressures at the state/provincial level in the two countries; and then India's large amount of debt. The last section draws from the experiences in China and India to lay out broader lessons about fiscal policy and the development process.

INITIAL CONDITIONS

India and China started their respective reform periods from very similar positions. For example, according to figures from the World Bank (WDI Online), per capita income in China in 1979 (in 2000 US$) was $175, while per capita income in India in 1991 was $215.

Prior to the reforms, both governments had maintained a dominant position overseeing economic allocations. State-owned enterprises played a major role in both economies. Both countries focused on building up heavy industries, which was a surprising choice considering they were poor, labor-intensive countries. State-owned banks controlled the allocation of a large fraction of the credit, and these allocation decisions were subject to direct government monitoring. State-owned firms received subsidized loans. They were also pressed by the government to hire more workers.

Why did the two countries choose to focus on heavy industry and to favor state-owned enterprises? A variety of potential explanations can be proposed. For example, heavy industry is needed as support for the military, and government officials can extract rents more easily from state-owned firms. One additional explanation explored in Gordon and Li (2009) is that heavy industries are much easier to monitor and tax than other sectors in the economy. If as a result governments rely on heavy industry for tax revenue, then they have a strong fiscal incentive to encourage its growth. Yet if these industries face high tax rates just because they are the only sectors that can be monitored and taxed, then market forces would cause them to be unusually small rather than unusually large. To protect their tax base, governments can give these firms subsidized inputs, and they can impose labor regulations that discourage layoffs. State ownership is yet another mechanism, with its own costs, for inducing these firms to expand even when the resulting after-tax rate of return is low. High prices (and accordingly high profits) in these industries can be encouraged through restrictions on entry of smaller nonstate firms.

Although state-owned enterprises played a dominant role in both economies prior to their reforms, India at least did have an active nonstate sector. Given the difficulties of taxing these firms, however, the government faced fiscal pressures to discourage their growth. Certainly, nonstate firms faced many legal restrictions, requiring licenses to enter into business, to invest, to produce new products, to have access to foreign exchange, and so on.

Both China and India had very little international trade prior to the reforms, and what trade existed was heavily under government control. Since imports competed with the output of domestic heavy industry, trade restrictions protected the government's tax base.

Prior to the reforms, one key difference in policies dealt with the treatment of agriculture. China collectivized agriculture in the 1950s and maintained these controls until 1979. India, however, maintained private agriculture throughout its history. At the same time, neither country invested many resources in improving agricultural productivity.

Given the pervasive range of government controls, allocation decisions were largely under the aegis of the government. As a result, the tax system played only a limited role in affecting allocations. An aphorism in China was that "money is neither necessary nor sufficient to buy goods." In particular, government controls over the economy went far beyond its control over the use of tax revenue: firms were not free to make use of after-tax profits without government approval. As a result, there was little need to worry about the tax distortions created by existing tax structures. In fact, the controls likely existed just because these tax distortions would otherwise have been extremely costly.

INITIAL ECONOMIC REFORMS

NONTAX CHANGES

The initial reforms in China focused partly on dismantling controls that India never had. In particular, farmers were allocated land and allowed to grow what they wished and to sell the resulting output in newly formed private markets, subject to required crop deliveries to the government. Indian farmers already had such flexibility. In addition, China's controls tightly restricting the creation of nonstate firms were largely eliminated.

Otherwise, the initial reforms were very similar. Both countries initiated the reforms by relaxing the controls that had previously existed on the nonagricultural sector. Firms could now make many decisions without government approval. While state-owned banks remained important, other banks started playing an increasingly important role in the allocation of credit.

With this relaxation of controls, the size of the state-owned sector started to decrease. China initially prevented large-scale layoffs by fiat, though the unemployment rate in India quickly grew under the reforms.

Controls over international trade were also eased substantially. For the most part, explicit tariff rates were scaled back. Even when particular tariff rates rose, as happened with consumer durables in China, this largely reflected a substitution of explicit tariffs for even higher nontariff barriers. In addition, controls on exchange rates were substantially eased. Although capital controls remained, current account convertibility was quickly in place in both countries. As a result, firms started to face serious competition from abroad.

Results in both countries were also very similar. After 14 years of the reforms, China's per capita GDP had grown to $535, whereas India's was $548. Since China started from a slightly poorer position, this represented an 8.3 percent growth rate in China and a 6.9 percent growth rate in India. Given the large informal sectors in both economies and the resulting substantial measurement errors in these figures, outcomes seem very close.

THE TAX STRUCTURE AT THE BEGINNING OF THE REFORMS

Unlike India, China did not have an explicit tax structure at the beginning of the reforms. Firms simply transferred all of their profits to the government and received back whatever funds were needed to finance projects that the government authorized. With the reforms, the government quickly set up an explicit tax structure, choosing one that was very similar to the tax system that India already had in place at the beginning of its reforms. Following the introduction of this tax system in China, the tax structure remained relatively stable until 1994. In India, rates changed somewhat, but the overall tax structure was also very stable during the first 15 years of the reform period.

The key sources of tax revenue in both countries were various excise, sales, and turnover taxes, with rates varying dramatically by industry. At the beginning of the reform process, China collected 10.6 percent of GDP in excise tax revenue, compared with 8.4 percent in India. In China, the national government received the taxes paid by state-owned enterprises, while local governments received the excise taxes paid by nonstate firms. Similarly, in India, the national government received the excise tax revenue from manufacturing firms and the state governments received revenue from retail sales of goods.

The other key source of revenue for the national government was corporate income taxes. China introduced a corporate tax at a 55 percent rate in 1983, with revenue from state-owned firms going to the national government and revenue from nonstate firms going to the jurisdiction that oversaw each firm. India started the reforms with a basic corporate rate of 50 percent, with closely held firms taxed at 55 percent. Given the more extensive government oversight of firms that survived into the initial years of the reforms, China was able to collect 7.8 percent of GDP in corporate taxes in 1985, whereas in India revenue was only 1.4 percent of GDP as of 1996, even though the statutory tax rates were very close. These differences in revenue may be more apparent than real, however, because China provided large subsidies to state-owned firms (e.g., through grants or very cheap credit for new investment), whereas India provided extensive tax preferences to firms, reducing reported corporate tax revenue in India but not China.

These statutory provisions imply large differences in effective tax rates by type of firm. From the perspective of the national government, for example, excise tax revenue came only from manufacturing, while wholesale and retail trade, services, and agriculture were tax exempt. In China, the national government instead collected taxes only from existing state-owned firms, so in practice again collecting largely from the manufacturing sector. Prior to the reforms, these governments made use of direct controls to protect this tax base, allocating more resources to the highly taxed sectors than these firms would have acquired on their own and imposing many regulations limiting access to inputs by the nonstate sector. As a result of these controls, the preexisting distortions created by the statutory tax system made little difference.

With the relaxation of economic controls at the beginning of the reform process, however, these tax distortions suddenly started to matter. Resources quickly shifted from sectors facing high tax rates to those facing low tax rates (or evading taxes entirely), resulting in a loss in revenue at least relative to GDP. With the relaxation of controls, the government simultaneously lost access to various sources of information about firm sales and profits, making it harder to enforce the existing taxes.

In China, for example, corporate tax revenue dropped quickly, so that by 15 years into the reforms, China was collecting only 1.5 percent of GDP in corporate revenue.[1] Similarly, excise tax revenue fell from 10.6 percent of GDP in 1985 to 6.4 percent by 1994.[2]

Tax revenue in India proved to be somewhat less vulnerable to these new opportunities to reallocate resources to save on taxes. Tariffs collected 3.6 percent of GDP in revenue as of the beginning of the reform period, but only 1.8 percent of GDP by 2003.[3] Excise tax revenue also fell, from 8.4 percent of GDP in 1991 to 7.7 percent in 2003. However, corporate tax revenue grew quite quickly, from 1.4 percent in 1995 to 2.3 percent in 2003.

The data suggest an important shift in resources under the reforms away from the most heavily taxed sectors. The (initially tax-exempt) service sector, for example, grew from 42 to 53 percent of GDP, while Mathur (2001) reports that capital goods production shrank from 25 to 7.1 percent of overall industrial production. According to the figures in Topalova (2004), state-owned firms had 74 percent of the paid-in capital in 1985, but only 28 percent by 2002. Nonetheless, the fraction of tax revenue coming from state-owned firms grew from 23 percent in 1991 to 38 percent in 2002, as reported in Rao and Rao (2006). Increasing effective tax rates on state-owned firms protected the government from enduring a large fall in overall tax revenue.

Another possible explanation of why government revenue in India did not fall more in response to these large changes in resource allocation is that the government gradually became more effective at tax enforcement. For example, the government began linking deductions for purchases of inputs by one firm with revenue that should be reported by another firm for sales of these goods. In addition, with the reforms, the financial sector became much more important in India and generated considerable tax revenue. At the beginning of the reforms, 67 percent of corporate tax revenues came from manufacturing, even while it represented only 16 percent of GDP. By 2003, revenue from manufacturing had fallen to only 33 percent of corporate tax revenue, a decline in real terms. During the same time period, however, the fraction of corporate tax revenue coming from the financial sector grew from 12 to 29 percent.

In spite of any improvements in tax enforcement in India, tax evasion remains very high. For example, Chai and Roy (2006) quote the *Economic Survey* from the Government of India as reporting that only 9 percent of workers are employed in the organized sector, with the rest in the informal economy.

IMPLICATIONS OF TAX DISTORTIONS FOR FIRM AND GOVERNMENT BEHAVIOR

With the reforms, the distortions inherent in the tax structure existing at the beginning of the reforms became much more important for firm behavior. Given the sharply different tax rates faced in different sectors, the resulting misallocations could be very costly on efficiency grounds. Firms could find it attractive to undertake quite costly changes in behavior, given the potential tax savings. These costs would be immediately salient to the government, since any tax savings to the firm reflect revenue losses to the government. Given that services and agriculture had effectively been untaxed, at least at the beginning of the reform period in India, high-taxed firms could acquire subsidiaries in these other industries and then use transfer pricing to shift sales and profits to these lightly taxed subsidiaries. Since the tax was on turnover rather than value added, firms could also avoid taxes through vertical mergers. Corporate groups may have played an important role in India in part because they are in an effective position to quickly shift sales and profits across sectors in response to differences in tax rates.

Governments continued to face distorted incentives when setting economic policies, since effective tax rates differed by sector. Any policies that induce a shift in resources from a lightly taxed to a heavily taxed use to that extent result in both a revenue gain and an efficiency gain.[4] Tariffs, for example, can be used to prevent imports from undermining domestic production in the more heavily taxed manufacturing sector. Regulations requiring licenses and fees for many decisions made by more lightly taxed firms hinder these firms' activities, shifting resources into sectors facing higher tax rates. Government control over bank loans can be used to direct new investment toward more heavily taxed firms. To make this new investment profitable for these firms, loans may need to be subsidized, with the resulting tax revenue collected on the new investment helping to offset the cost of these subsidies. The government may also impose regulations making it difficult for highly taxed firms to shed labor. In China, the government even forced state-owned firms to hire more workers than they wanted.

On net, given the offsetting distortions faced by both firms and the government, it is unclear in principle whether the highly taxed sectors will be smaller or larger than they would be with undistorted market allocations. Because of the tax distortions, highly taxed firms would like to shift resources elsewhere, whereas the government would prefer to see more resources allocated to these firms. Kochhar et al. (2006) argue that heavy industry played a more important role in India than it would have with undistorted market allocations, and the same can undoubtedly be said about China. This suggests that high tax rates led on net to *more* activity in the sector.

Even if these remaining controls result in an efficiency gain, by reducing the misallocations otherwise caused by existing statutory tax distortions, they can easily come at a high long-run cost. By hindering the entry and growth of new small firms, the government may be undermining the testing of new ideas and the training of new entrepreneurs. The favored firms, those with high tax rates, have little incentive to innovate just because of their heavy taxation. Any short-run improvements in efficiency then come at a high long-run cost in anemic growth.

The reform process in both countries seemed to reflect a conscious decision to relax the regulations protecting the government's tax base. The resulting loss in tax revenue would create not only immediate budgetary problems, but also a higher growth rate. The immediate budgetary problems, however, can be an important issue and one we return to in the section on state/provincial fiscal problems.

SUBSEQUENT TAX REFORMS

The efficiency (and revenue) losses resulting from the distortions inherent in the tax system prevailing during the initial years of the economic reforms in China and India grew quickly as firms took advantage of the relaxation of controls and learned how to rearrange their activities in order to save on taxes. This initial tax system proved to be incompatible with a market economy.

Faced with these pressures, China initially chose to reimpose the types of government controls that had existed prior to the reforms, closing down many nonstate firms and intensifying government controls over the allocation of credit. This policy retrenchment in part precipitated the Tienanmen student demonstrations in 1989. However, while revenue increased in response, the economic stagnation that resulted proved to be too costly to be sustainable, and the new controls were quickly eliminated. However, the basic incompatibility between tax policy and a market economy remained.

Fifteen years into the reform period, in response to these pressures, both India and China felt pressed to undertake a major tax reform. The specifics of these reforms, as well as their timing, were remarkably similar. To begin with, both countries replaced most of their excise taxes with a value-added tax—in China at a 17 percent rate and in India at a 16 percent basic rate. By eliminating the sharp differences in excise tax rates by product, and the possible compounding of tax liabilities as goods were traded between firms, economic incentives became much more neutral.

In addition, both countries tried to broaden the base of these taxes on sales. In China, the key change was to extend the national government's control over tax administration and collection from just state-owned firms to nonstate firms as well. In India, the government is in the process of extending the tax base to include services, which had previously been tax exempt and yet comprise 52 percent of GDP. In addition, India has worked toward a uniform VAT rate in all states.[5] There is still a 4 percent supplementary tax for all cross-state sales of goods between firms, though there is discussion of phasing this out as well.

In addition, the corporate tax rate has been cut dramatically. In China, the tax rate was reduced to 33 percent as part of the same tax reform, while India more gradually reduced its corporate rate to just the same 33 percent rate. With a lower tax rate, tax distortions discouraging capital-intensive sectors are reduced.

An interesting remaining difference, however, is that China maintained a lower corporate tax rate for foreign-owned firms until very recently, whereas India has a higher rate.[6] The lower rate in China may be compensation for contracts that facilitate technology transfer to domestic firms. Perhaps foreign direct investment in India is more likely to compete with the most heavily taxed domestic firms?

Even if the statutory tax rates became much more uniform, however, effective tax rates still varied substantially. The Chinese national government had not previously taxed nonstate firms in part because it did not have the sources of information available to enforce such a tax. India has also faced very high evasion rates, particularly outside of manufacturing. The high tax rates that previously existed reflected the need to rely on a narrow tax base for government revenue, given the inability to monitor and tax activity outside the manufacturing sector.

The immediate response to these tax reforms in China was a drop in tax revenue from 12.6 to 9.3 percent of GDP, as statutory tax rates fell on the firms that could easily be taxed but effective tax rates did not rise that much on firms that were hard to tax. In part this also reflected teething problems (e.g., firms filed claims for VAT tax credits for far more in exports than in fact were recorded at the border). In the case of India, it is too soon to judge the effects of the VAT reform on revenue.[7]

In order to lower tax rates on those firms that are easy to tax while still maintaining government revenue, the key issue is improving the government's ability to monitor and enforce taxes on a broader set of firms. Here, both countries have been actively working to improve tax administration.

China has had a unique source of information on firm performance, through appointing a party representative in each firm whose job in part is to monitor the taxable activity of the firm. Part of the reform extending the VAT to nonstate firms was a decision to have this party representative report to the national government rather than the local government. As financial transactions have become more complicated, however, the ability of this representative to monitor activity becomes increasingly difficult. To improve the financial information available to the Chinese government, the reforms in 1994 also included a major change in the accounting conventions, shifting from a focus on recording quantities of inputs and outputs (as was needed under planning) to recording monetary transactions in much more detail. With better information from accounting reports, tax administration became easier. By the late 1990s, the government also focused much more on monitoring each firm's bank transactions in order to double check the accounting reports on receipts and payments.[8]

India has also focused on reducing tax evasion in order both to collect more revenue and to "level the playing field" across sectors. The VAT that was introduced is invoice-based rather than accounts-based, so that firms can claim a credit for VAT paid on input only with a receipt that can then be traced to the selling firm, thereby ensuring that VAT was also paid on the sale.[9] Much more use is being made of withholding taxes, eliminating the need to trace payments in order to impose tax. Partly in an attempt to tax profitable activity in the informal sector, the government has become much more aggressive in enforcing the personal income tax, requiring anyone with a house, a telephone, a credit card, a car, membership in an exclusive club, or expenditures on foreign travel, to file a personal income tax. By monitoring these big-ticket expenditures, the government is making use of readily available information to infer information that is otherwise hard to monitor.

Evasion rates still remain high, however. For example, according to Gordon and Li (2005), the average VAT rate among developed economies is 16.2 percent, while the average statutory corporate tax rate is 29.6 percent, which is at or below the statutory tax rates in India and China. Yet among developed economies these two taxes alone on average collected 17.9 percent of GDP in revenue, compared with 6.6 percent in India as of 2005 and 7.4 percent in China in 1995.

IMPLICATIONS OF THESE TAX REFORMS

These tax reforms have dramatically reduced the differences in statutory tax rates on different uses of resources within the economy. Since tax rates fell on sectors that are easy to tax, effective tax rates must also have become more similar even if effective rates did not rise much among sectors that are hard to tax.

With more equal tax rates by sector, we should see important changes in both firm behavior and government behavior. Firms' allocation decisions are now much less distorted by the tax law and so should be based to an increasing extent on economic payoffs. This implies a reallocation of resources from activities that had been lightly taxed to activities that had been heavily taxed. This behavioral response therefore raises revenue, helping to compensate for the initial loss in revenue caused by the tax reforms.

As importantly, government incentives become less distorted. Only with these more neutral incentives regarding resource allocation do these governments have an economic incentive to focus on policy reforms that eliminate any government interference with market allocations. As a result, these tax reforms seem essential to induce the other types of policy reforms essential in establishing a well-functioning market economy.

Consistent with this picture, in China these tax reforms were quickly accompanied by a drop in government oversight over the allocation of bank loans, allowing banks to choose where to lend based simply on the likelihood of repayment. After these reforms, China quickly opened up discussions about joining the World Trade Organization, resulting in a sharp drop in tariff rates. The inference is that there was less concern to protect the heavily taxed sectors, since tax rates no longer differed much by sector. Remaining controls limiting the entry and growth of private and other nonstate firms were quickly relaxed. The government also sold off many of the smaller state-owned firms, while the layoff rate from the larger state-owned firms has been very high.

In India, it is too soon to see how government policy will respond more broadly to the more neutral incentives the government now faces as a result of the recent tax reforms. Some of the reforms seen in China after 1994 have already occurred in India, however. According to Mathur (2001), for example, government regulations on interest rates on loans to large firms were relaxed as of 1994, and to small firms in 1998. Tariff rates have fallen dramatically, even prior to the recent tax reforms.

Because of the restrictions on tax policy coming from the Indian constitution, however, important distortions to government incentives remain. In particular, the national government still collects VAT solely from the manufacturing sector, with some supplementary taxes now coming from the service sector. As a result, the national government still has an incentive to favor manufacturing when setting other policies. Although these distortions to government incentives remain, it is still the case that fiscal incentives are less distorted than they were prior to these tax reforms.

STATE/PROVINCIAL FISCAL PROBLEMS

DISTORTIONS CREATED BY THE TAX SYSTEM

State and provincial governments play an important role in India and China. Understanding the fiscal situation of these lower tiers of government is therefore as important as understanding the situation of the national governments.

In India, among state and local governments, state governments have the dominant role. Until recently, their main source of revenue was excise taxes on intrastate sales of goods, with rates varying dramatically by good. In 2005, most states agreed to shift to a VAT on intrastate sales, with most goods taxed at the same rate. In addition, states collect revenue from sales of goods to other states, though here the rate is constrained by the national government to 4 percent. State tax revenue has been stable over time at roughly 6 percent of GDP.

China is more decentralized than India. While provincial governments collected taxes from firms they set up, so did counties, townships, and even villages. Although in principle this revenue was supposed to be shared with the national government, in practice local governments helped firms to hide their profits from the national government. As of 1994, however, the national government took over control of assessing and collecting corporate taxes on these nonstate firms. The result was a sharp jump in the amount of revenue going to the national government, from roughly 30 to 50 percent of overall tax revenue, with local revenue dropping from 9.8 percent of GDP to only 4.9 percent.

In China, at least statutory tax provisions were the same across locations. In India, however, statutory excise tax rates varied substantially by location, creating distortions in both firm and government behavior.

These tax structures also distorted the incentives each state and local government faced when setting nontax policies. On fiscal grounds, a government should be indifferent to the entry or exit of a firm if its tax payments just equal the marginal cost of the extra public services required by the firm (and new employees that the firm brings to the location). Statutory tax rates, however, had no link to the cost of these services, creating incentives for governments to favor firms that pay more in taxes than they cost in services.

In India, excise tax rates varied dramatically by good, creating strong incentives to favor one industry over another. In particular, agriculture and services were very lightly taxed relative to sales of goods. Taxes were also higher to the extent that local firms engaged in interstate trade, since exports were taxable while imports were not tax deductible. Tax competition to attract such firms led to a loss of revenue, to the point that the national government intervened to set a uniform tax rate in all jurisdictions on interstate trade.

Given the use of turnover taxes, jurisdictions also had an incentive to discourage imports of goods that crowded out sales of locally produced inputs. Final sales to consumers would be taxable regardless. However, sales of locally produced but not imported inputs to the retail firm would also be taxable. In fact, Indian cities made use of a separate tax, called an Octroi, on imports of goods from other locations.

In China, local governments seem to have been yet more entrepreneurial. They often imposed controls preventing the imports into the jurisdiction of goods that crowded out highly taxed local goods, as documented in Young (2000). The national government did its best to break down these trade barriers. To encourage more output of highly taxed goods, local governments would provide these firms cheap inputs and cheap credit. Since agricultural taxes were low relative to the taxes collected from other uses of the same land, local governments often intervened to seize agricultural land, transferring it to nonagricultural firms. This is another example of a low tax rate discouraging rather than encouraging an activity.

Complicating any discussion of the fiscal incentives faced by local governments is the fact that the national government provided substantial transfers to local governments in both countries. This system of course encourages any action by the local governments that induces a larger transfer from the national government. For example, China provided low-interest loans to local banks that local governments could then lend out to firms. Local governments found that if they lent out more funds than they had, the national government provided yet more low-interest loans, in effect providing an extra transfer to the jurisdiction. The result was excessive lending and an overheated economy. For the most part, those jurisdictions that contributed more in taxes got back more revenue from the national government, providing an incentive to encourage revenue-generating activities.

In India, transfers from the national government are based in part on a formula that changes every few years and in part on grants whose allocation is more discretionary. These grants have tended to go to jurisdictions facing the greatest fiscal needs, encouraging jurisdictions to appear needy (e.g., collecting little in taxes and spending a lot). We return to this issue in the section Role of Debt Finance.

BUDGETARY LIMITS ON STATE AND LOCAL SPENDING

Even with the transfers from the national government, state and local spending faces tight fiscal constraints in India. While state and local current expenditures, for example, are 12.9 percent of GDP in the United States, local government revenue plus transfers from the national government total to only 9.7 percent of GDP in India.

Perhaps because of this tight budget, the quality of the services provided by state and local governments seems abysmal. For example, the national constitution requires that everyone receive at least eight years of education, which is to be provided without charge, but according to Mathur (2001), the average years of education received is only two. The overall literacy rate is only 61 percent, with sharp differences by gender. Only 84 percent of children complete primary school, and only 35 percent are enrolled in secondary school.

Health care is also very poor. As one indicator of the state of India's health care system, around a third of children are born with low birth weight.

The quality of public utilities is also extremely poor, with major problems in the quality of telecommunications, transportation, port facilities, access to clean water, and frequent power failures. These problems with the current infrastructure are now imposing serious limits on further economic growth.

What can be done to improve the quality of local public services? The easy answer is to provide state and local governments a larger fraction of overall tax revenue. Yet state and local governments already receive two-thirds of the overall tax revenue, given transfers from the national government. This is about the same figure as in China. The comparable figure in the United States for the fraction of overall government consumption expenditures undertaken by state and local governments is 61 percent. The issue therefore does not seem to be a poor division of revenue between state and national governments but instead either too low overall revenue or poor uses of the available funds.

If the problem is simply that overall tax revenue is low, by restricting all types of government expenditures this problem should gradually solve itself. While at 15 years into its reform period government revenue in China was only 9.3 percent of GDP, so much lower than in India, within another 10 years this figure had grown to 17.2 percent. This growth reflects the improved administration of the tax system, as financial records are increasingly available to help provide independent documentation of firm sales and profits. Similar growth in the size of government should be feasible in India as well. However, 10 years is a long time to wait. The long-run costs of 10 more cohorts of schoolchildren with poor education and 10 more years of restricted trade due to poor quality port facilities, for example, can be very high.

Another alternative is for the government to borrow extra funds to finance improved local public services now, aiming to repay these funds in the future out of the resulting economic growth. This is the very route India has been pursuing. According to Mathur (2001), the combined current fiscal deficits of the national and state governments together come to an astounding 10.3 percent of GDP, of which 54 percent is national deficits and 46 percent is deficits of state and local governments. According to Rajaraman (2006), as of 2003 over 40 percent of current tax revenue was used to cover interest payments on the accumulated debt. Given this large-scale borrowing, state and local expenditures net of interest payments are already comparable as a fraction of GDP to that seen in the United States or China.

Yet even with this massive borrowing, the quality of public services is still very poor. It is hard to see how this level of borrowing can be maintained, let alone increased in order to improve the quality of services.

One other strategy, and one that the Chinese have used aggressively, is to introduce user fees to finance local public services such as education or health care. The Chinese have also encouraged private firms to provide infrastructure investments. Contracts have been signed with private firms to build new roads and port facilities in exchange for receiving the resulting tolls for a period of years. Prices for electricity have been raised so as to give electric-generating firms an incentive to invest so that they can provide the amount of power demanded. Private entry has been encouraged to improve telecommunications.

When user fees finance public services where the marginal cost of an extra user is below the average cost of provision, then these fees inordinately discourage use of the services on efficiency grounds. Alternative sources of revenue also create efficiency costs, however. For those public services where nonpayers can be excluded, user fees do provide an easily enforced source of revenue.

Pang (2006) recommends that India should also turn to the private sector to invest in improved infrastructure. Is this a good strategy? The arguments against this strategy are in part distributional, in part constitutional, and in part political. The distributional concern is that any nontrivial user fees will impose a sizeable burden on the poor, large enough to cause them to forego education and health care. If this were the only concern, then the available government budget could be focused on providing full or partial tuition credits for the poorest households, with richer households then paying the required fees themselves.[10] The constitutional problem arises because the constitution promises free education up through grade eight. China faces the same problem, and "solved" it by charging no tuition but instead charging various fees for books, uniforms, and other essential inputs to education. The political problem is that if private firms choose to proceed with a project, based on the promise of future user fees, once the project is complete the government may renege on the promise and force a reduction in these user fees, impose a new tax on these fees, or otherwise try to intervene to aid users of the facilities at the expense of the private firm.[11]

POOR INCENTIVES TO PROVIDE LOCAL PUBLIC SERVICES

The other possible direction to pursue in enhancing the quality of local public services is to improve the incentives for state and local governments to provide higher quality services.

Residents can pressure local governments to improve the quality of local public services either through voice or through exit. Voice should be a much more effective mechanism in India than in China, given that state and local governments are elected in India but appointed by higher levels of government in China. However, voters face a free-rider problem that not only discourages them from voting but also, more importantly, discourages them from becoming informed about any malfeasance by state and local officials.[12]

The other source of pressure on local officials is exit. Residents who are unhappy with the quality of local services and local public utilities can leave. This imposes a fiscal cost on local officials to the extent that the departing residents paid more in taxes than they imposed in marginal costs for extra local public services. Thus, with a VAT being the main source of state and local tax revenue, losing higher spending residents is a net fiscal cost, while losing poorer residents could even be a net fiscal gain. The greater the mobility of residents in response to poor quality services, the greater the need for local officials to take account of the exit threat.

To strengthen incentives, the threat of mobility in response to poor quality of public services would need to be greater, and the fiscal implications of this mobility should be greater. Yet in India at least, state governments face very little threat of exit, given the language barriers to moving within India as well as the substantial cultural differences between different regions. How then can incentives be strengthened?

One possible mechanism would be to shift funding and responsibility to provide local public services to local governments (*panchayats*). Mobility between panchayats should be much greater than between states, since distances are smaller, languages are shared within an area, and cultural differences can be minimal. Mathur (2001) presents a very successful example of a shift of funding in Kerala from the state government to local panchayats, with a clear improvement in the quality of local public services.

To strengthen the fiscal incentives created by mobility, the funding from the state government to panchayats should be tied to the number of residents, so that departures have clear fiscal costs for the local government. Since the cost of providing public services to residents varies across people (e.g., only school-aged children require education), the funding could vary as well with the demographic composition of the residents. Otherwise, local governments have an incentive to provide those services that attract residents who bring in more funding than they cost in extra services, and to withhold services from those (with school-aged children) who cost more than they bring with them in extra funding.

Local funding for public services could also come from user fees. With user fees, the departure of local residents implies a loss of those user fees. If the user fees cover the full marginal costs, then local officials have a fiscal incentive to provide these services even without any pressures from voice or exit. This role of user fees in providing incentives for officials to provide a service can be at least as important as their role in helping to finance these services.

Although mobility between panchayats should be much greater than that between Indian states, these mobility costs could be reduced further. People who choose to move need to sell any local land they own and then find housing elsewhere. To ease this process, land markets and rental markets should operate smoothly. Yet currently, land markets work poorly, given the very high stamp duties paid on sales and given the high property tax payments due in the future linked to the reported sales price. Reducing these taxes would be helpful in generating a more liquid market for land.[13]

Similarly, any regulations on the rental market (e.g., rent controls) make it harder for people to find housing elsewhere, again hindering mobility.

There is also a question about how to induce local officials to provide services to firms. The Chinese reforms were particularly effective in this regard, since they tied local revenue to the profits of local firms. As a result, local governments got a sizeable share of any extra future profits generated by, say, improved infrastructure. To the extent that benefits from local public services go to firms as well as to households, tying the funding of local governments to the profits of local firms—for example, through sharing some fraction of corporate tax revenues with local governments—could make sense as well.

This link between future profits and future funding for the local government helps provide incentives for current officials to improve the quality of infrastructure, though only to the extent that these officials will remain in office in the future when this extra revenue accrues to the local government. In China, there has been little turnover of local officials, so that this link between current expenditures and future revenue can provide strong fiscal incentives. It may be less effective in India, where local officials can quickly be voted out of office.

ROLE OF DEBT FINANCE

One striking observation regarding the current fiscal situation in India is the large deficits at both the national and the state levels. This debt overhang is growing quickly, and interest charges require around 40 percent of current tax revenue. Is this high debt a cause for concern?

One can argue, for example, that tax revenue will grow quickly in the future in India, not only because of the rapid growth in the economy but also because of further improvements in tax enforcement. This certainly has been the experience in China. Anticipating this future growth in revenue, it may be reasonable to borrow against this future revenue, particularly to finance current government expenditures such as education and infrastructure projects that help generate this future growth in revenue.

So the question is not whether any debt should exist but whether there is currently too much debt. The discussion in Heller and Rao (2006) suggests that India currently has too much debt. The question that arises is why both national and local governments have borrowed so heavily.

Alesina and Drazen (1991), for example, argue that the political party currently in power has an incentive to spend not only current tax revenue but also future tax revenue on its own pet projects. Any remaining resources will likely be spent by the opposition party on projects that the party currently in power finds of little value. This could easily be the rationale for the current runup in debt in the United States and may also explain some of the accumulating debt in India as well. It may be mutually advantageous for the political parties to commit themselves to avoid adding to the debt. The question is how to do so. Restricting the use of debt to capital projects is one device that state and local governments often use, but this formula is likely too restrictive at the national level.

The runup of state government debt raises other possible concerns. If a state government maintains an unsustainable level of expenditures, what will happen? As emphasized by IMF (2006), the national government has simply provided extra transfers to cover the shortfall, generating a soft-budget constraint. With a soft-budget constraint, extra spending simply generates extra transfers, implying a large implicit subsidy rate for this extra spending and a major distortion to the incentives faced by state governments.

To reduce or eliminate this distortion, transfers from the national government should be set based on a formula that does not depend directly or indirectly on state fiscal deficits. Linking transfers to local population or local corporate tax revenue, for example, eliminates any link between extra spending and fiscal transfers.

For this commitment to be credible, a workable legal means must be in place to deal with defaults by state and local governments. According to IMF (2006), however, there have been no defaults by state or city governments in India, in spite of the large debt overhang. Therefore, there is no experience to fall back on in dealing with such defaults. If a clear legal structure existed, the threat of default would become more plausible and would help eliminate these distortions in fiscal incentives.

SUMMARY AND BROADER IMPLICATIONS FOR TAXES AND DEVELOPMENT

When comparing the history of fiscal policies in India versus China during their reform periods, what jumps out are the remarkable similarities. Prior to the economic reforms, both countries had tax systems typical of poor countries generally, relying primarily on excise taxes, corporate income taxes, and tariffs for revenue. In practice, revenue was collected primarily from firms in manufacturing and even within manufacturing primarily from state-owned firms.

With a narrow tax base and high tax rates, both countries had in place many controls protecting this tax base. Tariff and nontariff barriers protected the domestic tax base from foreign competition. Both countries also used a variety of controls over the allocation of resources within the domestic economy to favor state-owned firms and heavily taxed firms more broadly. Among other policies, the government influenced the allocation of credit, in part through state-owned banks, and imposed regulations limiting the activity of firms in lightly taxed sectors.

The economic reforms relaxed many of these controls on the lightly taxed sectors and reduced effective tariff rates. With the relaxation of controls, firms could now more easily respond to economic incentives, leading to a major reallocation of resources and a jump in the rate of economic growth.

Part of this reallocation, however, was a shift in activity away from the most heavily taxed industries toward services and other more lightly taxed industries. The result was a drop in tax revenue. In China in particular, tax revenue fell in half during the first few years of the reform process. The large differential tax rates by sector generated increasingly important efficiency costs, since firms now had more flexibility to respond to these tax distortions.

Fifteen years into their economic reforms both countries undertook major tax reforms, shifting from differential excise taxes to a VAT and reducing corporate tax rates substantially. Although it is feasible to cut the high tax rates on sectors that are easy to tax, it is more difficult to raise the effective tax rate on sectors that are hard to tax. The result in China was a further decline in revenue for a few years until the government was able to monitor and tax a broader range of economic activity.

This inevitable decline in government expenditures as a result of the reform process creates a major difficulty, potentially undermining the economic reforms. Given the narrow tax base and high rates, only two options are available to deal with this fall in revenue: cut expenditures or increase government borrowing in an attempt to maintain expenditures.

China largely cut expenditures, shifting to user fees for education and health and contracts with private firms to provide infrastructure. The result has been poor-quality education and health care, at least in rural areas. The low quality of education in rural areas will inevitably be a drag on China's long-term growth. While infrastructure investment has been strong, user fees are often far above the marginal cost of provision, leading to insufficient use of this infrastructure on efficiency grounds.

Another problem with cutting government expenditures in response to declining tax revenue is a political risk. Many residents may gain enough from the reforms to be willing to accept a drop in government expenditures. For those who lose from the reforms, however, a drop in government expenditures only exacerbates the economic pressures they face. Poor education in particular can reduce the hope that at least their children can gain from the reforms. The result can be a loss of political support for the reform process. China has experienced a sharp increase in political unrest, mainly in rural areas that have benefited less from the economic reforms. This unrest does not create a serious political threat to the Chinese government, but in other countries undergoing economic reforms such unrest has in many cases produced a change in government, leading to a reversal of the economic reforms.

India has instead relied heavily on government borrowing to try to maintain public expenditures. At this point, its fiscal deficit is around 10 percent of GDP. The question is whether this heavy borrowing is sustainable as a means of dealing with the fall in tax revenue.

Tax revenue as a fraction of GDP should eventually grow in India, giving it the resources to repay accumulating debt. As the data show, tax revenue/GDP is much higher among developed than among developing countries. In practice, tax revenue in China (as a fraction of GDP) did eventually recover to its level prior to the reforms, but this occurred roughly 25 years into the reform process. The expectation of this future revenue can encourage foreign and domestic creditors to lend to the government. However, any new doubts about future economic growth and future revenue collection could make lenders reluctant to extend further credit, generating a financial crisis. Such financial crises have undone the reforms of many developing countries.[14]

At least based on the experiences in China and India, fiscal pressures seem to be an inevitable part of the reform process. Whether countries undergoing economic reforms deal with these fiscal pressures by cutting expenditures or increasing government borrowing, there are risks to the future of the economic reforms. Finding better ways to deal with these fiscal pressures should be a major priority in future academic research on tax policy in developing countries.

NOTES

An earlier version of this chapter was presented at a conference on "Growth in India and the World," held in New Delhi during December 14-15, 2006. I thank conference participants, especially Govinda Rao, for comments.

1. This drop would have been even larger had the government not intervened and replaced the initial structure of the corporate tax with contracts between the government and each firm, starting in 1987. Under these contracts, tax payments were based on projections of the firm's future profits rather than actual reported profits. The aim in part was to reduce effective *marginal* tax rates on firm profits by basing taxes on past activity.

2. This fall in revenue also reflected widespread tax evasion that became easier as controls were relaxed. State-owned firms, for example, would often open up a neighboring nonstate firm and use transfer pricing to shift profits into the nonstate firm, thereby avoiding tax payments at least to the national government.

3. The equivalent reported figures for China were 2.3 percent of GDP in 1985, falling to 0.6 percent in 1994. These figures are not really comparable to those for India, however. Government-owned trading firms controlled much of the international trade, so that their profits in part reflected implicit tariff revenue.

4. When firms are just willing to shift resources in response to a policy change, after-tax profits are largely unaffected. However, tax revenue changes, and this change therefore reflects the overall change in efficiency.

5. Here, the national government can only recommend changes, since each state ultimately controls its tax policy. Almost all states at this point have agreed to adopt the uniform rates recommended by the national government.

6. As part of its agreement when joining the WTO, China pledged to eliminate the differential tax rates on foreign vs. domestic firms.

7. However, corporate tax revenue has increased even while tax rates have fallen, likely due to improved tax enforcement.

8. A key part of this reform has been a requirement that each firm maintain only one tax number on its bank accounts, so that all bank transactions can be linked to the firm.

9. Of course, this tracing is not easy, so that the benefits to date have been limited.

10. These tuition subsidies probably should be paid by the national government, out of funds otherwise transferred to state and local governments. If they were paid by state and local governments, they would create an incentive to push poor residents out of the jurisdiction.

11. See Wallack and Singh (2007) for evidence that this fear has hindered attempts in India to contract with private firms to invest in major infrastructure projects.

12. See Banerjee et al. (2006), for example, for evidence on the limitations of voice in India, given the poor information available to local residents.

13. A property tax is often argued to be an attractive tax to finance local governments (e.g., see Wilson and Gordon, 2003), in part because it links the budget of local officials more closely to their performance. The intuition is that land values quickly reflect any changes in the quality of local public services. Without effective

assessments, however, land taxes do not respond to mobility and so create no incentives to retain residents.

14. At this point, however, India's debt is largely internal, so that the country may not be immediately vulnerable to a financial crisis.

REFERENCES

Alberto, A. and Drazen, A. (1991). "Why Are Stabilizations Delayed?" *American Economic Review,* 81, pp. 1170–88.
Banerjee, A., et al. (2006). "Can Information Campaigns Spark Local Participation and Improve Outcomes? A Study of Primary Education in Uttar Pradesh, India." World Bank Policy Research Working Paper No. 3967.
Chai, J.C.H., and Roy, K. C. (2006). *Economic Reform in China and India.* Northampton, MA: Edward Elgar.
Gordon, R. H., and Li, W. (2005). "Taxation and Economic Growth in China." In *Critical Issues in China's Growth and Development,* Y. K. Kwan and E.S.H. Yu, eds. Burlington, VT: Ashgate.
———. (2009). "Tax Structures in Developing Countries: Many Puzzles and a Possible Explanation." *Journal of Public Economics,* 93, pp. 855–66.
Heller, P. S., and Rao, M. G. (2006). *A Sustainable Fiscal Policy for India: An International Perspective.* New York: Oxford University Press.
IMF. (2006). "India: Selected Issues." IMF Country Report No. 06/56.
Kochhar, K., et al. (2006). "India's Pattern of Development: What Happened? What Follows?" IMF Working Paper No. 06/22.
Mathur, K.B.L. (2001). "India: Fiscal Reforms and Public Expenditure Management." Japan Bank for International Cooperation Research Paper No. 11.
Pang, G. (2006). "India—East Asian Growth, Latin American Deficits." Mimeo.
Rajaraman, I. (2006). "Fiscal Developments and Outlook in India." In *A Sustainable Fiscal Policy for India,* P. S. Heller and M. G. Rao, eds. New York: Oxford University Press.
Rao, M. G., and Rao, R. K. (2006). "Trends and Issues in Tax Policy and Reform in India." Mimeo.
Topalova, P. (2004). "Overview of the Indian Corporate Sector, 1989–2002." IMF Working Paper No. 04/64.
Wallack, J., and Singh, N. K. (2007). *Piecemeal Politics: Infrastructure Development in India.* Mimeo.
Wilson, J. D., and Gordon, R. H. (2003). "Expenditure Competition." *Journal of Public Economic Theory,* 5, pp. 399–417.
World Bank. "WDI Online." http://devdata.worldbank.org/dataonline/.
Young, A. (2000). "The Razor's Edge: Distortions and Incremental Reform in the People's Republic of China." *Quarterly Journal of Economics,* 115, pp. 1091–35.

CHAPTER 3

Tax Policy in Argentina: Between Solvency and Emergency

Oscar Cetrángolo and Juan Carlos Gómez Sabaini

At the turn of the century, Argentina experienced a serious economic crisis, brought about by the forced abandonment of the monetary convertibility regime and characterized by sharp changes in relative prices and income, as well as by widespread breaches of contracts.[1] This economic crisis proved to be different from previous crises, however, as Argentina managed to recover quickly and significantly (see Figure 3.1).

The recovery presents some exceptional features. At few times in Argentina's economic history has the country experienced such external and fiscal surpluses. More importantly for the purposes of this study, Argentina's tax burden is far higher than ever before. Understanding these historic trends is necessary to our study of the characteristics, strengths, weaknesses, and reforms of Argentina's tax system. The second section of this chapter, which serves as an introduction to this study, examines the central features of Argentina's fiscal situation from a historical viewpoint. Next, we present an explanation of the particular institutional characteristics of Argentina's federalism, which is necessary to the study of Argentina's tax system. Lastly, the next section places the Argentine tax system in context, introducing the principal features of taxation in Latin America.

The main body of this chapter includes a detailed analysis of the evolution of Argentine tax level and structure, the key stylized characteristics of this structure, and the principal challenges that Argentina continues to face.

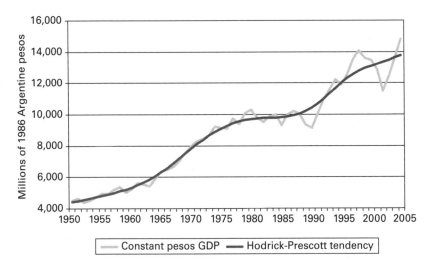

Figure 3.1   GDP Evolution, 1950–2005.

Source: ECLAC, on the basis of data from Secretaría de Programación Económica.

THE ECONOMIC EVOLUTION AND ITS IMPACT ON THE FINANCING OF THE PUBLIC SECTOR: THE FISCAL DEFICIT

THE FISCAL SITUATION: A HISTORICAL PERSPECTIVE

A proper evaluation of Argentina's fiscal situation in the 1990s requires a wide historical perspective. Argentina's public sector reached the 1990s with long-standing structural imbalances and brief periods of surpluses, which, as a result of successful stabilization programs, generally coincided with extraordinary increased revenues. This increase in revenues was due, in large part, to improved tax collection during periods characterized by sharp decreases in inflation rates and some lags in tax payments (the Tanzi effect). Likewise, the highest deficits have coincided with the deterioration of revenues during macroeconomic crises, considering the relative stability of primary spending due to budget rigidity. In sum, fiscal evolution has been closely associated with the macroeconomic evolution.

An examination of the evolution of primary and total revenues since 1961 demonstrates the magnitude of the long-term fiscal deficits. In addition to the deep deficits that coincided with serious macroeconomic crises (1975, 1981–1983, 1989–1990, and 2001–2002), primary and total deficits

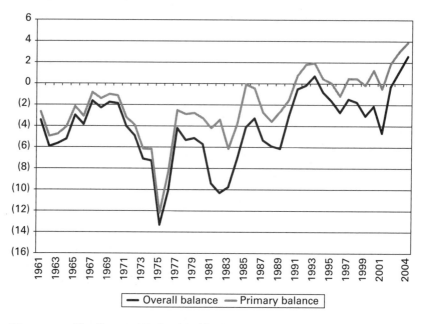

Figure 3.2   Nonfinancial Federal Public Sector Balance (on an Accrual Basis, as a Percentage of GDP).

Source: Own elaboration on the basis of data from the Ministry of Economy and ECLAC, Buenos Aires office.

constituted approximately 2.1 percent and 4.1 percent of GDP, respectively. However, this was due to two clearly different situations.

Until 1990, the deficit without privatizations, with partial financing from the inflationary tax, hovered around 5.8 percent of GDP. During the 1990s, the deficit dropped to 2.1 percent of GDP, and revenues from privatizations were 1.7 percent of GDP. At the same time, the primary balance improved from –3.5 percent of GDP for the 1961–1990 period (annual average) to 0.5 percent surplus of GDP. On the basis of the information presented in Table 3.1 and Figure 3.2, it may be concluded that the public sector has shown an important adjustment process of its imbalances in the long term. This does not mean that the persistent imbalances, especially those resulting from debt service, were easier to finance in the convertibility period, when there was no inflationary tax.

Throughout the four decades prior to the 2001 crisis, the government undertook various attempts to restrict the level of capital spending and, in some periods, operating spending (personnel and assets and services).[2] In addition to debt service, another two sets of spending exerted increased

Table 3.1   Nonfinancial Federal Public Sector Balance, 1961–2000 *(annual average as a percentage of GDP)*

Period	Total	Primary	Total without Capital Revenue	Primary without Capital Revenue
1961–1970	(3.46)	(2.61)	(3.86)	(3.01)
1971–1980	(6.70)	(5.13)	(6.91)	(5.34)
1981–1990	(6.43)	(2.85)	(6.61)	(3.03)
1991–2001	(1.65)	0.50	(2.14)	0.01
2002–2004	1.16	2.94	1.15	2.93
1961–1990	(5.53)	(3.53)	(5.79)	(3.79)
1961–2004	(4.11)	(2.08)	(4.41)	(2.38)

Source: Own elaboration on the basis of data from the Ministry of Economy and ECLAC, Buenos Aires office.

pressure: pensions and spending related to fiscal and financial relations with the provinces. Taking into account the federal nature of Argentina, we believe the evolution of federal and province accounts should be disaggregated. Regardless of the seriousness of many fiscal problems affecting the provinces, we can better understand the dominant character of the fiscal evolution of the central government through an explanation of the evolution of the consolidated public accounts[3] (Figure 3.3).

THE FISCAL SITUATION SINCE THE EARLY 1990S

The evolution of fiscal revenues in the 1990s was a determining factor in the late 2001 economic crisis. But since fiscal problems cannot be attributed to a single factor, tax policy and traditional difficulties in dealing with tax evasion share the menu of fiscal deficiencies together with finances of the provinces, privatizations, pension reform, and debt management among others. While the early 1990s were considered a period of sizeable reforms in terms of public intervention, long-standing public policy problems in education, health, the pension system, and infrastructure (to mention the most important) persisted. Thus the extent to which reforms helped should be questioned.[4]

In aggregate terms, the following phenomena stand out: the importance of revenues from privatizations in the first half of the 1990s,[5] the growing deficits that began in 1993, and the growing gap between total and primary balance, which highlights increased debt interests.

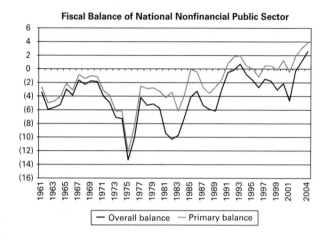

Fiscal Balance of National Nonfinancial Public Sector

— Overall balance — Primary balance

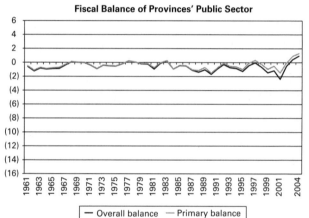

Fiscal Balance of Provinces' Public Sector

— Overall balance — Primary balance

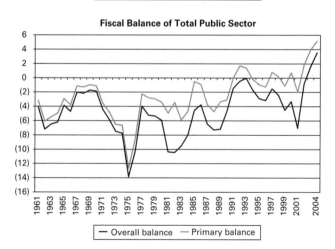

Fiscal Balance of Total Public Sector

— Overall balance — Primary balance

Some of the macroeconomic factors that helped create a solvent fiscal situation during the early 1990s were reversed after 1994—international interest rates bounced back slightly, and the recession, unleashed by the unfavorable external shock that followed Mexico's devaluation, greatly influenced collection trends, especially after 1995. However, two other factors closely linked to fiscal policy decisions explain fiscal imbalances. First, the government was unable to manipulate the nominal exchange rate and thus sought to partially offset the trade sector's loss of competitiveness by reducing taxes and resuming tax reimbursements on exports. The most important measure undertaken was the reduction in employers' taxes that financed social security. The second factor resulted from the negative impact of pension system reform, which will be discussed in a later section. Despite these emergency measures and the temporary recovery of the economic activity that began in 1996, the public sector continued to show imbalances that it tried to counter with a series of various and partial tax reforms.

THE FISCAL SITUATION AFTER THE CRISIS

The features that characterized Argentina's fiscal policy before the 2001 crisis are different from those that have prevailed in the period after the crisis, during which exceptional growth in the trade balance and in the net fiscal surplus were achieved. In 2004, the public sector's fiscal income showed a surplus at 2.6 percent[6] of GDP, and such surplus was estimated to have increased to 3.5 percent of GDP in 2005. These data show the vast improvement in public accounts after the 2001–2002 crisis. In 2002, this improvement resulted from a decrease in spending as a percentage of GDP in proportion to revenue growth. Such spending cuts arose primarily from a reduction in the real value of public sector wages, pension payments, and debt interests. The first two changes resulted from the depreciation of the exchange rate that occurred when the convertibility system was abandoned. Between 2001 and 2002, the nominal exchange rate increased by 200 percent and 130 percent in real terms, while the public

---

Figure 3.3   Evolution of the Consolidated Balance of the Nation and the Provinces (as a Percentage of GDP).

Source: Own elaboration on the basis of data from the Ministry of Economy and ECLAC, Buenos Aires office.

sector's salaries and pension payments remained virtually constant. Improvement subsequent to 2002 resulted from the increased growth of tax revenues relative to spending.

Together, these factors generated the previously mentioned primary surplus, despite the creation of a new social assistance program to deal with the social costs of the crisis.

Never before in Argentina's history has its tax burden been so high. This is due, in part, to emergency taxes, half of which came from export duties, which amounted to a total of 4.6 percent of GDP in 2004. However, the significant growth of traditional taxation (e.g., VAT, income, and payroll taxes) confirms the usual assumption that tax administration efforts are more efficient during periods of economic recovery.

POLITICAL STRUCTURE OF THE FEDERAL GOVERNMENT: THE TAX POWERS OF EACH LEVEL OF GOVERNMENT AND THE REVENUE-SHARING SYSTEM

A complete discussion of the Argentine tax system must include certain relevant characteristics of Argentina's institutional organization. Argentina is a federal country comprised of 24 highly autonomous provinces, 14 of which existed before the national organization that occurred in the mid-nineteenth century. Argentina's National Constitution stipulates that the provinces retain all powers not specifically delegated to the federal government. As a consequence, the federal government has full responsibility in matters of foreign affairs, minting, trade regulations, domestic and international navigation, and defense. Powers in certain other policy areas— among them, justice, primary education, and social security—are shared. Because the institutional framework is imprecise in its delegation of these powers to the varying levels of government, responsibilities have been reallocated numerous times during the past three decades. These processes of reallocation, which are not always orderly and transparent, have made the nation–provinces–municipalities relationship more complex.

With respect to the powers of taxation, the National Constitution, in article 75, subsection 2, defines federal and provincial tax powers by stating that indirect taxes, with the exception of import and export fees that are exclusively federal, are shared by both levels of government. Direct taxes fall exclusively under the auspices of the provinces, but the federal government is not precluded from levying direct taxes during a limited term and on condition that national security and defense requires it.

In practice, the federal government collects most taxes while revenues are shared. The provinces retain four main taxes (the real estate tax, automobile tax, stamp tax, and gross income tax), which allow them to collect enough revenue to cover, on average, approximately 40 percent of their expenses, and they finance the rest of their expenses through indebtedness and transfers from the central government. In Argentina, the tax revenue collected by subnational governments has not grown in proportion to their spending. This has resulted in a growing gap between spending and revenues at a subnational level, which has increased tensions between the nation and the provinces.

From a long-term perspective, the imbalances between jurisdictional structures of spending and revenues (tax and nontax revenues) were not very significant until the 1980s (Figure 3.4). Before the decentralization of schools and hospitals in the late 1960s, the central government collected and spent similar percentages of the total budget. Since the 1980s, however, the highest concentration of revenues managed by the federal government and the decentralization of spending has given rise to pressure on the tax-sharing system and increased tension between the federal and provincial governments, as the federal government controls three-quarters of revenue but only half of consolidated spending.

The allocation of taxes between levels of government should attempt to meet the needs of often divergent goals. On one hand, it is true that, in theory, subnational governments can better meet their citizens' preferences when local taxes allow costs of providing certain assets and services by the local government to be internalized. However, various reasons make it difficult to allocate tax powers to subnational governments in such a proportion to fully finance their growing delivery of assets and services. Therefore, although there is a theoretical agreement about a necessary symmetry between spending and tax powers, in practice, few taxes can be decentralized without a significant loss of efficiency and fairness.

This point is of particular importance in almost every country in the region, whose economies are characterized by deep regional productivity disparities. As Figure 3.5 shows, Argentina presents an extremely imbalanced regional productive structure. The relation between the per capita income of the Province of Santa Cruz (the richest in terms of this indicator) and the Province of Formosa (the poorest) in Argentina is 8.6 times.[7] This disparity in regional terms not only impacts the construction of equalization schemes, but also limits certain decentralization attempts. Thus, such disparities among regions translate into different tax bases and

Resources

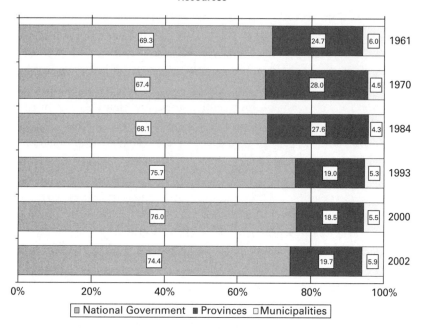

	1961
69.3 / 24.7 / 6.0	1961
67.4 / 28.0 / 4.5	1970
68.1 / 27.6 / 4.3	1984
75.7 / 19.0 / 5.3	1993
76.0 / 18.5 / 5.5	2000
74.4 / 19.7 / 5.9	2002

0%   20%   40%   60%   80%   100%

☐ National Government   ■ Provinces   ☐ Municipalities

Expenditures

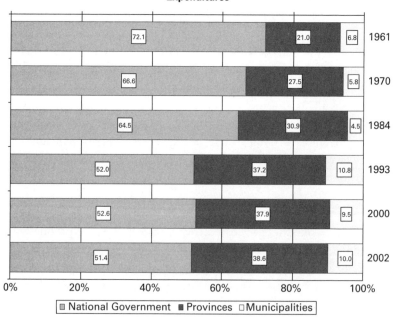

72.1 / 21.0 / 6.8	1961
66.6 / 27.5 / 5.8	1970
64.5 / 30.9 / 4.5	1984
52.0 / 37.2 / 10.8	1993
52.6 / 37.9 / 9.5	2000
51.4 / 38.6 / 10.0	2002

0%   20%   40%   60%   80%   100%

☐ National Government   ■ Provinces   ☐ Municipalities

Figure 3.4 Structure of Revenues and Spending in Percentages by Level of Government.

Source: Cetrángolo and Jiménez (2003).

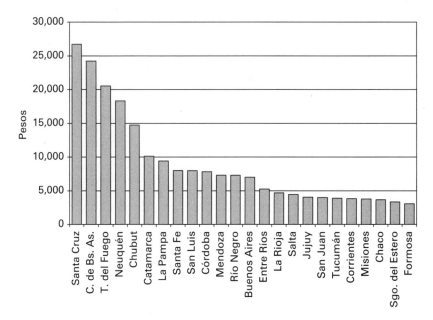

Figure 3.5   Regional GDP per Capita, 2002.
Source: Graphic regional overview. ECLAC, Buenos Aires.

institutional capabilities. All these factors highlight the importance of revenue-transfer schemes to subnational governments.

In addition, the process of decentralization of social expenditures and the concentration of revenues in the central government exert pressure on financial transfer systems to homogeneously provide public goods while paying attention to fairness. These data rule out any attempt to make any headway in fiscal co-responsibility projects (which does not mean ignoring the need to transfer some tax powers to provinces). Figure 3.6 shows the high degree of correlation between the quality standards in the public provision of health and education and the degree of development relative to each jurisdiction.[8]

Consequently, it is essential that any alternative policy attempting to improve fairness in Argentina should include mechanisms that help equalize regional differences, in particular those related to decentralized social spending. An efficient tax-sharing system, with explicit goals and with adequate incentives, can make up for the deficiency present in subnational tax systems and thus finance the functions assigned to these governments.

In order to complete this introduction to Argentina's federalism, the role of local governments will be briefly mentioned. The National Constitution

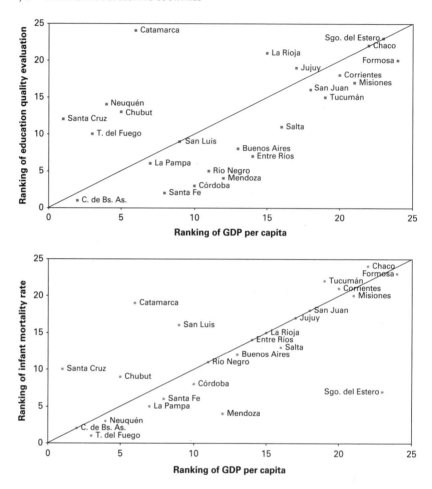

Figure 3.6   Regional Product and Schooling Quality and Infant Mortality Rate, by Ranking.

Source: Own elaboration on the basis of data from Ministerio de Educación, Ciencia y Técnica, Ministerio de Salud y Ambiente de la Nación and ECLAC, Buenos Aires Office.

defines for each province the elements of its own municipal regime. The provinces' constitutions and municipal organic laws set forth different areas of competence for municipalities—the goals and policies of the local governments deal mainly with basic urban services such as garbage collection and public lighting. With regard to taxes, only municipalities of certain provinces are authorized to collect them (see Table 3.2).

Table 3.2 Municipalities' Tax Powers

	Own Taxes as % of Revenues	Urban Real Estate	Rural Real Estate	Automobiles	Gross Income	Others
Buenos Aires	0.0					
Catamarca	0.9					X
Chaco	12.5	X	X	X		
Chubut	37.5	X	X	X	X	
Córdoba	5.5			X		
Corrientes	1.3					X
Entre Ríos	0.0					
Formosa	10.5	X		X		
Jujuy	4.5			X		
La Pampa	0.0					
La Rioja	0.0					
Mendoza	0.0					
Misiones	4.1					X
Neuquén	12.4			X		
Río Negro	0.0					
Salta	8.2	X		X		
San Juan	0.0					
San Luis	0.0					
Santa Cruz	18.8	X		X		
Santa Fe	0.0					
Stgo. del Estero	0.0					
Tierra del Fuego	18.5	X		X		
Tucumán	0.0					
Total	**1.5**					

THE LEVEL AND STRUCTURE OF TAXATION

A GLOBAL OVERVIEW OF THE TAX BURDEN 1932 AND 2004

An overview of the level of the tax burden since 1950 is presented in Figure 3.7, which shows that Argentina may be considered to have a medium to high tax revenue coefficient relative to those of other Latin American countries, especially until the early 1990s, when it first exceeded 20 percent of GDP. A global analysis of the evolution of Argentina's tax system cannot be performed without taking into consideration tax revenues from subnational governments, particularly at the province level,[9] which have represented approximately 3.5 percent of GDP and which have exhibited a trend of growth.

From a longer-term perspective, the federal tax revenue[10] remained below 10 percent of GDP until the mid-1940s, moving to a new level of 14 percent between 1950 and 1990 and increasing again thereafter (see Table 3.3).

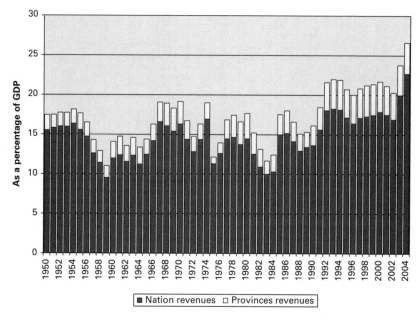

Figure 3.7   Level of Total Collection (Federal and Provincial Revenues Including Social Security Contributions), 1950–2004.

This is in contrast with the early expansion of government activities and the consolidation of the Argentine welfare state throughout the twentieth century. An important aspect that should therefore be pointed out is that such expansion of the state was not in line with a similar evolution in traditional tax collection. Throughout Argentina's history, customs revenues, taxes on fuels to finance road building and the construction of hydroelectric plants, the initial surplus of the pension system, the inflationary tax, the indebtedness, and privatization have been important sources of revenues that made the expansion of the public sector possible without the concurrent development of tax collection. In the past few years, extraordinary revenue sources gradually faded away, which made it even more important to take steps to strengthen traditional taxes. Export duties may be the last of this kind of resource and will be explained later in this chapter.

After a sharp reduction during the crisis in late 2001, tax revenue showed a strong expansion during 2003 and 2004 (Figure 3.8), owing to the economic policies adopted (and analyzed in more detail later on), especially owing to export duties and other regulations that impacted corporate income.

Some aspects regarding Argentina's tax structure should be highlighted (Table 3.3), especially the fluctuations in social security contributions, which peaked in the 1950s and the 1970s, after which they declined. These contributions went down from 30 percent of total income to a mere 15 percent of present-day income. This issue will be dealt with in a later section of this chapter.

We also can observe that the evolution of Argentina's income tax, unlike that of other Latin American countries, reached its heyday during the 1940s and 1950s, then virtually disappeared in the 1980s, after which it resumed an upward trend.

Table 3.3   Average Collection by Decades

	1932–1940	1941–1950	1951–1960	1961–1970	1971–1980	1981–1990	1991–2001	2002–2004
As a percentage of GDP								
Income, benefits, and capital gains	0.95	2.56	3.37	2.35	1.37	1.02	2.54	3.93
Assets	0.32	0.25	0.47	0.54	0.61	0.54	0.35	0.59
Taxes on goods and services	3.52	3.69	4.73	4.85	5.47	6.17	8.74	9.57
Taxes on international trade and transactions	3.27	1.03	0.44	1.77	1.83	1.73	0.92	2.71
Social security contributions	1.37	3.01	4.86	4.20	4.51	2.94	4.31	2.90
Others	0.00	0.06	0.12	0.15	0.17	0.40	0.49	0.15
Federal gross tax revenues	**9.43**	**10.60**	**14.01**	**13.86**	**13.97**	**12.80**	**17.36**	**19.86**
As a percentage of the total								
Income, benefits, and capital gains	10.0	24.2	24.1	17.0	9.8	8.0	14.6	19.8
Assets	3.4	2.3	3.4	3.9	4.4	4.2	2.0	3.0
Taxes on goods and services	37.3	34.9	33.8	35.0	39.2	48.2	50.4	48.2
Taxes on international trade and transactions	34.7	9.7	3.2	12.7	13.1	13.5	5.3	13.6
Social security contributions	14.5	28.4	34.7	30.3	32.3	23.0	24.8	14.6
Others	0.0	0.5	0.9	1.1	1.2	3.1	2.9	0.7
Federal gross tax revenues	**100.0**	**100.0**	**100.0**	**100.0**	**100.0**	**100.0**	**100.0**	**100.0**

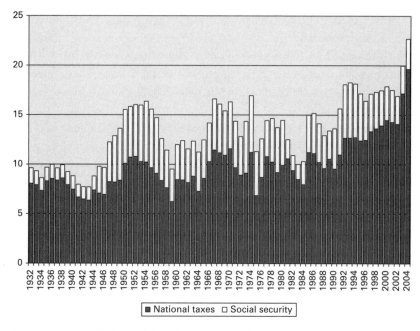

**Figure 3.8   Level of Federal Collection (Federal Taxes and Social Security),
1932–2004 (as a Percentage of GDP).**

THE CURRENCY BOARD PERIOD 1991–2001: AN ENDLESS
PROCESS OF TAX REFORMS

During the period of the convertibility regime (1991–2001) the federal government's tax revenue reached around 17 percent of GDP (on average), and the consolidated tax burden—including provinces and municipalities—reached an average of 21 percent, with a decrease after the tequila crisis (1995). Tax revenue subsequently increased to 21 percent of GDP, however, highlighting the fact that collection is very sensitive to macroeconomic shocks.

Since the beginning of this period, tax collection has shown a substantial change. Initially, the convertibility plan coexisted with the tax structure, resulting from the reforms performed during the hyperinflation years (1989 and 1990), which benefited from the sharp drop in the inflation rate. In subsequent years, economic authorities began introducing constant reforms in the tax system.[11]

In the 1990s, the tax structure was characterized by its deep initial concentration. In 1993, the first main taxes (VAT, income, and contributions to the social security system) represented between 7 and 80 percent of the total tax revenues. Of this total amount, VAT represented 40 percent. The most important measures taken in the first years of the 1990s were the broadening of the VAT base (more widespread than in 1980); lowering income tax rates; abolishing taxes on exports; reforming the tax on fuels accompanying the deregulation of the sector (which led to the gradual simplification of the system of specific allocation funds), and abolishing minor taxes.

As the reforms progressed, the government became more pragmatic. While maintaining the basic orientation, it ruled out the proposal of reducing tax rates inspired by the Laffer effect and, on several occasions, increased the rates of VAT and the income tax shared with the most important provinces. As a result, federal tax revenues grew by 64 percent between 1991 and 1992—VAT collection grew by 160 percent while the income tax quadrupled, encouraging the concentration mentioned earlier.

In addition, tax reform was sustained by a strengthening program that included information generated by a sales-invoicing system, new penalty provisions, and a broad withholding-at-source system that facilitated the collection of the two taxes previously mentioned. The concentration of collection in these taxes made revenues highly sensitive to the evolution of macroeconomic variables. This sensitivity was costly after 1995, when the domestic economy suffered from the unfavorable external shock that followed Mexico's devaluation.

After mid-1994, a new phase of public accounts started. In the third quarter of 1994, the first negative fiscal results were observed, which coincided with pension reform (detailed later in this chapter) and which occurred months before the drop in traditional tax revenues that was due to the recession.

The federal government was forced to take emergency measures, which in some cases meant reviewing actions previously undertaken. Such measures included an increase in VAT rates (from 18 to 21 percent), the partial review of the initial decrease in payroll taxes paid by employers, an increase in import fees, a reduction of reimbursements for exports and the subsidy on capital assets, and a broadening of the income and personal assets tax base. Despite these measures and the gradual recovery of the economic activity level, which began during the second half of 1996, the public sector continued to show imbalances. The persistence of the deficit led to additional measures applied mainly to revenues. These measures included an increase in taxes on fuel and the resumption of the tax on diesel fuel. The additional revenues resulting from these reforms were then applied to the social security system. The 1998 tax reform was aimed at strengthening tax revenues. To achieve this goal, the government broadened the VAT base and created taxes on minimum presumed income, on paid interest and on the cost of corporate indebtedness, on automobiles, motorcycles, ships, and planes (destined to increase teachers' salaries), and the *Monotributo* (a tax paid by the self-employed). Through this reform, the government could increase tax revenues by an amount closer to 1 percent of GDP. Although some of the adopted measures have significant importance in enhancing taxation (as the broadening of VAT base), others, on the contrary, have to be discounted sooner or later as they imply an increase in the investment cost for enterprises (tax on paid interest, for example). In addition, the tax on minimum presumed income and the *Monotributo* have remained in the tax system; their pertinence is highly debatable.

Thus, the initial attempt to create a tax system that concentrated on only a few taxes had to be reversed in order to deal with the fiscal crisis. By late 1999, the newly inaugurated government passed a tax package that included several reforms of VAT, which broadened the VAT base and abolished certain exemptions. In addition, the use of differential rates was extended, levying 10.5 percent on several services. The evolution of this tax during the 1990s shows that once the positive effect in the first years of the decade—coinciding with the launching of the convertibility plan—had passed, the subsequent, significant increases in tax rates and bases only managed to maintain the level of collection.

In 2000, the government reformed the income tax, broadening the tax base through reduction of the nontaxable minimum income, tax deductions for family benefits, and special deductions. An emergency tax on high income was created, and tax rates on personal assets exceeding $200,000 were increased. In addition, some internal tax rates were increased. These reforms generated additional tax revenues of around 1.8 percent of GDP.

In May 2001, the government introduced new tax reforms whose goals were not quite clear. On the one hand, the government created a tax on debits and credits in current accounts; it simultaneously launched competitiveness plans. These plans were based on agreements signed by chambers of commerce, the federal government, and provincial governments, through which some productive activities were aided in order to stimulate the economy, but which reduced collection at a faster pace than the drop in consumption. In addition to such plans, the tax paid by sectors producing capital assets was reduced by half, and the export regime was applied to all the producers of such assets in respect to the VAT tax credit.[12]

In sum, regardless of the Argentine government's initial intention to simplify the tax system, subsequent fiscal emergency situations forced the government to enact several reforms that resulted in a heterogeneous and highly complex tax system, which also affected the distribution of the funds. Both pension reform and the troubled financial relations between the nation and the provinces are two central factors in this story.

COMING OUT OF THE CRISIS, 2002–2004

Beginning in 2002 and continuing to the present day, as a consequence of the measures adopted due to the economic "crisis" following the government's recognition of financial insolvency, the Argentine government adopted several tax measures that strongly impacted tax collection. These measures moved tax collection from the characteristic 20–22 percent of GDP in the 1990s to 26.5 percent in 2004.

A significant part of this increase is due to the introduction of export duties that generated almost 2.5 percent of GDP. This emergency tax responds to the federal government's need to address the peso's extraordinary devaluation that occurred after the crisis.

The strong increase in VAT and the broadening of the financial debit and credit tax base and its rate rise also exerted some influence on the increase of tax revenue as a percentage of GDP; other influential measures included a strong increase in the corporate income revenue of around 2 percentage points of GDP. Corporate tax revenue was up by close to 70 percent relative to the pre-crisis period, partly because the government refused to apply regulations regarding balance adjustments, as a result of inflation in 2002, and partly because of the higher income of oil companies, as a result of an increase in oil prices.

We can therefore see that the increase in the tax burden is sustained by single-occurrence impacts on permanent taxes (corporate income) or by increases that arise from temporary taxes (export duties and banking debits). This reinforces the thesis that the volatility of the tax system increases in response to changes in macroeconomic circumstances.

Nevertheless, since mid-2003, this increase in revenue has been sustained, perhaps as a result of the greater efforts made to improve the efficiency of tax administration that accompanied the economic recovery.

This long-term analysis allows us to find the structural roots of Argentina's financing problem, from which we infer that the structural imbalances observed from a long-term perspective have not been covered by an adequate tax structure, even with constant and stable revenues over the course of time (Table 3.3).

MAIN FEATURES OF THE PRESENT SITUATION

Before embarking on an analysis of the specific challenges that face Argentina's tax system, we turn to a discussion of eight stylized factors that characterized the evolution of the country's tax structure throughout history.

SUSTAINED GROWTH OF CONSUMERS' TAXES

Until the 1950s, consumer goods taxes were not highly significant; in time, however, they increased to total approximately 2 to 2.5 percent of GDP in the late 1980s and subsequently increased to a new level, crossing the 6 percent threshold in 1993. See Figure 3.9, as well as Table 3.4.

Thus, it is clear that the government, when faced with a constant lack of resources, systematically resorted to indirect taxation to improve the

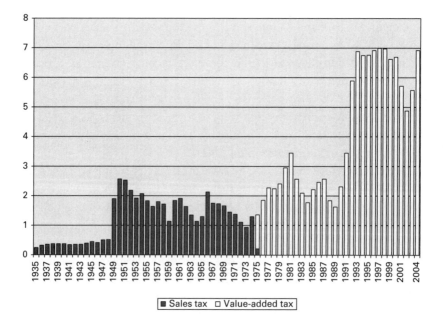

Figure 3.9   Sales Tax and VAT, 1935–2004 (as a Percentage of GDP).

Table 3.4   VAT Productivity,[1] 1991–2004

	1991	1994	1997	2001	2002	2003	2004[3]
Revenue (as % of GDP)	3.75	6.75	6.99	5.71	4.88	5.57	6.92
Tax rate[2] (%)	16.00	18.00	21.00	21.00	21.00	21.00	21.00
Productivity	0.235	0.375	0.333	0.272	0.232	0.265	0.330

Source: Based on data from Dirección Nacional de Investigaciones y Analisis Fiscal (Ministry of Economy).

1. Productivity is defined as the ratio of VAT revenues to GDP divided by the standard rate (expressed as a percentage). This coefficient, also called "efficiency rate," has been used as a summary indicator of the performance of the VAT.
2. From 11/1/90 to 2/20/91 the tax rate was 15.6 percent; from 2/21/91 to 2/29/92 it was 16 percent; from 3/1/92 to 3/31/95 it was 18 percent; from 4/1/95 to 11/17/02 it was 21 percent; from 11/18/02 to 1/17/03 it was 19 percent; and from 1/18/03 it was 21 percent.
3. Provisional data.

level of tax revenues. In this context, we should highlight the behavior of VAT, which, although implemented in 1975, only experienced a dramatic increase in revenues as of 1992.

Following the beginning of 1990, the evolution of VAT rates was dominated by an overall rate, which at that time reached a minimum level of 13 percent, which was around the level established in the first months following implementation of the VAT. In the last few years, the dominant trend in designing the VAT has been toward increasing both its base and rates, allowing revenues to increase significantly, both in absolute terms and in relation to other taxes. After reaching 13 percent in February 1990, the tax rate rose to its current 21 percent level in 1997.

As for the tax base, a new reform eliminated almost every tax exemption on goods, with the exception of books, magazines, newspapers, bread, milk, and medicine. The VAT was also extended to services performed by banks and other financial institutions,[13] insurance, private health insurance plans, artistic, cultural, sporting and cinematographic events, and personal services related to these events, and transportation of people and freights. Services provided by the state, provinces, municipalities, educational entities, as well as by public health insurance plans and stock exchanges, were excluded.

In recent years, due to a combination of base-broadening and increased tax rates, revenues reached levels close to 7 percent of GDP. In addition, we must mention the relevance of the turnover taxes applied by provincial governments, which are identified as "Tax on Gross Sales" and are applied to each stage of the production process, with the exception of agriculture and cattle breeding.

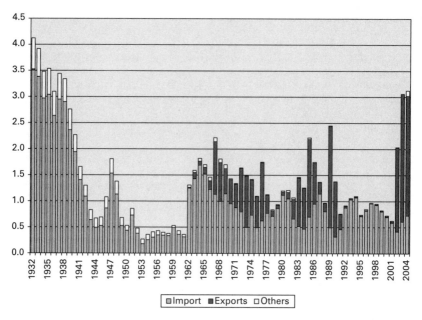

Figure 3.10   Foreign Trade Taxes, 1932–2004 (as a Percentage of GDP).

GRADUAL LOSS OF RESOURCES FROM IMPORT DUTIES

The gradual loss of resources from import duties since the mid-1940s became accentuated during the 1950s and, subsequently with the trade expansion, was promoted by the convertibility period. This general pattern
first occurred in Argentina before emerging in several other countries of
the region (Figure 3.10).

INTERMITTENT BUT SIGNIFICANT PRESENCE
OF EXPORT TAXES

Throughout Argentine history, revenues resulting primarily from the export of agricultural goods have contributed substantially to the financing
of the state. In the days following the 2001 crisis, this took the shape of
export duties charged by customs, similarly to other historic periods when
the rate of exchange was extraordinarily devalued to meet the foreign crisis, as was observed in Figure 3.10. In other periods of history, the Central
Bank generated these resources through the introduction of multiple exchange rates.

This emergency tax has two additional advantages: first, it reduces the impact of devaluation on the domestic price of commodities, many of which make up a substantial part of the mass consumer basket. This results in the improvement in real wages. Second, because these revenues are, in accordance with the Constitution, not shared with the provinces, they bring quick relief to the central government's accounts.

POOR PERFORMANCE OF INCOME TAXATION

Despite possessing an expanded middle class, a high level of urban concentration, a reasonable level of income per capita, and a Gini coefficient below 0.4, Argentina has never managed to develop an income tax that generates much revenue (Figure 3.11). Although the tax had some relevance between 1945 and 1955, after that it lost its relative share in the tax structure. Only after the 1990s did the tax begin to recover its previous standing. We should note that a substantial portion of its growth was due to privatized companies.

Considering it is a common characteristic in the whole region, the weight of the income tax burden has rested primarily on the strong

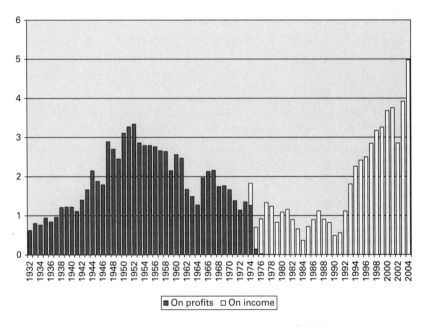

On profits On income

Figure 3.11   Income Tax, 1932–2004 (as a Percentage of GDP).

contribution of the corporate income tax; as regards the personal income tax, most of its revenue comes from wages. Income from financial activities (dividends, interest, and others) has scarce contribution to the total personal income tax. Table 3.5 describes this phenomenon and shows the weakness of the system in achieving its goals with regard to income distribution, since the state can do little with a personal income tax that has no incidence on nonwage income.

IRRELEVANCE OF THE WEALTH TAXES

As in most countries in the region, taxes at the federal level levied on personal assets have not had much importance in Argentina, though to judge their impact, we must also consider the role played by provinces and municipalities in this respect. Property taxes or taxes on the holding of real estate account for 25 to 30 percent of revenues at the lower levels of government, demonstrating that the weight of these provincial taxes on personal assets is close to 1.5 percent of GDP. See Table 3.6.

LOSS OF IMPORTANCE OF PAYROLL TAXES

After an important increase in payroll tax revenue from the 1930s to the mid-1980s, it began to decrease, partly due to the growth of the informal employment market and the structural reform to the pension system that introduced individually capitalized accounts in 1994. This point is explored in more detail later in the chapter.

Nonetheless, this factor of production should be examined because not only is it taxed by social security contributions, but also the main weight of the tax on personal income is levied almost exclusively on salaries. See Table 3.7.

USE OF EMERGENCY OR EXTRAORDINARY TAXES

The structural weakness of traditional taxes in obtaining sufficient revenues to ensure fiscal solvency has resulted in the search for emergency or extraordinary revenues by means of nontraditional sources. These supplementary taxes, such as taxes on corporate assets and financial transactions, have been an important source of financing for Argentina's public sector at various times in history. As explained earlier, many countries in

Table 3.5 Personal and Corporate Income Tax, 1992–2004

Tax Revenues[1]	1992	1993	1994	1995	1996	1997	1998	1999	2000	2001	2002	2003	2004[2]
As a percentage of GDP													
Taxes on income, profits, and capital gains	1.61	2.03	2.44	2.51	2.57	2.90	3.21	3.56	3.98	3.99	3.04	4.30	5.26
Individuals	0.33	0.57	0.75	0.79	0.98	0.92	0.99	1.08	1.39	1.38	1.13	1.33	1.38
Corporations and other enterprises	1.21	1.35	1.56	1.58	1.49	1.78	2.00	2.18	2.31	2.32	1.56	2.64	3.64
Others unidentifiable	0.07	0.11	0.13	0.14	0.10	0.20	0.23	0.30	0.28	0.29	0.35	0.33	0.24
As a percentage of total taxes on income, profits, and capital gains													
Taxes on income, profits, and capital gains	100.0	100.0	100.0	100.0	100.0	100.0	100.0	100.0	100.0	100.0	100.0	100.0	100.0
Individuals	20.3	28.2	30.6	31.4	38.1	31.9	30.8	30.3	34.8	34.5	37.2	30.9	26.2
Corporations and other enterprises	75.3	66.5	64.0	63.0	58.2	61.3	62.1	61.3	58.2	58.2	51.4	61.4	69.2
Others unidentifiable	4.4	5.3	5.4	5.6	3.7	6.9	7.0	8.4	7.0	7.2	11.4	7.7	4.6
As a percentage of total gross tax revenues													
Taxes on income, profits, and capital gains	7.5	9.2	11.1	12.1	12.8	13.9	15.2	16.6	18.3	18.9	15.0	18.1	19.8
Individuals	1.5	2.6	3.4	3.8	4.9	4.4	4.7	5.0	6.4	6.5	5.6	5.6	5.2
Corporations and other enterprises	5.6	6.1	7.1	7.6	7.5	8.5	9.4	10.2	10.7	11.0	7.7	11.1	13.7
Others unidentifiable	0.3	0.5	0.6	0.7	0.5	1.0	1.1	1.4	1.3	1.4	1.7	1.4	0.9

Source: Based on data from Dirección Nacional de Investigaciones y Analisis Fiscal (Ministry of Economy).

1. Based on IMF-Government Finance Statistics Manual classification.
2. Provisional data.

Table 3.6   Provincial Taxation, 1990–2004 *(as a percentage of GDP)*

Year	Gross Income Tax	Real Estate Tax	Automobiles Tax	Stamp Tax	Others	Total
1990	1.32	0.64	0.21	0.25	0.07	**2.48**
1991	1.51	0.66	0.29	0.31	0.06	**2.82**
1992	1.95	0.66	0.31	0.37	0.24	**3.54**
1993	2.12	0.63	0.31	0.40	0.25	**3.72**
1994	2.14	0.64	0.33	0.40	0.26	**3.76**
1995	2.02	0.61	0.31	0.35	0.26	**3.55**
1996	2.02	0.60	0.30	0.35	0.33	**3.60**
1997	2.05	0.62	0.32	0.32	0.41	**3.72**
1998	2.19	0.63	0.33	0.33	0.42	**3.90**
1999	2.20	0.63	0.32	0.32	0.43	**3.90**
2000	2.15	0.64	0.29	0.28	0.46	**3.82**
2001	2.08	0.61	0.29	0.28	0.37	**3.64**
2002	1.97	0.53	0.21	0.23	0.46	**3.39**
2003	2.35	0.58	0.23	0.27	0.37	**3.81**
2004	2.58	0.59	0.23	0.29	0.35	**4.04**

Source: Based on data from Dirección Nacional de Investigaciones y Analisis Fiscal con las Provincias (Ministry of Economy).

Table 3.7   Taxes on Wage and Salaries, 1992–2004

	1992		1996		2000		2004	
Tax Revenues	% of GDP	% of total	% of GDP	% of total	% of GDP	% of total	% of GDP	% of total
Total taxes on wage and salaries	5.72	100.00	4.93	100.00	4.79	100.00	4.42	100.00
Personal income tax	0.33	5.71	0.98	19.85	1.39	28.93	1.38	31.18
Social security contributions	5.39	94.29	3.95	80.15	3.40	71.07	3.04	68.82

Latin America share this use of supplementary taxes. This issue is also treated in more detail in a later section.

SIGNIFICANT TAX EXPENDITURES

Another characteristic of the Argentine tax system is its lack of transparency in providing promotional tax measures. The amount of benefits granted, which are significant in terms of the country's tax burden, and the methods employed—which include the approval of private sector projects, the application of tax deferrals, and the inclusion of VAT among the various tax measures implemented—have made the system highly vulnerable to evasion and corruption. Moreover, while determining the tax impact of the different systems employed is a complex task, it is even more difficult to identify the effects that arise from those regimes, since they have never been subject to careful scrutiny and evaluation.

THE SIX MAIN CHALLENGES OF ARGENTINA'S TAX SYSTEM

Future Argentine tax discussions must resolve six challenges. To ensure long-term solvency, the government must undertake the following:

a. Providing an adequate response to problems related to financing the social security system

b. Replacing emergency taxes on corporate assets and taxes on financial operations

c. Substituting export taxes

d. Reducing tax expenditures

e. Strengthening the fairness and equity of the tax system

f. Improving the tax administration

PROVIDING AN ADEQUATE RESPONSE TO PROBLEMS RELATED TO FINANCING THE SOCIAL SECURITY SYSTEM

Argentina was one of the first Latin American countries to develop a contribution-based social security system that was financed by payroll taxes. The system consists of retirement contributions, unemployment insurance, family subsidies, and health plans for active and retired employees and their families. Until 1984, when a major tax reform was introduced, total charges against salaries for social security financing (including employer contributions and employee deductions) accounted for up to 50 percent of the gross salary.

It is impossible to understand the dynamics and magnitude of the Argentine fiscal crisis in the last quarter century without making a careful analysis of the retirement crisis.[14] We must emphasize the importance of tax resources reassigned to financing the retirement system, due to insufficient revenues collected from specific charges and, at the same time, to the impact of these allowances on subnational finances and the conflict between the state and the provinces.

Several tax assignments for the financing of retirement pensions were introduced to improve the sector's financial situation. During the 1990s, a significant portion of tax revenues was assigned to finance the retirement system, substantially affecting tax co-participation. In Figure 3.12, we see the evolution of retirement contributions as of 1987, when they were financed entirely by payroll contributions and deductions. We observe both an important increase in retirement expenses during the first years of the decade and a significant loss experienced by taxes against salaries for financing retirement payments.

In the last years of the convertibility program, almost 70 percent of social security expenditures were financed by taxes other than payroll taxes. The gap between revenues from the taxes intended to finance the social security system and the expenditures of the system was one of the primary causes of the solvency problem of the public sector. To clarify this point, Table 3.8 shows a decomposition of the deficit of the social security system into several sources. It can be seen that the transfer of funds (employee contributions) to the new capitalization scheme and a reduction in employer contributions together account for close to 3 percent of the GDP deficit.

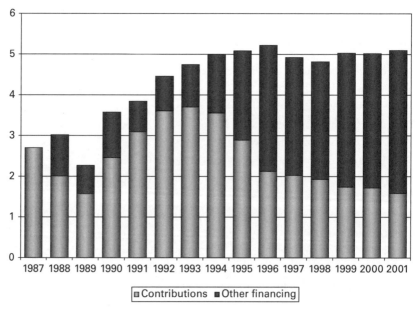

Figure 3.12   Retirement Payments and Their Financing (as a Percentage of GDP).

Table 3.8 Determining Factors of the Pension System Deficit, 2000

	Billion $	% of Total	% of GDP
Pension system deficit	9.4	100.0	3.30
Capitalization system	4.3	45.9	1.52
Reduction in			
contributions	3.8	40.6	1.34
Other reasons	1.3	13.5	0.44

Source: Cetrángolo and Grushka (2005).

The future configuration of the retirement system and its impact on public accounts has yet to be defined—in particular, the real level of public sector benefits and the future coverage of the senior population. At the time of the system reform, it was officially expected that coverage would increase. Instead, coverage dropped from 39 percent in October 1994 (measured by the percentage of contributors to the system against employment) to 36 percent in May 2000. Consequently, coming up with alternative sources of financing has become imperative.

REPLACING EMERGENCY TAXES ON CORPORATE ASSETS AND TAXES ON FINANCIAL OPERATIONS

An aspect particular to Argentina's tax system, which also reflects a more general trend observed in many countries in the region, is the use of extraordinary taxes in emergency situations. The structural difficulties faced by Argentina's tax situation—highlighted by both the lack of sufficient revenues for financing expenditures and the unsatisfactory development of tax on income, as well as the difficulties in improving efficiency—has led different administrations to resort to applying extraordinary or emergency taxes, such as the tax on corporate assets and the tax on financial transactions.

Emergency Taxes on Corporate Assets

Argentina's attempts to increase the collection of corporate income tax have resulted in extensive legal and administrative difficulties. As a result, Argentina and several other countries in the region have implemented alternative determination methods that, in some cases, will substitute or complement the assessment of the corporate tax base, with the purpose of improving revenues.

In certain instances, these alternative methods have been based on the application of a minimum tax based on assets or, more recently, on gross sales.[15] As a result, a larger fraction of economic activity is subject to the corporate tax, with the individual tax applying almost exclusively to revenue from personal work at a company.

Although in most cases a rate of around 1 percent on the value of gross assets has been used (see Table 3.9), more recently the use of the value of sales or gross income as a substitute base has been favored, which has given rise to even more discriminatory treatments than the tax itself created.

The application of these taxes is the undeniable result of the limitations Argentina has faced in enforcing the corporate tax. These minimum taxes have largely replaced the corporate tax, making allocation problems and efficiency worse.

On the other hand, strengthening the income tax would require the ability to broaden the base of such a tax by eliminating exemptions and discriminatory treatment benefiting certain individuals and/or sectors of activity and by creating an improved tax administration.

Taxes on Financial Operations

Argentina was one of the first countries to implement a tax on "banking debits," doing so in 1983 and again in 2001; other countries in the region (Peru, Brazil, Venezuela, Colombia, and Ecuador) followed shortly thereafter.[16] Table 3.10 shows the evolution of the rates applied in these countries. It should also be mentioned that in some cases, such taxes were applied to both debits and credits, which explains why the collection of this type of tax varies between 0.3 percent of GDP for Argentina in 1990 or 1992 and 3.5 percent for Ecuador in 1999.

These taxes have essentially been used as an easy source of revenue, transferring the collection responsibility from the government to financial institutions, so that fiscal administrators play a minor role in its collection. Although such taxes were introduced with the specific purpose of improving revenues in the short term and had an emergency nature, their success in generating revenue has resulted in their continued use.

As pointed out by Coelho, Ebrill, and Summers,[17] however, the market response shows that there are adverse effects, including a significant degree of financial disintermediation. In the case of Argentina, for example, the tax administration found that some large companies were using armored trucks to make payments of large amounts of money in

Table 3.9 Tax on Net Worth, Assets, and Gross Income *(in percentage points)*

	1986	1992	1997	2000	2001	2004
Argentina	1.5 on net wealth	2.0 on gross assets	1.0 on assets	1.0 on assets	1.0 on assets	1.0 on assets
Brazil	–	–	–	–	–	–
Chile	–	–	–	–	–	–
Colombia	8.0 on net wealth	7.0 on net wealth	5.0 on net wealth or 1.5 on gross wealth	5.0 on net wealth	5.0 on net wealth	5.0 on net wealth
Costa Rica	0.36–1.17 on fixed assets	0.36–1.17 on fixed assets	1.0 on assets	1.0 on assets	1.0 on assets	Rebated
Dominican Rep.	–	–	–	–	n/a	1.0 on assets
Ecuador	0.15 on assets	0.15 on net wealth	0.15 on net wealth	0.15 on net wealth	–	–
El Salvador	0.1–1.4 on net wealth	0.9–2.0 on assets	–	–	–	–
Guatemala	0.3–0.8 on unmovable wealth	0.3–0.9 on unmovable wealth	0.2–0.9 on unmovable wealth	1.5 on assets	0.2–0.9 on unmovable wealth and 3.5 on assets	Rebated and substituted by a 5% on gross incomes in place of the corporate income tax.
Honduras	–	–	–	0.75 on assets	0.25 on assets	1.0 on assets
Mexico	–	2.0 on gross assets	1.8 on assets	1.8 on assets	1.8 on assets	1.8 on assets
Nicaragua	1.0 on unmovable wealth	1.5–2.5 on net wealth	1.0 on unmovable wealth	1.0 on unmovable wealth	1.0 on unmovable wealth	1.0 on assets
Panama	1.0 on net wealth	1.0 on net wealth	1.0 on net wealth	1.0 on net wealth	1.0 on net wealth	2.0 on net wealth
Paraguay	1.0 on unmovable wealth	1.0 on unmovable wealth	1.0 on unmovable wealth	1.0 on unmovable wealth	–	–
Peru	1.0–2.5 on net wealth	2.0 on net wealth	0.5 on net wealth	–	–	–
Uruguay	2.8 on net wealth	2.0 on net wealth	1.5–3.5 on net wealth	1.5–3.5 on net wealth	–	–
Venezuela	–	–	–	1.0 on assets	–	–

Source: Gómez Sabaini (2005).

Note: (n/a) Not available.

cash in order to avoid paying this tax. The information presented in Table 3.10 refers to the different collection productivities in those countries that applied such a tax. In this sense, Brazil, Colombia, and Ecuador have managed to obtain substantially higher results than those obtained by Argentina (although in 2001 collection productivity improved), Peru, and Venezuela.

Table 3.10 Debit and Credit Operations Taxes

Country/Year	Rate	Revenue[1]	Productivity[2]
Argentina			
1989	0.70	0.66	0.94
1990	0.30	0.30	0.99
1991	1.05[3]	0.91	0.86
1992	0.60[3]	0.29	0.97[4]
2001	0.60[5]	1.46[4]	2.43
Brazil			
1994	0.25	1.06	4.24
1997	0.20	0.80	4.00
1998	0.20	0.90	4.50
1999	0.22[3]	0.83	3.79
2000	0.34[3]	1.33	3.96
2001	0.36[3]	1.45	3.97
Colombia			
1999	0.20	0.73	3.66
2000	0.20	0.60	3.00
2001	0.30	0.76	2.53
Ecuador			
1999	1.00	3.50[6]	3.50
2000	0.80	2.33[6]	2.91
Peru			
1990	1.41[3]	0.59	0.42
1991	0.81[3]	0.46	0.57
Venezuela			
1994	0.75	1.30	2.60[4]
1999–2000	0.50	1.12	2.24
2002	0.75	1.07	1.43

Source: Kirilenko and Summers, in *Taxation of Financial Intermediation: Theory and Practice for Emerging Economies*, edited by Patrick Honohan. World Bank, June 2003.

1. In percentage of GDP.
2. Tax revenues in percentage of GDP divided by average legal tax rate.
3. Average of rates adjusted by the time that each rate was valid.
4. Adjusted by the time that each rate was valid.
5. On each side of a transaction. Total rate is 1.2 percent.
6. The tax applied to debits and credits.

There are several reasons for this behavior. First, the productivity ratio seems to be in inverse proportion with the rate. Second, revenue will be lower when there are close substitutes abroad for domestic banks, as in the case of Uruguay for the Argentine financial market. Tax avoidance is also more difficult when the use of bank checks as a form of payment is more entrenched, as in Brazil.

Although this tax has not proved to be very effective as a revenue source, at present, tax authorities consider it an efficient way to capture useful information to control other taxes. Essentially, this tax is a selective tax applied to a specific activity—the use of the bank checks—though in Argentina, it has come to include not only bank debits but also credits with the financial system. This characteristic affects the productivity of the tax since in an operation of transfers among accounts, one transaction is being taxed twice, which increases collection.

Experience has shown that as the tax is maintained in the short term, its rate is low, and there is a low elasticity in the use of the check, attempts to avoid such a tax are expected to be few and far between. If there is a perception that such a tax will become permanent and rates will be increased, however, the economic "damage" will be significant and the number of transactions performed in cash will increase. In turn, this has led governments to adopt measures to counteract these deviations, such as the limitation of banking endorsements, by establishing maximum amounts for the operations of recorded assets and other measures that finally affect the efficiency of the economy.

SUBSTITUTING EXPORT TAXES

Argentina has often used export taxes to soften the domestic impact of currency devaluations on the price of goods and salaries or to prevent the export sectors from reaping extraordinary benefits. During some periods, these resources were not considered taxes, but were the result of introducing multiple foreign exchange schemes that generated quasi-fiscal income in the hands of the Central Bank.

Although these measures represented considerable fiscal income (see Figure 3.10), they have never generated the massive fiscal revenues such as those revenues collected following the 2002 currency devaluation, which increased the rate of exchange from one to three with respect to the U.S. dollar.

The elimination of this extraordinary source of revenue, which amounted to almost 3 percent of GDP, poses a serious challenge for the next few years and will also impact provincial finances. While export duties are only collected by the state treasury, all other taxes are subject to a co-participation system and thus affect both the national and provincial spheres.

REDUCING TAX EXPENDITURES

It is evident that tax expenditures in force modify tax fairness and equity. They create regional or sector "fiscal paradises"; they arbitrarily transfer the tax burden from one group of economic agents to others (who are not necessarily in a better position); they undermine the ability of some non-promoted provinces to obtain financing; and they open the door to tax evasion and fiscal fraud, all of which complicate tax administration.

Notwithstanding this group of provisos, Argentina has made substantial use of tax policy, granting some economic sectors (automotive, paper, aluminum, and steel industries) and other regional advantages to certain areas of the country, often on the basis of geopolitical or social factors (the provinces of La Rioja, Catamarca, San Luis, San Juan, and Tierra del Fuego, among others).

Unlike promotion systems granted by developed countries (Table 3.11), Argentina's policies have been based on the VAT, shifting the neutrality of the tax and opening opportunities for fiscal fraud, which has been substantial in recent times. Originally, the system of granting tax benefits was established on the basis of the approval of specific projects, instead of utilizing automatic mechanisms, which has encouraged administrative corruption and weakened the transparency of the system. Similarly, within the provincial systems, local authorities responsible for the application of these projects have often been the very same provincial entities that gain from the tax incentives. In fact, they converted them into a method for transferring revenues that accounts for one of the more complex aspects of the Argentine federal regime.

From the aforementioned, we can conclude that the fiscal cost of promotion (in terms of decreased potential revenues) is merely one of the problems the tax system generates and is not the most significant one. Noncompliance, fiscal fraud, modifications to economic neutrality, and the negative impact on the relative price of factors (effectively lowering the relative cost of capital) constitute economic effects that have not been

Table 3.11   FDI Incentives in Developing Countries and Members of the OECD

FDI Incentive	% OECD Countries	% Developing Countries
Capital goods import duties exempted	5	56
Tax exemption/holiday	20	55
Investment/reinvestment allowance	30	49
Lower tax rate	5	45
VAT exemption for capital goods	0	34
Accelerated depreciation	30	30
Raw material import duties exempted	5	30
VAT exemption for raw materials	5	24
Duty drawback	5	24
Export income treated preferentially	0	20
Loss write-off	0	18
Reduction in local, municipal taxes/duties	30	18
VAT exemption on exported inputs	10	18
Subsidized loans	45	18

Source: Goodspeed (2004).

quantified but are, in the long run, much more important than the loss in fiscal revenues.

We therefore consider it necessary to sanction, in an especially vigorous way, all detected noncompliance and, at the same time, avoid new investments through dossiers that belong to old projects whose benefits have supposedly lapsed. In order to achieve this, substantial changes should be made, such as establishing the Argentine Ministry of Economy as the regulatory authority for the entire promotion system regarding all matters related to taxation. Through the tax collection agency (the Federal Agency for Public Income—AFIP), the Ministry should exercise the primary faculty of establishing information criteria, performing inspections and controls according to estimates, initiating legal proceedings, and sanctioning noncompliance. At the same time, the Ministry must reorganize the administrative entity and establish a department specializing in the control of promoted companies nationwide. It is fundamental to ensure that tax administrators have appropriate incentives because the control of promoted activities, though not conducive to immediate fiscal revenues, is the only way to ensure that these benefits produce the desired effects and do not simply become tax evasion pockets.

With regard to tax deferrals, required warranties should be adopted to ensure future payments. Such an undertaking demands the dedication of a great number of people and substantial resources. Thus, an alternative to

Table 3.12   Tax Expenditures in Selected Latin American Countries

Countries	Year	Total Tax Revenue (A) (% of GDP)	Tax Expenditures (B) Total (% of GDP)	Direct Taxes (% of total)	Indirect Taxes (% of total)	(B)/(A) (%)
Latin America						
Argentina[2]	2001	17.3	3.0	36.1	63.9	17.5
	2003	19.6	2.5	32.7	67.3	12.8
	2004	22.6	2.4	27.4	72.6	10.5
	2005[4]	22.4	2.6	28.6	71.4	11.4
Brazil[2,3]	2001[1]	13.5	1.5	66.7	16.7	11.1
	2002	15.3	1.8	65.2	34.8	11.6
	2003	16.0	1.7	65.3	34.7	10.6
	2004	16.5	1.4	68.6	31.4	8.5
Chile	1998	17.8	4.2	73.8	26.2	23.6
	2002	18.1	4.2	74.0	26.0	23.2
	2005[4]	17.8	4.2	79.0	21.0	23.6
Colombia	1998	14.4	7.4	35.0	65.0	51.4
	1999	14.2	9.2			64.8
Ecuador	2000	11.6	4.9	47.0	53.0	42.1
Guatemala	2000	9.7	7.3	28.0	72.0	75.2
Mexico[2]	2002	13.2	5.3	51.0	49.0	40.2
	2003	12.6	6.3			50.0
	2005[4]	10.9	6.7			61.5
Peru	2003	14.7	2.5	34.0	66.0	17.0
Uruguay	1999[1]	24.1	6.6	20.0	76.0	27.4
	2000	23.6	5.3	11.0	89.0	22.3
OECD						
Australia[2]	1999–2002	24.2	4.3			17.8
Canada[2]	1999–2002	17.6	7.9			44.9
Netherlands	2002	39.2	2.4			6.1
USA[2]	2001–2004	18.5	7.5			40.5

Source: Gómez Sabaini (2005). "Evolución y situación tributaria actual en América Latina: Una serie de temas para la discusión."

1. The sum is less than 100 percent because there are tax expenditures included as other taxes.
2. Does not include tax expenditures other than federal government.
3. Direct taxes include the Income Tax, CSLL, and CFSS.
4. Forecasted.

the granting of tax deferrals should be found—a more transparent means that will not hinder administrative actions.

Beyond these general considerations, an in-depth, detailed analysis of the existing situation should be made because the matter is administratively complex. In addition, a series of anomalous situations have appeared and continue to appear in this field (such as the granting of benefits by decree, the "substitution" of beneficiaries and objectives in the approved contracts, the "renegotiation" of benefits originally granted, and a long series of political, regulatory, and administrative anomalies that justify evaluation and an in-depth audit).

Some countries in the region have begun to include an official estimate of so-called tax expenditures in their annual budgets, even when their comparison in time and among countries is limited by the different methodologies adopted and the quality of the data utilized. Therefore, Table 3.12 provides only a rough comparison of the magnitude of tax expenditures in the countries in the region, relative to both GDP and total revenues. To illustrate this point further, we include information on some OECD countries, where this type of tax expenditure also seems to be significant.

In Table 3.13, we observe the disaggregation of the calculations for Argentina and the significance of tax expenditures related to VAT, which account for 50 percent of the total estimate. For this purpose, tax expenditures are defined as the amount of tax revenue that the government sets aside, as a consequence of a special treatment to specific areas, economic sectors, or certain taxpayers. Estimates of tax expenditures are computed on a cash basis, meaning that the revenue loss is only related to the fiscal year.

The information presented leads us to inquire about the consequences of promotion regimes that were in force in the region during the last decade; further studies of these expenditures are clearly needed.

STRENGTHENING THE FAIRNESS AND EQUITY OF THE SYSTEM

Income inequality has increased in this region since World War II, and since the 1990s this tendency has not been uniform among countries. On average, inequality has increased in South America but has remained stable in Central America and the Caribbean, as we can observe in Table 3.14. Evidence suggests that there is a converging movement toward unequal income in the entire region. We can also observe that among the countries included here, Argentina has the highest increase in inequality (measured through Gini coefficients), moving from third place in the early 1990s to seventh place in the region at the beginning of the current decade.

As is well known, in Latin America the effects of the tax system on income distribution have always presented great conceptual and methodological problems. Perceptions of the role of taxation on income have not only changed during the past decades, but the effects of taxation policies

Table 3.13   Tax Expenditures in Argentina

Tax	2003		2004		2005	
	Thousands of $	% of GDP	Thousands of $	% of GDP	Thousands of $	% of GDP
Total	9437	2.51	10096	2.37	12157	2.55
Included in the tax laws	7360	1.96	8040	1.89	8946	1.88
Included in incentives laws	2077	0.55	2056	0.48	3211	0.67
VAT	4493	1.20	4941	1.16	5924	1.24
Included in the tax laws	3115	0.83	3709	0.87	4103	0.86
Included in incentives laws	1378	0.37	1232	0.29	1821	0.38
Income	2254	0.60	1767	0.42	2392	0.50
Included in the tax laws	2122	0.56	1640	0.39	1765	0.37
Included in specific incentives laws	132	0.04	127	0.03	627	0.13
Fuels	1287	0.34	1662	0.39	1910	0.40
Included in the tax laws	1287	0.34	1662	0.39	1910	0.40
Social Security Contributions	763	0.20	935	0.22	1067	0.22
Included in the tax laws	763	0.20	935	0.22	1067	0.22
International Trade and Transactions	253	0.07	315	0.07	336	0.07
Included in incentives laws	253	0.07	315	0.07	336	0.07
Personal Goods	44	0.01	59	0.01	62	0.01
Included in the tax laws	44	0.01	59	0.01	62	0.01
Excises	30	0.01	34	0.01	38	0.01
Included in the tax laws	30	0.01	34	0.01	38	0.01
Presumed Minimum Income	90	0.02	21	0.01	24	0.01
Included in incentives laws	90	0.02	21	0.01	24	0.01
Others	224	0.06	362	0.09	403	0.08
Included in incentives laws	224	0.06	362	0.09	403	0.08

Source: Dirección Nacional de Investigaciones y Analisis Fiscal.

continue to be discussed, since many studies of such policies have encountered great conceptual and empirical limitations.

Answering the question "Who pays taxes?" is difficult, despite the decades of work in this field.[18] As indicated later in this chapter, a more optimistic message can be obtained from the economic policy viewpoint: it is more convenient to analyze the marginal effects of tax reforms than to look at the average of existing structures.

Table 3.14 Gini Coefficients: Distribution of Equivalent Family Income in Latin American Countries

Country	Early 1990s (A)	Mid-1990s (B)	Early 2000s (C)	Variation (D)=(C) – (A)
Argentina	0.426	0.458	0.504	0.078
Bolivia	0.543	0.558	0.559	0.016
Brazil	0.595	0.583	0.572	−0.023
Chile	0.547	0.549	0.561	0.014
Colombia	0.559	0.543	0.558	−0.001
Costa Rica	0.439	0.440	0.446	0.007
El Salvador	0.505	0.494	0.518	0.013
Honduras	0.556	0.541	0.530	−0.026
Jamaica	0.496	0.515	0.490	−0.006
Mexico	0.539	0.525	0.527	−0.012
Nicaragua	0.542	n/a	0.541	−0.001
Panama	0.547	0.540	0.544	−0.003
Peru	0.457	0.464	0.477	0.020
Uruguay	0.408	0.409	0.425	0.017
Venezuela	0.417	0.445	0.455	0.038
Simple average	**0.505**	**0.507**	**0.514**	**0.009**
Weighted average	**0.519**	**0.512**	**0.515**	**−0.004**
Dominican Rep.		0.502	0.481	
Ecuador		0.530	0.543	
Guatemala		n/a	0.560	
Paraguay		0.578	0.549	

Source: Gasparini (2003).

In the case of Argentina, several studies indicate that progressiveness has declined over the years—a trend that is contrary to expected changes in income distribution.[19] In this sense, the tax structure is the most important factor determining this result, since taxes on income are basically progressive and taxes on consumer goods are not. Although the global level of taxation has increased throughout the last few decades, as indicated previously, taxes on income have not evolved accordingly. Thus, given the relatively low burden of taxes on personal income, the distributive effects of the tax system have been low, and the evidence shows that no redistribution changes have been produced as a result.

This poses a question regarding the ability of the tax system to capture an increasing percentage of revenues through taxes on personal income, selective taxes on luxury items, or equity taxes. In this respect, the orientation of changes in the Argentine tax system has not been favorable.

Taxes on personal income have not increased; in fact, they have decreased slightly, since taxable bases did not expand at the same time as tax rates dropped. Similarly, we have observed a growing participation of general consumer taxes (VAT), which have suffered a process of taxable base expansion as well as a sustained increase in the overall tax rate. Selective taxes have concentrated on items of low price flexibility (beverages, tobacco, etc.), whereas taxes on luxury items were eliminated. Lastly, taxation on equity has been low, as coverage of these taxes is reduced; in the case of fixed assets, valuation does not match market price, and collection coefficients are not adequate.

Table 3.15 shows the results of the 1997 tax distribution incidence, based on studies of the Argentine case. This demonstrates the existence of a regressive tax system, in contrast with the behavior of industrialized countries.

The information gathered allows us to define a slightly regressive tax system, with a tendency toward proportionality. This definition is confirmed by estimates of the inequality index, which, in the case of the Gini increases its value when inequality grows. The proportionality condition is not positive from the point of view of equality because we expect a developed tax system to comply with the requirement for vertical equality, according to which those with larger incomes should face a higher tax

Table 3.15   Tax Burden in Income Deciles for the Total Tax System, Argentina 1997

Economic Classification of Taxes	Overall Average	*Percentage of Cases Corresponding to Each Group*		
		20% Lower Income	70% Middle Income	10% Higher Income
Income taxes	4.91	2.52	3.08	7.17
Social security contributions and withholdings	11.34	16.30	13.78	8.19
Wealth taxes	2.83	2.21	2.41	3.36
Goods and services	19.59	25.93	20.81	17.76
Foreign trade	1.66	2.30	1.76	1.51
Other taxes	2.07	3.03	2.23	1.81
Total	**42.39**[1]	**52.29**	**44.06**	**39.80**

Source: Santiere, Gómez Sabaini, and Rossignolo (2000).

1. The Average Tax Burden of the System is 42.39 percent, a particularly high figure, as a result of several factors, including: (i) the tax concept adopted encompasses more than is usual in other investigations; (ii) the GDP suffered a reduction in the recent National Accounts estimate; (iii) the definition of Family Available Net Income is notably more restricted than the one applied in previous investigations; (iv) in every case, Available Income is a figure that reflects values that are much lower than GDP and therefore, tax pressure with respect to GDP (conventional tax burden) has to be lower than the quotient between the same mass of taxes and Available Income.

burden than those with lower incomes. In other words: we would expect the tax/income quotient to be lower on average in the lowest income groups and higher than average in the groups with higher economic capacity. This condition did not prove true in Argentina in 1997.

Lastly, we must indicate that investigations on the matter of tax distribution conducted in Argentina have, actually, been limited to the evaluation of several taxes (VAT, income, etc.), but the first overall effort dates back to 1965 and was part of the general analysis of taxation in the country. Then, the average tax burden (taxes / family income) was 19.5 percent, and individualized by sectors showed a relative proportionality around the mean, with a small increase in the last section. The second study takes data centered on the year 1986 (Santiere, 1989). The methodology of this study was to analyze the tax burden on different deciles of the population, as classified by their income levels. In 1999, Santiere and Gómez Sabaini recalculated the year 1986 to make it as compatible as possible with the methodology employed and allow dynamic comparison with the studies in 1993 and 1997. The analysis of this 11-year period served to demonstrate the regressiveness of the Argentine tax system in regards to the selected well-being indicator, total family income. The trend is more marked in 1993 and 1997.

Toward the end of 1998, an investigation was published by Leonardo Gasparini who, after elaborating an extensive series of alternatives, presented a wholly regressive system in reference to per capita family income, which is slightly more progressive if the well-being pattern adopted is the family's or individual's global consumption.

The above-mentioned endeavors and their results offer a rather coherent picture, leaving us with little doubt as to the regressiveness of the tax package in force in Argentina, always taking into account that the contrast variable is available income. Finally, the latest investigations confirm renewed interest in the distribution and equality aspects of the taxation system, following a period in which this matter was largely ignored and attention was paid to the phenomena of automatic development of the economy, globalization, and other aspects related to economic policy.

STRENGTHENING THE TAX ADMINISTRATION

The weakness of the tax administration has always been one of the main problems affecting the Argentine taxation system, and the response to this issue has been the least positive. This weakness is evident in the sphere of provincial tax administration (24 jurisdictions) and even more so when one examines municipal tax administration (1,500 municipalities).

To this end, the Argentine government set up AFIP in 1997 and took over unified control of national taxes (domestic resources, social security, and customs duties), following the guidelines viewed at the time as a solution for all Latin American tax administrations. The AFIP, which employs nearly 20,000 people, was granted administrative independence, and its budget was financed by a predetermined percentage of the entity's total revenues.

A decade after its establishment, it is significant that one of AFIP's future objectives is to deepen the process of integration among its constitutive entities, since uniting the General Tax Bureau (DGI) and the General Customs Bureau (DGA) has still been more of a proposal than a fact.

Together with these administrative measures, the administration was supported by legal regulations that allowed for the honorable exit of a great mass of contributors who were not subject to any type of control by the entity, both regarding their statement and payment of income tax and compliance with social security obligations. With this in mind, legislation was passed on the Monotributista regime, which consisted of a fixed-payment system that accorded different levels or categories under which contributors were enrolled. The payment system was a substitute for all other taxes (personal income tax, VAT, and social security contributions) and currently encompasses 1,200,000 cases, over which the AFIP wields minimum controls. This system, seemingly benign, is one of the most serious problems faced by the tax system, as it has permitted the incorporation of a mass of potential income tax and VAT contributors, which affects both the equality and the economic efficiency of the system.

In the past few years, tax administrators, not only in Argentina, but in Latin America as a whole, have consistently placed the weight of tax administration on controlling VAT compliance. In this regard, we observe that countries have invested large amounts of money to improve tax compliance—and perhaps tax evasion is in decline; however, investigation of this phenomenon is limited. Tax noncompliance involves the performance of illegal actions, with the purpose of reducing tax payments, defined as evasion, and the temporary deferment of payments, known as arrears. Although arrears imply a delay in the availability of funds for the state, evasion results in the loss of state revenues and inequality in the distribution of the tax burden. This generates disloyal competition among evaders and those who are in compliance, as well as the inefficient distribution of economic resources. In order to estimate VAT compliance, the AFIP[20] calculated potential revenues, corresponding to VAT revenues that would have been collected if all those responsible had liquidated and paid their obligations in full and compared it to revenues actually collected. Through this methodology, potential revenues were determined by adding VAT contained in purchases that do not generate fiscal credit—that is, end consumer purchases and those of contributors who are tax-exempt or to whom this tax does not apply. During the period examined, noncompliance reached a maximum of 34.8 percent in 2002. Between 2003 and 2004, there was a marked drop in noncompliance, and last year, VAT noncompliance was down to 24 percent, the lowest in the series (Figure 3.13).[21]

The improvement in tax compliance is mainly the result of two factors: the procyclicity of tax collection and the increased efficiency of the tax administration. An increase in tax revenues tends to follow closely intensified economic activity, if all other variables conditioning this activity hold stable (tax rates, taxable base scope, etc.). The second factor is part of

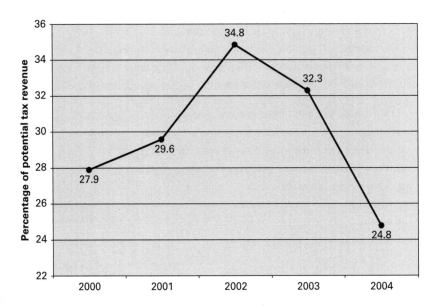

Figure 3.13   VAT Evasion.

the group of new measures implemented by the tax administration to reduce noncompliance.

Several imbalances affect the Argentine taxation system. First, the public sector's financial situation has become highly unstable owing to erratic revenues and its dependence on the economic cycle. Second, a structure that leans too heavily on direct taxation and that is extremely "allergic" to taxing personal income and equity affects the equality vital to any tax system.

The disorderly process of decentralizing expenses toward subnational jurisdictions with significant productive development differences has resulted in an accentuated lack of correspondence between expenses and income at the federal level. This has been resolved by a significant dependence of asset transfer systems between jurisdictions that are not sufficiently transparent. Similarly, we see a predominance of exception mechanisms, which, under the relatively light burden of income tax, have been granted to VAT and thus lead to severe inefficiency in the assignment of resources.

Lastly, the great significance of the informal economy, added to the weakness of the administration at both the state and provincial tax levels, not only involves the loss of resources, but also aggravates existing differences in equality and domestic competitiveness.

Specifically, throughout this work, eight main features of the present situation and six main challenges facing Argentina's tax system have been identified. In summary, the main characteristics or stylized factors quoted are:

a. Sustained growth of consumers' taxes
b. Gradual loss of resources from import duties
c. Intermittent but significant presence of export taxes
d. Poor performance of income taxation
e. Irrelevance of wealth taxes
f. Importance of payroll taxes
g. Use of emergency or extraordinary taxes
h. Importance of tax expenditures

Finally, the main challenges ahead that have been identified in relation to the Argentine tax system are:

a. Financing the social security system and its effects at the different levels of government

b. Replacing emergency taxes on corporate assets and taxes on financial operations

c. Substituting export taxes

d. Reducing tax expenditures

e. Strengthening the fairness of the system

f. Strengthening the tax administration

NOTES

1. For a review of the macroeconomic aspects in this period, see Heymann (forthcoming).

2. These aspects are fully reviewed in Carciofi (1990) and Cetrángolo et al. (1997).

3. It is common to see analyses of Argentina's situation in which the provinces' governments are ascribed the highest responsibility when the aggregate fiscal problem is explained.

4. These aspects are discussed by Cetrángolo and Jiménez (2003).

5. Between 1991 and 1995, cumulative revenues from privatizations accounted for 2.7 percent of GDP.

6. In addition, if we consider the consolidated result (including that of provinces' governments), the surplus amounts to 3.5 percent for 2004.

7. This relation in Brazil is 7.2 (between Federal District and the State of Maranhão), and in Mexico 6.2 times (between Federal District and Chiapas). This same relation in the case of Canada is only 1.7 times.

8. The figure shows the provinces ranked by GDP per capita and by education evaluation results, from high to low, and infant mortality rate, from low to high. For a further analysis of these matters, see Gatto and Cetrángolo (2003).

9. There are no series of tax resources from governments of municipalities. Between 1993 and 2000, tax collection from municipalities was 0.07 percent of GDP.

10. During the first three years of the convertibility regime, consolidated tax revenue grew fast and reached 22 percent of GDP in 1993, as a consequence of the plan of stabilization and its impact on revenues due to collection lags ("Tanzi effect").

11. There are no series of tax revenues from provinces before 1950.

12. Cetrángolo and Jiménez (2003), Chapter 3.

13. This reform modified the previous system of VAT determination on these institutions. Till then, the tax had been calculated on the basis of the remuneration of factors and the reform implied the adoption of the usual system of determination through debits and credits.

14. An in-depth analysis of this problem is found in Cetrángolo and Grushka (2005).

15. In practice, the corporate income tax is a payment in advance of those taxes, in order to allow transnational enterprises to fully use the tax credit granted by foreign tax authorities. In other circumstances, and especially in more recent experience, these alternative methods have tended to provide options to the taxpayer as to the

criterion of the determination to be used, with prior authorization from the tax authority.

16. Outside the region, in 1983, Australia also implemented a tax on debit banking, which subsequently reached a provincial level and which currently is under consideration for its abolishment.

17. Coelho, Ebrill, and Summers (2001), p. 24.

18. De Ferranti, Perry, Ferreira, F., and Walton (2004), Chapter 9.

19. Gómez Sabaini, Santiere, and Rossignolo (2002) and Santiere, Gómez Sabaini, and Rossignolo (2000).

20. AFIP (2005).

21. The information utilized came primarily from the National Accounts System. They used the supply-product matrix for 1997, updating it with value indexes for the years of the series being analyzed. In order to determine potential revenues, first, the theoretical tax base was calculated according to taxable household consumption (household consumption less consumption that is exempt or nontaxable), to which they added intermediate consumption and taxable investment for production of exempt goods and services, and the consumption of public sector taxable goods and services and investments, since their VAT content cannot be deducted at later stages. Following that, they estimated potential revenues by applying the most appropriate VAT rates to each item. Thus, a general 21 percent taxable base rate is applied to household consumption, and, in specific cases, this rate drops to 10.5 percent for some products and services (some agricultural products, passenger transport, and health care services, among others). For intermediate taxable consumption for the production of exempt or nontaxable goods, the VAT is 10.5 percent for capital goods and services such as soil preparation and rotation, 27 percent for some public services, and 21 percent for the remaining goods and services acquired during the production process. In the case of taxable investment for the production of tax-exempt and nontaxable items, the overall rate is 21 percent, except for purchases of capital goods, where the rate is 10.5 percent. The same 10.5 percent rate is also applied to new construction and household improvements. Finally, in regards to the state taxable base, made up of goods and services expenses and taxable investments, the VAT rates applied are the same as those used for aforementioned goods and services.

REFERENCES

AFIP (Administración Federal de Ingresos Públicos). (2005). *Calculo del incumplimiento del IVA 2002–2004*. Buenos Aires, Argentina: AFIP.

Agosin, M., Barreix, A., Gómez Sabaini, J. C., and Machado, R. (2006). "Reforma tributaria para el Desarrollo Humano en Centroamérica." *Revista de la CEPAL,* 87. Santiago, Chile: ECLAC (Economic Commission for Latin America and the Caribbean).

Carciofi, R. (1990). "La desarticulación del pacto fiscal. Una interpretación sobre la evolución del sector público argentino en las dos últimas décadas." Documento de trabajo 36. Buenos Aires, Argentina: ECLAC.

Carciofi, R., Barris, G., and Cetrángolo, O. (1994). *Reformas Tributarias en América Latina*. Santiago, Chile: ECLAC/Gobierno de los Países Bajos.

Cetrángolo, O., Frenkel, R., Damil, M., and Jiménez, J. P. (1997). *La Sostenibilidad de la Política Fiscal en América Latina. El Caso Argentino*. Washington, DC: Banco Interamericano de Desarrollo.

Cetrángolo, O., and Grushka, C. (2005). "Sistema previsional argentino: Crisis, reforma y crisis de la reforma." *Serie financiamiento del desarrollo 151*. Santiago, Chile: Unidad de Estudios Especiales, ECLAC.

Cetrángolo, O., and Jiménez, J. P. (2003). "Política fiscal en Argentina durante el régimen de convertibilidad." *Serie Gestión Pública 35*. Santiago, Chile: ECLAC.

Coelho, I., Ebrill, L., and Summers, V. (2001). "Bank Debit Taxes in Latin America: An Analysis of Recent Trends." Working Paper 01/67. Washington, DC: IMF.

De Ferranti, D. M., Perry, G. E., Ferreira, F.H.G., and Walton, M. 2004. *Inequality in Latin America: Breaking with History?* Washington, DC: World Bank.

Dirección Nacional de Investigaciones y Analisis Fiscal (Ministry of the Economy). (2000 and 2002). *Informe de Recaudación Tributaria*. Buenos Aires, Argentina: Ministry of the Economy.

ECLAC. (2006). *Graphic Regional Overview*. Buenos Aires, Argentina: ECLAC.

Gaggero, J., and Gómez Sabaini, J. (2003). *Argentina: La Cuestión Fiscal Bajo la Convertibilidad y la Reforma Tributaria Pendiente*. Buenos Aires, Argentina: Fundación OSDE (Obra Social de Ejecutivos).

Gasparini, L. (2003). *Income Inequality in Latin America and the Caribbean: Evidence from Household Surveys*. University of La Plata: CEDLAS (Centro de Estudios Distributivos Laborales y Sociales).

Gatto, F., and Cetrángolo, O. (2003). "Dinámica productiva provincial a fines de los noventa." *Serie estudios y perspectivas, No. 14*. Buenos Aires, Argentina: ECLAC.

Gómez Sabaini, J. C. (2005). "Evolución y situación tributaria actual en América Latina: Una serie de temas para la discusión." Santiago, Chile: ECLAC.

Gómez Sabaini, J. C., Santiere, J. J., and Rossignolo, D. (2002). "La equidad distributiva y el sistema tributario: Un análisis para el caso argentino." *Serie Gestión Pública, 20*. Santiago, Chile: ECLAC.

Goodspeed, T. J. (2004, May 24–25). "Taxation and FDI in Developed and Developing Countries." Paper presented at Andrew Young School Annual Conference on Public Finance Issues, at the Andrew Young School of Policy Studies, Georgia State University.

Herschel, F. J., et al. (1963). "Política Fiscal en la Argentina." In *Programa Conjunto de Tributación*, Consejo Nacional de Desarrollo, ed., p. vi. Buenos Aires, Argentina: OEA/BID.

Heymann, D. (forthcoming). "Buscando la Tendencia." *Work Study*. Buenos Aires, Argentina: ECLAC.

Kirilenko, A., and Summers, V. (2003). *Taxation of Financial Intermediation: Theory and Practice for Emerging Economies*, P. Honohan, ed. Washington, DC: World Bank.

———. (2004). "Bank Debit Taxes: Yield and Disintermediation." Chapter 10, in *Taxing the Financial Sector*, H. Zee. Washington, DC: IMF.

Mesa Lago, C. (2000). "Estudio comparativo de los costos fiscales en la transición de ocho reformas de pensiones en América Latina." *Serie financiamiento del desarrollo, No. 93.* Santiago, Chile: ECLAC.

———. (2005). *Las reformas de salud en América Latina y su impacto en los principios de la seguridad social.* Mimeo. Santiago, Chile: ECLAC.

Santiere, J. J. 1989. *Distribución de la carga tributaria por niveles de ingreso.* Banco Mundial, Buenos Aires.

Santiere, J., Gómez Sabaini, J. C., and Rossignolo, D. (2000). *Impacto de los Impuestos Sobre la Distribución del Ingreso en Argentina en 1997.* Project 3958. Buenos Aires, Argentina: World Bank and Ministry of Economics.

CHAPTER 4

Tax System Reform in India

M. Govinda Rao and R. Kavita Rao

Many developing countries have embarked on tax reforms in recent years. Such reforms have been motivated both by local factors and by rapid internationalization of economic activities. The need to correct fiscal imbalances and the transition from a centralized plan to a market economy were the important local factors hastening tax reforms. Difficulties in compressing expenditures necessitated that tax system reform take an important role in fiscal adjustment strategy. The transition from plan to market required the substitution of administered prices with market-determined prices, the replacement of physical controls with financial controls, and the substitution of public enterprise profits with tax revenues. Similarly, tax reforms become imperative in a globalizing environment. Enhancing competitiveness and attracting foreign investment require minimizing both the efficiency and compliance costs of the tax system. Globalization also involves loss of revenue from customs, which needs to be replaced with domestic taxes.

The Indian tax system also had to be reformed in response to changes in development strategy. In the initial years, tax policy was used as an instrument to achieve a variety of diverse goals. Among these goals were increasing the level of saving and correcting for inequalities arising from an oligopolistic market structure created by a centralized planning regime, including a licensing system, exchange control, and administered prices (Bagchi and Nayak, 1994). While the history of taxation in India is peppered with efforts for tax reform, especially in the form of various expert committees, the fiscal crisis of 1991 provided the first major window of opportunity for a serious rethink, followed by action.

This chapter analyzes both the structure and the operations of the Indian tax system. The first section discusses the evolution of the Indian tax system and tax collections and the impact of historical and institutional factors in shaping Indian tax policy. Next, we provide a critical analysis of some key features of the tax regime and its reform options. An analysis of the observed trends in tax revenue is presented in the following section, highlighting the possible efficiency and equity implications of the tax system. The final section pulls together the various suggestions for consolidation of tax reforms in India.

EVOLUTION OF INDIAN TAX SYSTEM

THE ASSIGNMENT SYSTEM

The assignment of tax powers in the constitution provides the framework for the evolution of the tax system in India. It assigns most of the broad-based and mobile tax bases to the center. These are taxes on nonagricultural incomes and wealth, corporation taxes, customs duties, and excise duties on manufactured goods. The tax powers of the states include taxes on agricultural incomes and wealth, sales taxes, excises on alcohol, taxes on motor vehicles, passengers, and goods, stamp duties, registration fees on transfer of property, and taxes and duties on electricity. Of these, the sales tax is the most important and contributes 60 percent of states' tax revenue.

The evolution of tax policy within the framework of planned development strategy had important implications. First, tax policy was directed to raise resources for the public sector without regard to efficiency implications. Second, the objective of achieving a socialistic pattern of society on the one hand and the attempt to tax large oligopolistic rents generated by the system of licenses, quotas, and restrictions on the other called for a steeply progressive tax structure. Third, pursuit of a multiplicity of objectives complicated the tax system, with adverse effects on both efficiency and horizontal equity. This also opened up large avenues for evasion and avoidance of taxes. Fourth, the above considerations complicated the tax system, and selectivity and discretion became a legitimate part of the tax policy and administration. Fifth, the influence of special interest groups, changing priorities, and lack of an information system and scientific analysis led to an ad hoc and often inconsistent calibration of policies. Finally, a poor information system was both the cause of selective application of the tax system and its effect.

RECENT TRENDS IN INDIAN TAX REFORMS

While India has had a history of periodically assessing the tax structure through the constitution of tax reform committees (India, 1971, 1977), actual reform attempts were largely ad hoc. It required a crisis of some severity before systematic tax reforms were implemented. The fiscal and balance-of-payments crises of 1991 warranted systematic reform not only to improve the revenue productivity of the tax system to phase out fiscal imbalance, but also to reorient the tax system to the requirements of a market economy. Tax reforms were an integral part of this larger reform initiative.

The Tax Reform Committee (TRC; India, 1991) laid out a framework and a road map for the reform of direct and indirect taxes as part of the structural reform process. The paradigmatic shift in tax reforms adopted by the TRC was in keeping with the best practice approach of broadening the base, lowering marginal tax rates, reducing rate differentiation, simplifying the tax structure, and adopting measures to make the administration and enforcement more effective.

The important proposals put forward by the TRC included reduction in the rates of all major taxes, that is, customs, individual and corporate income, and excise taxes, to reasonable levels, in order to maintain progressivity but not to induce evasion. The TRC recommended a number of measures designed to broaden the base of all the taxes by minimizing exemptions and concessions, drastically simplifying laws and procedures, building a proper information system and computerization of tax returns, and revamping and modernizing administrative and enforcement machinery. It also recommended that the taxes on domestic production should be fully converted into a value-added tax and that the VAT should be extended to the wholesale level, in agreement with the States, with additional revenues beyond the postmanufacturing stage passed on to the state governments. The tax reforms witnessed thereafter sought to follow the directions spelled out in this report.

While the TRC laid down the analytical foundations for the reform of the tax system in a liberalized environment, subsequent reports extended the road map for reforms to meet the demands of the emerging economic environment in the new millennium. These reports include the task force reports on the reform of direct and indirect taxes (India, 2002a, 2002b) and the report of the task force on the implementation of the Fiscal Responsibility of Budget Management Act, 2003 (India, 2004).

Reform of Direct Taxes

At the central level, the income tax evolved as a principal instrument to bring about redistribution until the mid-1970s. Thus, in 1973–1974, the personal income tax had 11 tax brackets, with rates monotonically rising from 10 to 85 percent. When the surcharge of 15 percent was taken into account, the highest marginal rate for persons above Rs. 200,000 income was 97.5 percent. Combined with the highest wealth tax rate of 5 percent, the budget speech for 1971–1972 argued that this tax rate would ensure a ceiling on income at Rs. 250,000, for income from capital alone.

In the case of company taxation, the classical system of taxation involved the taxation of the profits in the hands of the company and the dividends in the hands of the shareholders. The distinction was made for widely held companies and different types of closely held companies. The tax rate varied from the base rate of 45 to 65 percent in the case of some widely held companies. Although nominal rates were high, the effective rates were substantially lower due to generous tax preferences such as depreciation and investment allowance.[1]

Tax reforms initiated after 1991–1992 attempted to simplify tax rates considerably. The number of brackets was reduced to three for personal income tax. In 1992–1993, the prescribed rates were 20 percent, 30 percent, and 40 percent, respectively. Financial assets were excluded from the wealth tax, and the maximum marginal rate was reduced to 1 percent. Further simplification was achieved in 1997–1998 when the three bracket rates were reduced to 10-20-30 percent; they have remained steady thereafter, with some changes in the associated income brackets. The budget for 2005–2006 made some major changes in structure by raising the exemption limit to Rs. 100,000 and abolishing the provision for a standard deduction.[2] The exemption limit for women and senior citizens was higher, respectively, at Rs. 135,000 and Rs. 185,000. The other major change relates to the amalgamation of provisions under various incentive schemes into a blanket cap of Rs. 100,000, made deductible from income. This was proposed as a step toward introducing an Exempt-Exempt-Tax (EET)-based system of taxation of savings, investment, and income earned.[3] Exigencies of revenue have led to an additional surcharge of 10 percent of the tax paid and a 2 percent charge earmarked for primary education on all taxes.

In the case of corporate taxation too, the basic rate was brought down to 50 percent, and rates applicable to different categories of closely held companies were unified at 55 percent. The distinction between closely held and widely held companies was done away with, and the tax rates were unified at 40 percent in 1993–1994. In 1997–1998, when personal income tax rates were reduced, the company rate was brought down to 35 percent. The 2005–2006 budget finally achieved a much needed alignment of the highest marginal tax rate in personal income tax with the tax applicable on corporate income tax, thereby reducing the corporate income tax rate to 30 percent. This was topped by a 10 percent surcharge, as applicable to personal income tax for income beyond Rs. 1,000,000. With regard to a dividend tax, there has been a distinct lack of direction. Levy of a 10 percent tax on dividends was shifted from individuals to companies in 1997–1998. The tax rate was increased to 20 percent in 2000–2001, reduced again to 10 percent in 2001–2002, and in 2002–2003, the levy once again reverted to the shareholders.[4] This policy was reversed yet again in 2003–2004 with the levy of the tax on the company, ostensibly to encourage the debt and equity markets.

The system evolved from a high marginal tax rate regime to one of lower rates. Generous depreciation provisions and a large number of tax preferences in the tax statutes sought to cushion the impact of the former regime on taxpayers. The transition to a regime with more moderate tax rates has been witness to a scaling down of the investment allowance and depreciation provisions. The same cannot, however, be said about the tax incentives and preferences. In the case of the personal income tax, the Advisory Group on Tax Policy and Tax Administration lists the incentives in 25 pages of its report (India, 2001a: 125–150). These include incentives and concessions for savings, housing, retirement benefits, investment in and returns from certain types of financial assets, investments in retirement schemes, and income of charitable trusts. A variety of tax preferences have not only distorted the after-tax rates of return on various types of investments in unintended ways, but have also significantly eroded the tax base. The major tax preferences in the case of a corporate tax were investment allowance, an accelerated depreciation allowance, and tax incentives for investment in infrastructure (Section 80IA of the Income Tax Act), housing development (Section 80 HHBA of the Income Tax Act), investment in depressed areas (Section 80IC of the Income Tax Act), export incomes (Sections 10A, 10B, 10BA, and 80HHC of the Income Tax Act), small units (Section 80 HHA of the Income Tax Act), some sunrise industries (Section 10A of the Income Tax Act), and special economic zones (Section 80IAB of the Income Tax Act). The 2005–2006 budget sought to tone down the incentives embedded in the depreciation provisions by reducing the rate on general plant and machinery to 15 percent from the existing 25 percent cushioned by an increased investment allowance, that is, an initial depreciation allowance to 20 percent without conditionalities regarding installed capacity increases.

The wide-ranging tax preferences have led to large-scale avoidance of the tax by companies, resulting in several "zero-tax" companies. In order to correct this, a minimum alternate tax (MAT) was imposed in 1997–1998, at regular rates of tax on 30 percent of book profits. Presently, the liability arises when the tax payable on taxable income computed as per the Income Tax Act is less than 7.5 percent of the company's "book profit." Such a company is subject to a MAT of 7.5 percent of "book profit," as defined in the Income Tax Act. Like the regular income tax, this tax is also topped up by a surcharge of 2.5 percent and a cess (an additional earmarked charge) of 2 percent. The budget for 2006–2007 raised the MAT rate to 10 percent, with a provision to provide a partial tax credit against corporate income tax in subsequent years.[5]

The budgets of 2004–2005 and 2005–2006 saw the introduction of a few more stand-alone levies ostensibly to plug a few loopholes and garner resources at the same time. The Fringe Benefits Tax was introduced as a levy on companies having Indian employees. The tax is payable by the company on a part of its expenditures on certain identified items of fringe benefits; 17 such items have been identified, each associated with a number defining the extent of tax liability. Interestingly, this tax is over and above the provision for taxation of perquisites in the hands of the employee, as a part of the personal income tax regime. The second stand-alone levy introduced was a Banking Cash Transactions Tax, which was applicable on "large" cash withdrawals from current accounts operated in banks. This tax was rationalized on the grounds that it would help track "black economy" transactions, by creating a trail. A third such levy is a securities transaction tax, applicable on the sale of financial securities on the stock exchanges. This levy was introduced to capture a tax on financial transactions and effectively replace an evasion-prone provision for capital gains taxation. In the neighborhood of each of these activities, it may appear that the solution proposed is an effective one. This, however, results in a proliferation of taxes with unknown effects on equity and efficiency. Furthermore, it leaves unanswered the question of whether the underlying problems should be addressed head-on or whether a local solution should be found for every such loophole in the law.

The most important ongoing reform in recent years is in tax administration. Expansion of tax deduction at source (TDS) is one of the significant measures to reach the "hard to tax" groups. In addition, every individual living in large cities covered under any one of six conditions (ownership of house, cars, membership of a club, ownership of credit card, foreign travel, and subscriber of a telephone connection) is necessarily required to file a tax return.[6] The budget for 2004–2005 stipulated mandatory reporting by third parties on several high-value transactions, which can help strengthen the information on large taxpayers. While the issue of permanent account numbers (PANs) has been simplified by outsourcing it to the UTI Investors' Services Ltd., the work on Tax Information Networking (TIN) has been outsourced to the National Securities Depository Ltd. (NSDL). Strengthening the information system through the TIN, processing and matching the information from various sources on a selective basis, are part of an important initiative that is likely to improve tax compliance.

Reform of Indirect Taxes

By the mid-1970s, the structure of excise duties was complex and highly distortionary. The tax structure was a mix of specific and ad valorem taxes, and on the latter alone, there were 24 different rates varying from 2 to 100 percent (excluding tobacco and petroleum products, which were taxed at higher rates). The report of the Indirect Tax Enquiry Committee (India, 1977) recommended the conversion of specific duties into ad valorem taxes, the unification of tax rates, and the introduction of an input tax credit to convert the tax into a manufacturing stage value-added tax (MANVAT), but it was not implemented until 1986–1987. Not surprisingly, this piecemeal and gradualist approach led to a decline in the tax-GDP ratio after reforms.

A further reform impetus on excise duties came with implementation of the TRC's recommendations. The measures included gradual unification of rates and greater reliance on account-based administration. In 1999–2000, almost 11 tax rates were merged into 3, with a handful of "luxury" items subject to two non-VAT additional rates (6 and 16 percent). However, specific rates in respect of some commodities continued. These were further merged into a single rate in 2000–2001 to be called a Central VAT (CenVAT), along with three special additional excises (8 percent, 16 percent, and 24 percent) for a few commodities. Subsequent years have seen the stabilization of the primary rate of 16 percent, but a proliferation of multiple rates, especially below 16 percent, continues. It should be noted that apart from those excises that might be built into variations in rates, the central government imposes no explicit conventional "excises" in the present era.

Customs Duties. Contrary to the general patterns seen in low-income countries where international trade taxes generate the bulk of the revenues, revenue from this source was not very large in the initial years of independent India (Chelliah, 1986) owing to quantitative restrictions on imports. Furthermore, high and differentiated tariffs, varying rates with the stage of production (lower rates on inputs and higher rates on finished goods), and income elasticity of demand resulted not only in a high and varying effective rate of protection, but also a premium for inefficiency and unintended distortions in the allocation of resources.

By 1990–1991, the tariff structure was highly complex varying from 0 to 400 percent. Over 10 percent of imports were subject to more than 120 percent tariff. Wide-ranging exemptions granted by issuing notifications made the system complex and was a reflection of the influence of various special interest groups on tax policy. The TRC recommended a reduction in the number and level of tariffs to 5, 10, 15, 20, 25, 30, and 50 percent to be achieved by 1997–1998. The reform that followed resulted in the reduction in the peak rate from over 400 percent to 40 percent by 1997–1998 and further on to reach 12.5 percent in the budget for 2006–2007. However, the pattern of tariffs in which the rates vary with the stage of processing has continued, and this has caused very high effective rates on assembling consumer durable and luxury items of consumption. Along with relaxation of quantitative restrictions on imports and exchange rate depreciation, the change in the tariffs constituted a major shift in the foreign trade regime in the country.

Service Taxes. An interesting aspect of the assignment system in India was that except in the case of a few specified services assigned to the states such as the entertainment tax, the passengers and goods tax, and the electricity duty, services were not specifically assigned either to the center or to states. This violated the principle of neutrality in taxing consumption as it discriminated against goods. As services are relatively more income elastic, the tax system was also rendered less progressive. An even more important argument for taxing services is to enable a coordinated calibration of a consumption tax system on goods and services, as in the production chain services enter into goods and vice versa.

The introduction of a tax on services at the central level began in 1994–1995 with three services: non–life insurance, stock brokerage, and telecommunications. The list was expanded in succeeding years to include over 80 services at present.[7] Although initially taxed at 7 percent, the rate was increased to 10 percent in 2002–2003 and further to 12 percent in the budget of 2006–2007, with a case for convergence between the goods and services tax, where the goods are taxed at 16 percent. The Expert Group on Taxation of Services (India, 2001b) recommended the extension of the tax to all services along with the provision of an input tax credit for both goods and services and, subsequently, integration with the central VAT (CenVAT) on goods. However, while the government has yet to implement a general taxation of services, an input tax credit for goods entering into services and vice versa has been extended. In addition, the budget for 2006–2007 announced an intention to introduce a generalized goods and services tax by 2010.

State-Level Tax Reforms

Tax reforms at the state level have not coincided with those at the center. Although individual state governments tried to appoint committees from time to time and reform their tax structures, they made no systematic attempt to streamline the reform process even after 1991, when market-oriented reforms were introduced. Most of the reform attempts were ad hoc and were guided by exigencies of revenue rather than by attempts to modernize the tax system. Indeed, systematic studies were commissioned to show their reform orientation, but the recommendations were hardly implemented. The pace of tax reforms in the states accelerated in the latter half of the 1990s, with increasing pressures on their budgets and, in some cases, due to the conditionalities imposed by multilateral lending agencies or to meet the targets set by the medium-term fiscal reforms facility. The major landmark in tax reform at the state level was the simplification and rationalization of the sales tax system by introducing a value-added tax in 21 states on April 1, 2005. Subsequently, all other states also have switched to this new regime.[8]

The VAT reform adopted in April 2005 levies the tax at two rates, namely, 4 percent and 12.5 percent. Basic necessities are exempted. Petrol and diesel (which contribute about 40 percent of sales tax) are kept outside the VAT regime, and a floor rate on them is fixed at 20 percent. All dealers up to Rs. 500,000 are exempted. Those with turnover above Rs. 500,000 but below Rs. 5 million may pay a turnover-based tax and remain outside the VAT chain unless they voluntarily register and pay the tax at the prescribed rates. All importers and manufacturers as well as other dealers with turnover above Rs. 5 million are required to pay the VAT at prescribed rates and constitute the chain.

This design has two major limitations: (1) it applies only to intrastate transactions, and (2) it applies only to goods. For the taxation of interstate trade, the earlier origin-based system continues to apply. However, there is a provision for input tax credit, so as to ensure that the effective rate of tax on interstate transactions does not exceed the prescribed 4 percent. While the budget for 2006–2007 announced the transition to a generalized goods and services tax by 2010, a lot of details need to be worked out before such a transition can be implemented. The road map for the transition is expected to be announced within the next few months.

TRENDS IN INDIAN TAX REVENUES

This section presents an analysis of the trends in tax revenue in India. The focus is on the changes in the level and composition of tax revenue since 1991, when systematic reforms were set in motion. The analysis shows that despite initiating systematic reforms, the revenue productivity of the tax system has not shown an appreciable increase, and the decline in tax ratio due to reduction in customs duty could not be compensated by internal indirect taxes.

The trends in tax revenue in India show four distinct phases (Rao, 2000) (Table 4.1). First, there was a steady increase in the tax–GDP ratio from 6.3 percent in 1950–1951 to 16.1 percent in 1987–1988. In the initial years of planning, an increase in the tax ratio was necessitated by the need to finance large public sector plans. Thus, the tax ratio increased from a mere 6.3 percent in 1950–1951 to 10.4 percent in 1970–1971 and further to 13.8 percent in 1980–1981. The increase continued until it peaked at 16.1 percent in 1987–1988. The buoyancy of the tax in the later years of the first phase was fueled by the economy attaining a higher growth path and progressive substitution of quantitative restrictions with tariffs following initial attempts at liberalization in the late 1980s.

The second phase started with the economic recession following the severe drought of 1987 and was marked by stagnant revenues until 1992–1993. However, triggered by the pay revision of government employees,

Table 4.1 Fiscal Trends in India *(as a percentage of GDP)*

Year	Revenue Deficit[1] (Center)	Fiscal Deficit[1] (Center)	Primary Deficit	Debt Stock	Tax Ratio (Center)	Tax Ratio (States)	Tax Ratio (Total)	Transfer to States
1981–1982	(0.60)	6.4	4.1	46.4	9.4	4.9	14.3	n/a
1985–1986	1.8	8.8	5.7	51.9	10.6	5.3	15.6	n/a
1990–1991	4.2	9.3	4.9	61.4	10.1	5.3	15.4	4.9
1995–1996	3.2	6.5	1.6	60.1	9.4	5.4	14.8	4.3
1996–1997	3.6	6.3	1.1	58.0	9.5	5.2	14.7	4.3
1997–1998	4.2	7.2	2.0	56.5	9.1	5.3	14.5	4.9
1998–1999	6.4	9.0	3.6	58.6	8.3	5.1	13.4	3.7
1999–2000	6.3	9.5	3.8	58.9	8.9	5.3	14.2	3.8
2000–2001	6.5	9.2	3.3	61.5	9.0	5.6	14.6	3.9
2001–2002	6.9	9.6	3.4	63.2	8.2	5.6	13.8	3.8
2002–2003	6.7	9.9	3.4	69.5	8.8	5.9	14.6	3.8
2003–2004	5.8	9.2	2.9	72.4	9.2	6.0	15.2	n/a

Source: Public Finance Statistics, Ministry of Finance, Government of India; Annual Report, Reserve Bank of India, 2002–2003.

1. Revised estimates.

the expenditure–GDP ratio increased significantly after 1988–1989. This caused serious fiscal imbalances (Table 4.1), which led to an unprecedented economic crisis in 1991. The subsequent economic reform program led to a sharp reduction in import duties. Thus, in the third phase, the tax ratio declined from 15.8 percent in 1991–1992 to the lowest level of 13.4 percent in 1997–1998 and fluctuated around 13–14 percent until 2001–2002. The subsequent period has seen a gradual increase in the tax ratio. Thus, the tax–GDP ratio increased by over one percentage point to 15.2 percent in 2003–2004 (revised estimates for the center and budget estimates for the states). The aggregate tax–GDP ratio is yet to reach the levels that prevailed before systematic tax reforms were initiated in 1991.

Interestingly, the trends in tax ratios of direct and indirect taxes follow different paths. In the case of direct taxes, the tax ratio remained virtually stagnant throughout the period from 1950 to 1990 at about 2 percent of GDP. Thereafter, thanks to the reforms marked by significant reduction in the tax rates and simplification of the structure, revenue from direct taxes increased sharply to over 4 percent in 2003–2004 and is expected to be about 4.5 percent in 2004–2005. This is in sharp contrast to the steady increase in indirect taxes seen during the first 40 years of planned development, which, as a ratio of GDP, increased from 4 percent in 1950–1951 to 13.5 percent in 1991–1992 and declined thereafter to about 11 percent.

Table 4.2   Trends in Tax Revenue in India *(as a percentage of GDP)*

	Center			States			Total		
	Direct	Indirect	Total	Direct	Indirect	Total	Direct	Indirect	Total
1950–1951	1.8	2.3	4.1	0.6	1.7	2.2	2.3	4.0	6.3
1960–1961	1.7	3.5	5.2	0.6	2.0	2.7	2.3	5.5	7.9
1970–1971	1.9	5.1	7.0	0.3	3.1	3.4	2.2	8.2	10.4
1980–1981	2.1	7.1	9.2	0.2	4.4	4.6	2.3	11.5	13.8
1985–1986	2.0	8.3	10.3	0.2	5.0	5.3	2.2	13.3	15.0
1987–1988	1.9	8.7	10.6	0.2	5.2	5.4	2.1	14.0	16.1
1990–1991	1.9	8.2	10.1	0.2	5.1	5.3	2.2	13.3	15.4
1991–1992	2.4	8.0	10.3	0.2	5.3	5.5	2.6	13.3	15.8
1995–1996	2.8	6.5	9.4	0.2	5.2	5.4	3.0	11.7	14.8
2000–2001	3.3	5.8	9.0	0.2	5.4	5.6	3.4	11.2	14.6
2001–2002	3.0	5.2	8.2	0.2	5.4	5.6	3.2	10.6	13.8
2002–2003	3.4	5.4	8.8	0.2	5.7	5.9	3.5	11.1	14.6
2003–2004[1]	3.8	5.4	9.2	0.2	5.8	6.0	4.0	11.2	15.2
2004–2005[2]	4.3	5.6	9.9	n/a	n/a	n/a	n/a	n/a	n/a

Source: Public Finance Statistics, 2003–2004. Ministry of Finance, Government of India.

1. Actual for the center and revised estimate for states.
2. Revised estimates for center.

Fluctuations in the tax ratio are seen mainly at the central level. Central revenues constitute about 60 percent of the total; therefore, fluctuations in the central tax ratio significantly impact the aggregate tax ratio. During the first 35 years of planned development (1951 to 1986), the tax ratios at both central and state levels increased sharply. Thereafter, the ratio was stagnant at 5.5 percent at the state level until 2001–2002 and then increased marginally to 6 percent in 2003–2004. In contrast, the central tax ratio, which peaked in 1987, remained at that level until 1991–1992. In subsequent years, it declined until 2001–2002, but recovered to the pre-1991 level in 2004–2005 (revised estimates). At the central level, the share of direct taxes increased from 20 percent in 1990–1991 to over 43 percent in 2004–2005.

ANALYSIS OF CENTRAL TAXES

As mentioned earlier, over 60 percent of aggregate tax collections in the country are affected at the central level, as all broad-based taxes excluding the sales tax have been assigned to it. Furthermore, since the trends in central taxes have been decisive in determining the overall trends, it is useful to examine them in greater detail.

Bird (1993), after observing tax reforms in many countries, states that the "fiscal crisis has been proven to be the mother of tax reform," and Indian experience fits into this observation. However, unlike crisis-driven reforms, which are often ad hoc and address immediate exigencies of revenue, tax reform in India was undertaken after a detailed analysis. Interestingly, contrary to expectations, the period after the introduction of reforms has seen a decline in the tax–GDP ratio from 10.3 percent in 1991–1992 to 8.2 percent in 2001–2002 at the central level, before it recovered to about 10 percent in 2004–2005. This development has prompted many to ask whether the tax reforms caused the decline in the tax–GDP ratio.

The disaggregated analysis of the trends in central tax revenue presented in Table 4.3 shows that the sharpest decline in the tax–GDP ratio was in indirect taxes—both customs duties and central excise duty. Customs

Table 4.3   Level and Composition of Central Tax Revenue

	PIT	CIT	Direct Tax	Customs	Excise	Indirect	Total
As a percentage of GDP							
1985–1986	1.0	1.1	2.1	3.6	4.9	8.8	10.9
1990–1991	0.9	0.9	2.0	3.6	4.3	8.2	10.1
1995–1996	1.3	1.4	2.8	3.0	3.4	6.5	9.4
2000–2001	1.5	1.7	3.3	2.3	3.3	5.8	9.0
2001–2002	1.4	1.6	3.0	1.8	3.2	5.2	8.2
2002–2003	1.5	1.9	3.4	1.8	3.3	5.4	8.8
2003–2004	1.5	2.3	3.8	1.8	3.3	5.4	9.2
2004–2005[1]	1.6	2.7	4.3	1.8	3.3	5.6	9.9
2005–2006[2]	1.9	3.1	5.0	1.5	3.5	5.5	10.5
As a percentage of total tax revenue							
1985–1986	9.2	10.1	19.3	33.0	45.0	80.7	100
1990–1991	9.3	9.3	19.2	35.9	42.6	80.8	100
1995–1996	14.0	14.8	30.2	32.1	36.1	69.8	100
2000–2001	16.8	18.9	36.2	25.2	36.3	63.8	100
2001–2002	17.1	19.6	37.0	21.5	38.8	63.0	100
2002–2003	17.0	21.3	38.4	20.7	38.1	64.5	100
2003–2004	16.3	25.0	41.3	19.1	35.7	61.3	100
2004–2005[1]	16.6	27.1	43.9	18.4	32.9	56.1	100
2005–2006[2]	17.9	29.9	47.9	14.4	32.8	52.1	100

Source: Estimate of Revenues, Central Budget (various years).

1. Revised estimates.
2. Budget estimates.

duties declined by about 1.8 percentage points from 3.6 percent in 1991–1992 to 1.8 percent in 2004–2005, and the decline in the central excise duty during the period was by one percentage point from 4.3 percent to 3.3 percent. Interestingly, the tax ratio from both taxes declined until 2001–2002 and has stabilized at that level. This indicates that while the customs may continue to decline as tariff levels are further brought down, the tax ratio from internal indirect taxes is likely to increase if reforms toward improving the coverage of service tax and its integration with CenVAT are undertaken, and significant improvement in tax administration is achieved.

In contrast to indirect taxes, there has been a significant increase in the revenue from direct taxes. In fact, since the reforms were introduced, the direct tax–GDP ratio more than doubled from about 2 percent in 1991–1992 to 4.3 percent in 2004–2005. The increase was seen in both personal income and corporate income taxes, with the tax–GDP ratio in corporate income taxes increasing by more than three times, from 0.9 percent in 1991–1992 to 2.7 percent in 2004–2005. The revenue from the personal income tax increased from 0.9 percent to 1.6 percent during the period.

The decline in the share of customs revenue is to be expected when the tariff rates are significantly brought down in the wake of external liberalization. The decline could have been even faster but for the Finance Ministry's hesitancy in reducing the tariffs even more, owing mainly to the demands of the domestic industry. To some extent, it was expected that increasing imports due to liberalization would offset the effect of rate reduction. However, an increase in imports after liberalization was not enough to balance the revenues.

Excise duties declined throughout the 1980s in part because the rate structure assumed when the input tax credit was allowed was perhaps not revenue neutral. Continued exemption of the small-scale sector and widespread use of area-based exemptions are other important reasons for the decline in excise duties. In addition, due to a poor information system, it was possible to claim excessive input tax credit. Since 1997–1998, over 75 percent of the increase in GDP has been attributable to the growth in the services sector, and the manufacturing sector has been relatively stagnant, implying an automatic reduction in the ratio of taxes on the manufacturing base as a percentage of total GDP.

In contrast to indirect taxes, the revenues from both personal income tax and corporate income tax have steadily increased since 1991. The major reason attributed for the increase is improved tax compliance arising from a reduction in marginal tax rates (Das-Gupta and Mookherjee, 1997; Das-Gupta, 2002).

Level, Composition, and Trends in State Taxes

Table 4.4 presents the trends in states' tax revenues. As can be seen from the table, revenue from state taxes as a ratio of GDP was virtually stagnant throughout the 1990s, fluctuating at around 5 to 5.7 percent. In fact, from 1994–1995, the tax ratio declined to bottom out at 5.1 percent in 1998–1999, the year in which the states had to revise the pay scales, thereby exacerbating their fiscal problems. In subsequent years, there has been a steady improvement in the tax ratio to touch 6 percent in 2003–2004.

Among the different state taxes, the sales tax is predominant and constitutes about 60 percent of total state tax revenues. Therefore, not surprisingly, the overall trend in states' tax ratio follows closely the trends in sales tax revenue. Revenues from the sales tax after reaching a low of 3.1 percent in 1998–1999 increased marginally to 3.5 percent in 2000–2001, and it has remained at that level. Any attempt to improve the revenue productivity of the states' tax system has to deal with the reform of sales taxes. Therefore, the recent move toward destination-based VAT is extremely important.

The state excise duty is a sumptuary tax on alcoholic products and has always presented a problem of balancing regulatory and revenue considerations. The major components of the tax come from arrack, country liquor, and Indian Made Foreign Liquor (IMFL), including beer. The duty collected is by way of a license fee on the sale/auction of vends and taxes

Table 4.4 Trends in State-Level Taxes *(as a percentage of GDP)*

Year	Direct Taxes	Sales Tax	State Excise Duty	Stamps and Registration	Taxes on Transport	Other Indirect Taxes	Total Indirect Taxes	Total Taxes
1990–1991	0.2	3.2	0.9	0.4	0.5	0.3	5.1	5.5
1995–1996	0.2	3.0	0.7	0.5	0.4	0.5	5.2	5.4
1996–1997	0.2	3.2	0.7	0.5	0.4	0.3	5.1	5.2
1997–1998	0.1	3.2	0.8	0.5	0.4	0.3	5.2	5.4
1998–1999	0.1	3.1	0.8	0.4	0.4	0.3	5.0	5.1
1999–2000	0.1	3.2	0.8	0.4	0.4	0.3	5.2	5.3
2000–2001	0.2	3.5	0.8	0.4	0.4	0.4	5.4	5.7
2001–2002	0.2	3.4	0.8	0.5	0.5	0.4	5.4	5.7
2002–2003	0.2	3.5	0.8	0.6	0.5	0.3	5.7	5.9
2003–2004	0.2	3.6	0.8	0.5	0.6	0.3	5.8	6.0

Source: Public Finance Statistics, Ministry of Finance (relevant years).

on consumption. The problem in regard to country liquor is the brewing and consumption of illicit liquor. This has not only caused a loss of revenue, but has also been an important health hazard. With regard to IMFL, in one of the states, it was estimated that actual evasion of the tax may be as high as three times the revenue collected (Karnataka, 2001). The way to deal with this problem has more to do with strengthening the tax administration and information system and less to do with the structure of the tax.

The principal source of stamp duties and registration fees is the sale of immovable property transactions. The most important problem affecting this tax is undervaluation of the value of the property transacted. This is partially due to the high tax rates: until recently, the tax rates were as high as 12 to 15 percent on the value of transactions (Karnataka, 1996). Many of the states that reduced the rates have found the typical working of the Laffer curve phenomenon and have started reforms to reduce the rates in this direction. Undervaluation of immovable property is aided by the lack of an organized market.

At the local level, two taxes have some significance: the taxes on property, and in some states, Octroi—the tax on the entry of goods into a local area for consumption, use, or sale—levied by urban local bodies. The major problem with urban property taxes, as in the case of registration fees, is undervaluation. Alternative models of reform, using the capital value or rental value for valuing the property, have been suggested. The ultimate reform depends on development of an organized property market. In most cases, the recommendations suggested have been to use the guided value determined in some independent manner. As regards Octroi, this checkpost-based levy not only impedes internal trade and violates the principle of common market, but is also a source of corruption and rent seeking. Most states have eliminated this levy in recent years.

TAX POLICY: A CRITICAL REVIEW

DIRECT TAXES

Over the last decade and a half, thanks to simplifying reforms, the irritants in the tax system have been reduced significantly. The structure has been rationalized, in terms of both tax rates and associated brackets. Remaining issues relate to the plethora of tax preferences built into the tax regime. In some cases, these preferences took the form of deductions from taxable income—for instance, reimbursement of medical expenses and contributions to pension funds—and in others, rebate in tax payable.[9] The latter included a wide range of investment options. Each of these provisions was associated with a separate ceiling, suggesting significant scope and the need for tax planning in order to benefit from the variety of provisions. One sector that receives a significant degree of incentives within the personal income tax is the housing sector. For debt-financed investment in a residential accommodation by taxpaying individuals, the tax statutes provided for incentives on both interest payment and repayment of the principal. As a part of a major exercise to consolidate the tax structure, the budget of 2005–2006 consolidated a number of these preferences into a single broad provision of deduction from taxable income, with no individual ceilings prescribed. This was proposed as part of an initiative to make a transition from a regime of exempt-exempt-exempt mode[10] of treatment of savings and investment to one of exempt-exempt-tax mode. In the former regime, investments in designated savings instruments were exempt. The returns from these investments were also exempt, and even when the savings were liquidated following the lock-in period, tax was not payable. In the new regime, the tax will be paid when the savings instruments are liquidated. Another major change introduced was the elimination of the standard deduction provision. There was an increase in the exemption threshold to compensate for the change in the structure. Some debate has arisen regarding the equity implications of such a change. Although the change does reduce the complexity of the regime, it does imply a change in the balance of the tax regime in favor of self-employed as against salaried individuals.

A few issues remain, however. The transition to the EET regime is not yet complete, and no time path has been specified. Given the multiplicity of instruments for savings, there is a lack of clarity on whether investment in all forms would be subject to EET or whether the treatment would be limited to some specified instruments. The latter approach would require a mechanism for delineating future streams of incomes, as well as for taxation purposes, thereby introducing a degree of complexity into the tax regime.

Within corporate income taxation, there are two sets of issues: one relating to the rationale for a minimum alternate tax, and the other relating to the increasing number of stand-alone taxes incorporated into the tax regime, so as to plug existing loopholes in the tax structure. Some of these loopholes are discussed in the following sub-sections.

Minimum Alternate Tax

As mentioned in the earlier section, whenever the tax payable on taxable income computed as per the Income Tax Act is less than 7.5 percent of the book profit of the company, then this company is subject to a minimum alternate tax of 10 percent of the book profit, as defined in the Income Tax Act. Like regular income tax, this tax is also topped by a surcharge of 2.5 percent and an additional education charge of 2 percent. Certain incomes are exempt from this tax, notably income from certain infrastructure industries, income from units in specified economically backward areas, income of certain loss-making companies, and export profits. The primary implication of this tax is to place a ceiling on the incentive provided to companies by way of accelerated depreciation or incentives other than those mentioned above.

The tax preferences that are available can broadly be divided into two categories:

1. Provisions relating to depreciation, insofar as they are at variance with the prescriptions of the Companies Act. Until March 2005, the depreciation provisions in the Income Tax Act provided for a higher rate of depreciation of 20 percent on plant and machinery, a historical legacy from the times of significantly higher tax rates. While major corrections have been incorporated from the budget of 2005–2006, some differences persist.

2. Exemptions and concessions provided to address concerns of geographical equity or to encourage certain sectors of the economy.

The expert opinion is that the underlying causes for divergence between income as defined in the Income Tax Act and Companies Act should be corrected, so as to ensure a convergence between these two definitions of income, for reasons of both rational tax policy and transparency and good corporate governance.

In terms of depreciation, there is no clear rationale for continued differences between the Income Tax Act and the Companies Act. The Companies Act attempts to be faithful to the concept of depreciation—wear and tear of a machine or any other good. Given that depreciation gets intimately related to the expected life of the machine and the number of hours per day the machine is expected to run, the depreciation provisions in this act vary by the type of machine and the number of shifts it runs in a day. However, given that the resources so allocated are a notional entry in the books of account, and that depreciation has to attend to obsolescence of technology/equipment as well, it is desirable to explore a less information/monitoring intensive formula for depreciation. In this sense, the provisions as per the Income Tax Act require less detail in terms of application, especially in the case of machinery and plants.

Turning to the second category of tax preferences, exemptions and tax preferences, we find that broadly five categories of exemptions and tax preferences are available in the tax statutes, apart from the preferential treatment of agricultural income and income of charitable institutions: area-based exemptions for investment in backward areas; exemptions for exports and special economic zones (SEZs); exemptions for investment in power generation and other infrastructure sectors; investments in real estate development (especially for housing projects); and investments in the food-processing sector.

The effects of these incentives have been mixed. These incentive options have caused considerable distortion in economic decision making. In the case of backward-area incentives, for instance, investments are found to occur in industries with low investment requirements, low value-added, and hence, low employment potential (TECS, 2004). This also suggests the possibility that at the end of the incentive period, most of these industries may move out and return to the original location. On the one hand, this distorts resource allocation in the economy; on the other hand, it does not generate conditions for the sustainable growth of backward regions. Similarly, in the case of incentives for exports, there appears to be little ground for extending such benefits inasmuch as India has the unenviable status of being the country against whose goods the countervailing duty provisions have been invoked the most over the last five years (Bagchi et al., 2005).

Fringe Benefits Tax

The fringe benefits tax, as discussed earlier, is payable by the companies but is supposed to be a tax on the employees.[11] Also, this tax is payable even if the company is otherwise not liable to pay corporate income tax. This approach embodies a number of problems. First, through this provision, the government has introduced multiple measures for taxation of perquisites and fringe benefits provided by the employer to the employees. This provision is over and above the existing provision of taxation of perquisites as part of the personal income tax. Second, this tax is introduced through an additional act with its own rules and procedures and a separate return and assessments, making compliance tedious and costly. A simpler approach might be one involving expansion in the scope of taxation of perquisites where benefits can be assigned to identifiable beneficiaries within the income tax, alongside disallowing part or all of the expenditure deduction of other nonassignable items to capture the tax on such fringe benefits. Since, for most companies liable to this tax, personal income tax payable on the wages and salaries to employees would be deductible at source, this approach would involve no additional compliance costs. Furthermore, this would not require a separate act with its own rules and procedures, thereby easing the compliance requirements. The only situation where the liability might be reduced is in the case of loss-making companies, since the disallowed expenditure would only contribute to higher losses and hence no taxes; this situation alone does not merit a separate enactment.

Banking Cash Transactions Tax

This tax has been introduced in order to curtail cash transactions—a means by which a number of taxes, including income tax, are evaded. The tax, levied at 0.1 percent, is applicable on cash withdrawals from non-saving accounts held with banks, provided the amount of cash withdrawn is more than Rs. 25,000 in the case of individuals and Rs. 100,000 in the case of firms. While the rationale for the tax is fairly appealing, it is necessary to step back and analyze the factors that encourage cash transactions. For instance, it would be useful to determine the extent of overlap between the formal-sector banking institutions and the black economy. To the extent that income which becomes black or unaccounted for remains outside the network, this tax can only address the additions to the stock and not the stock itself. Without addressing the root cause, there is a good likelihood that alternative informal sector institutions will evolve to address the needs in this changed environment. For instance, since this tax is applicable only to transactions through scheduled commercial banks and not to cooperative sector banks, this may provide one of the many escape routes.

Securities Transactions Tax

The tax on transactions in securities in a recognized stock exchange in India was introduced in 2004–2005 at 0.15 percent. This tax is expected to reduce speculative trading in the stock markets and volatility in prices because this tax would be applicable to each such transaction. The rationale for this tax seems to stem from a perceived inability to appropriately tax the financial economy. One loophole that finds frequent mention in this context is the Double Taxation Avoidance Agreement (DTAA) of India with Mauritius. Under this treaty, corporate bodies registered in Mauritius would be taxed under Mauritian law rather than Indian law. Since Mauritius does not tax capital gains and dividends, it provides a viable routing option for avoiding taxes in India. Interestingly, this treatment has now been extended to the DTAA with Singapore as well. Moreover, given the impact of these agreements, the tax law was amended to eliminate taxation of long-term capital gains and reduce the taxation of short-term capital gains to 10 percent along with an STT of 0.15 percent. Although the solution appears appropriate in the limited context, it is not clear how a renegotiation of the DTAAs is not a better, more rational solution.

INDIRECT TAXES

The major issues related to indirect taxes can be classified into two categories: those relating to exemptions and tax preferences and those relating to the development of a coordinated system of domestic trade taxes.

Tax Preferences

Tax preferences within indirect taxes include, in addition to a list of exempt commodities in both excise and customs duties, exemptions for investment in depressed areas and for small-scale units in the case of the excise duty and a variety of duty-drawback schemes for exports in the case of customs duties.[12] Given the stated intent of reform to consolidate the taxes and reduce the number of rate brackets, there is an emergent need to reexamine the need for commodity-wise exemptions. This holds for both the excise duty and the customs duty. Similarly, in the case of the Service Tax, the tax continues to be structured as a levy on specified services. Implicit in this definition is a notion of exemption for all uncovered services. Although the list of taxable services is being expanded in every budget, it still remains selective. The limitations of such an arrangement are taken up in the discussion on a coordinated system of consumption taxes, in the following sub-section.

As mentioned in the discussion on direct taxes, tax exemptions and preferences tend to distort economic decision making. The excise exemptions provided, along with the income tax holidays for investment in depressed areas, do not induce sustainable economic activities. Given the substantial differential induced by these exemptions, activities that are subject to high tax rates tend to gravitate to these areas. Furthermore, anecdotal evidence suggests that such incentives are prone to evasion through appropriate accounting and billing, without inducing the corresponding scale of economic activity even in the short run. Thus, such incentives do not provide gains that are sustainable in the long run and that need to be reconsidered. Similarly, the incentives for small-scale units encourage artificial truncation of economic activities at the defining threshold. These units evolve into a strong interest group, which then lobbies for an enhancement of the qualifying threshold, thereby expanding the scope of the provision. While the intent is to incentivize only small units, which subsequently grow and move out of the incentive regime, the net impact at the margin at the time of transition is large enough to invoke significant resistance.

Coordinated System of Consumption Taxes

India's constitution assigns the power to tax domestic trade in the following manner:

a. The central government is assigned the power to levy an excise duty on manufactured goods.

b. The state governments are assigned the power to tax sale of goods within a state's geographical boundaries.

c. The central government is empowered to tax the sale of goods when the event spans two states.

d. Following a recent constitutional amendment, the central government is empowered to tax all services, except those explicitly assigned to the states such as railways, entertainment, and transportation by road.

This assignment clearly works against the evolution of a coordinated and comprehensive system of taxation of consumption in the country. The state sales taxes have made a transition from predominantly cascading-type first-point taxes to that of intrastate value-added taxes on goods—a transition that could be made while remaining within their constitutional assignment. On the other hand, the center made a transition from a manufacturing excise duty to a manufacturer's value-added tax, and subsequently attempted a limited integration of the tax on services with the tax on goods through the tax credit mechanism. The Union budget of 2006–2007 announced that by 2010 India would make a transition from the present structure to a generalized goods and services tax. A huge distance needs to be covered before such a transition can be completed. Some of the key issues that need to be resolved are as follows:

a. Will this be a single tax governing all taxes on goods and services? In other words, would it encompass both central and state-level taxes?

b. Should the country plan the transition directly to this prescribed state, or is a transition path necessary?

A single goods and services tax would be a harmonized domestic trade tax and would be desirable from the viewpoint of economic efficiency. Such a tax, however, would call for the states to surrender their fiscal autonomy. This part of the bargain would not be easy to achieve. The Kelkar Task Force Report (India, 2004) suggests a "Grand Bargain" between the center and states to achieve this. Even if such a bargain were to be effectively struck, there is a need for an institutional mechanism to enforce the new regime, unless it can take the form of a constitutional amendment. Once the bargain is struck, the next big question would be regarding administration of the new tax. With a single tax structure, it is not difficult to make a case for a single agency administering the tax. However, the problem of which level of government will administer the tax and how the tax administrators at the nonadministering level will be redeployed will have to be resolved. At a time when both center and states have embarked on fiscal adjustment, this issue does not yield an easy solution. Further complicating this whole matter are the coalition governments, where multiple parties have pivotal status.

The second set of issues relates to the transition from the present state to the proposed Goods and Services Tax (GST). The state-level VAT regimes are themselves considered to be a transition measure. Extending the prevailing intrastate VAT into an interstate VAT is necessary to make the tax system destination-based. For this transition to be complete, at least as far as the goods segment of the economy is concerned, the Central Sales Tax (CST)—the tax levied by the Union government on interstate sale of goods—will have to be phased out. Given that intrastate sales will be taxed at regular rates and interstate transactions will potentially suffer no tax burden, there is a need for an appropriate mechanism for monitoring interstate trade before the tax can be eliminated. Of the many alternatives available, especially ones that do not require an overarching presence of the Union government, the one that appears most suitable and least risky is zero-rating with prepayment as described below.

This model works on the principle of zero-rating, with the difference that the exporter in the exporting state will get the benefit of zero-rating his transaction provided the importer in the importing state has accounted for the transaction and paid the tax on it. This could either mean that the transaction is accounted for in the next tax period and the tax due is paid or that the importer agrees to pay the tax on every individual transaction at the time of placing the order and/or receipt of the goods. For instance, for an export transaction of Rs. 1000 from state A to state B, the exporter in state A verifies the registration number of the buyer from state B and claims zero-rating for this transaction as a part of his tax return. In state B, if the rate of tax is 10 percent, the buyer declares the purchase of Rs. 1000 and pays Rs. 100 as the tax due on the transaction, as a part of his tax return. There is verification of this information across the states, and any mismatch will invoke a reversal of the taxes refunded to the exporter.[13]

While this mechanism safeguards the revenues of both the exporting and the importing state, the cost of such a security is borne by either the exporter or the importer in the form of a higher interest burden and of verification of the buyer's credentials. The difference between this system and simply the zero-rating system is that in the present system the importer pays the tax at the time the goods are received, whereas in the case of zero-rating, the tax has to be paid at the time the goods are sold. Since local purchases would suffer tax up front, there is a level playing field between local purchases and interstate purchases in a prepayment system. (See Rao, 2005 for a discussion of the alternatives.)

Once these reforms are made, the only other major problem remaining will be the treatment of services within the state VAT regime. If services continue to be outside the state VAT base, a few immediately apparent services can add severely to the cost of manufacturing and trade: transportation and electricity. These are inputs into most manufacturing activities, use goods for the supply of services, and could suffer significant cascading. This issue is especially important, since petrol and diesel are being kept out of the VAT net, thereby perpetuating the possibility of a tax cascading in some form or the other.

In the context of the announced transition to a generalized GST, it is not clear how expansion of the scope of a state VAT to include services can be worked out. Inclusion of selective localized services, as the above example illustrates, would not address the basic problem of cascading within the tax system. The discussion of a comprehensive power to tax services, however, needs a definition of treatment of services of an inter-state nature. Here, the options available differ depending on whether or not there is an overarching central tax. Without reference to the context of the GST, therefore, it is difficult to discuss reform of the state VAT.

ANALYSIS OF THE TRENDS AND ECONOMIC IMPACT OF THE TAX SYSTEM

This section explains the observed trends in different central and state taxes in some detail and analyzes the possible efficiency and equity impli-cations of different taxes. Specifically, the analysis seeks to raise a number of questions, such as: has tax compliance improved over the years in re-sponse to a reduction in marginal tax rates? What other factors influence the revenue productivity of the tax system? What are the efficiency and equity implications of the tax system?

PERSONAL INCOME TAX

The increase in the revenue productivity of the personal income tax is at-tributed to the improvement in tax compliance arising from the sharp reduction in marginal tax rates in 1991–1992 and 1996–1997. This is re-flected in the negative correlation between effective tax rates and the ratio of income tax collections to GDP, akin to a Laffer curve.[14] Das-Gupta and Mookherjee (1997) attribute improvement in the overall performance of the tax system to the reduction in the marginal tax rates. In a more re-cent analysis based on 16 different structural, administrative, and institu-tional indicators, Das-Gupta (2002) concludes that the performance of the tax system has shown improvement and that tax compliance has in-deed improved after a reduction in marginal tax rates. Bhalla (2005) esti-mates the aggregate revenue elasticity at −1.43 percent and concludes that the 1996–1997 tax cut was a huge success in increasing revenues.

Can we attribute improved revenue performance of direct taxes solely to a reduction in marginal tax rates? A close scrutiny of the revenue gener-ated by the personal income tax shows that an increase in the scope of tax deduction at source (TDS) is the main contributor to the revenue increase (Table 4.5). The proportion of TDS to total revenue collections increased

Table 4.5   Contribution of TDS to Revenue, Personal Income Tax

	Tax Deduction at Source (%)	Advance Tax (%)	Gross Collections (Rs. crore)	Refunds (Rs. crore)	TDS/GDP (%)
1994–1995	22.18	56.87	17178.72	3357.76	0.37
1995–1996	22.21	50.01	22949.61	6462.48	0.42
1996–1997	50.87	27.30	20042.48	1808.49	0.75
1997–1998	50.87	24.10	19270.19	2169.60	0.64
1998–1999	52.44	23.59	22411.98	2171.83	0.67
1999–2000	53.69	24.58	28684.29	3029.79	0.80
2000–2001	63.22	20.89	35162.61	3398.63	1.06
2001–2002	67.10	19.23	35358.00	3354.00	1.04
2002–2003	65.55	20.26	42119	5253	1.12
2003–2004	64.03	20.04	48454	7067	1.12

Source: Report of the Comptroller and Auditor General (Direct Taxes) Government of India (various years).

from 22 percent in 1994–1995 to 50 percent in 1996–1997 and further to 67 percent in 2001–2002 before declining marginally to 64 percent in 2003–2004. As a proportion of GDP, the ratio of collections from TDS increased by 0.67 percentage points over the period considered. This suggests that improved compliance is largely, if not solely, due to improved coverage or greater effectiveness of TDS as a tool for collecting taxes. This observation, however, runs contrary to the results quoted above.

Interestingly, although it is tempting to attribute this increase to an increase in the scope of TDS on interest, dividends, payments to contractors, and insurance commissions, much of the increase has come about in TDS in salaries. Thus, an increase in tax revenue has possibly more to do with the expansion of the organized sector, financialization of the economy, and administrative measures on extending the TDS than on improved compliance due to a reduction in marginal tax rates. During the period from 1999–2000 to 2003–2004, the total number of personal income tax assessments increased from 19.6 million to 28.8 million. Broader coverage of PAN and expanded use of PAN and TIN have helped to create an extensive and reliable database to improve tax compliance. The above evidence, however, cannot be interpreted as presenting a case for increasing the marginal tax rates, since such increases would be associated with significant efficiency costs.

It is important to understand the impact of a reduction in the marginal tax rate and a reduction in the number of rate categories since 1991–1992 on the overall progressivity and equity of the tax system. With the reduction in the marginal tax rates, the effective rate declines as the level of income increases. From this fact, it would be tempting to conclude that progressivity has declined and that overall equity has worsened over the years. Such a conclusion would be inappropriate; what this shows rather is that among income taxpayers, the progressivity has declined. But this is also a period when income tax coverage increased substantially. In 2003–2004, as many as 29 million people paid income tax as compared to 3.9 million in 1989–1990. The tax–GDP ratio has doubled to more than 2 percent of GDP. This expansion in coverage would suggest that by bringing in a larger proportion of people into the tax net, there would be some improvement in horizontal equity: people with similar incomes remaining outside the tax net are possibly now paying taxes.

CORPORATE INCOME TAX

Of the four major taxes considered in this chapter, revenues from the corporation tax grew at the fastest rate during the 1990s. As a ratio of GDP, the revenue from the tax increased by three times from 0.9 percent in 1990–1991 to 2.7 percent in 2003–2004, despite a significant reduction in the rates. The reforms focused mainly on doing away with the distinction between closely held and widely held companies, reducing the marginal tax rates to align them with the top marginal tax rate of the personal income tax, and rationalizing tax preferences—investment allowance and depreciation allowance—to a considerable extent.

It is instructive to analyze the contribution of different sectors to the corporation tax. The contribution of the manufacturing sector according to the Prowess database accounts for two-thirds of corporate tax collections (Table 4.6). The analysis shows that the manufacturing sector contributed 40 percent of the corporation tax in 2003–2004. Within the manufacturing sector, the petroleum sector contributed the most (12.5 percent), followed by chemicals (6.5 percent), and basic metal industry (6.1 percent). In contrast, the contribution of textiles was just about 0.5 percent. In fact, in 1994–1995, industries such as chemicals, machinery, and transport equipment contributed the overwhelming proportion of the corporation tax, but their share declined sharply over the years. While part of the decline can be attributed to changes in the shares of these industries in total profits, this does not seem to be the only factor. For financial intermediation, for instance, while the share in total profits increased

Table 4.6 Sectoral Composition of Corporate Income Tax (CIT) Collections (as a percentage of total CIT collections)

	1994–1995	1995–1996	1996–1997	1997–1998	1998–1999	1999–2000	2000–2001	2001–2002	2002–2003	2003–2004
Mining	2.41	5.20	10.55	11.47	12.88	18.66	22.45	18.27	21.97	13.92
Manufacturing										
Food products	6.75	3.69	2.96	3.88	4.55	4.77	4.76	3.67	3.43	3.46
Textiles	1.92	0.83	0.81	0.72	0.56	0.55	0.64	0.37	0.47	0.52
Leather	0.04	0.04	0.04	0.04	0.05	0.11	0.07	0.02	0.02	0.03
Paper and wood	1.61	2.29	0.78	0.53	0.44	0.75	0.89	0.94	0.58	0.74
Petro products	11.75	12.21	7.55	5.50	9.42	6.28	4.97	7.46	11.13	12.48
Chemicals	17.21	13.98	8.67	7.58	6.89	5.74	5.41	5.43	6.00	6.46
Rubber and plastics	0.87	0.63	0.70	0.64	0.93	0.80	0.51	0.47	0.61	0.50
Nonmetallic minerals	1.20	1.82	0.82	0.53	0.46	0.38	0.57	0.40	0.30	0.48
Basic metals and products	3.84	4.70	4.32	3.08	3.60	4.45	4.22	2.95	2.86	6.09
Machinery	13.34	9.90	8.68	6.40	6.35	5.75	3.51	3.92	3.63	3.88
Transport equipment	8.80	10.84	9.41	6.37	5.65	4.61	2.41	3.06	3.96	5.31
Total: Manufacturing	67.33	60.93	44.74	35.27	38.9	34.19	27.96	28.69	32.99	39.95
Electricity, gas, and steam	0.34	1.70	1.70	8.80	11.49	7.51	9.09	6.49	5.57	1.91
Construction	2.44	1.73	1.38	1.17	1.38	1.27	1.17	0.97	0.89	1.31
Wholesale and retail trade	3.29	2.27	3.31	3.41	2.23	1.89	3.00	2.94	3.03	2.99
Hotels and restaurants	1.15	1.37	0.97	0.62	0.53	0.35	0.38	0.23	0.21	0.21
Transport services	0.36	2.27	2.12	2.07	1.39	1.42	1.91	1.50	1.49	1.27
Post and telecom	10.07	7.91	6.13	5.95	7.58	4.29	5.72	6.35	2.61	6.50
Financial intermediation	11.89	15.95	28.34	30.39	22.37	28.54	25.83	32.01	28.67	29.74
Real estate	0.01	0.03	0.03	0.02	0.01	0.02	0.01	0.02	0.02	0.03
Computer, R&D, and other business services	0.67	0.60	0.64	0.72	1.06	1.46	2.19	2.21	2.13	1.79
Social services	0.04	0.05	0.09	0.13	0.19	0.39	0.31	0.32	0.40	0.40
Proportion of Total CIT Collections	50.06	62.16	77.39	80.82	64.54	62.21	61.95	72.62	80.38	65.09

Source: Prowess database.

from 18 to 28 percent between 1994–1995 and 2003–2004, its share in total corporate tax collections changed from 12 to 30 percent during the same period. On the other hand, while the share of manufacturing declined from 67 to 40 percent in profits, its share in tax revenue changed only from 52 to 36 percent.

Another important issue examined here refers to the contribution of the public sector enterprises. Curiously, the contribution by public enterprises has shown a significant increase since 1991. The share fell from 23 percent in 1990–1991 to 19 percent in 1994–1995, but increased thereafter to constitute about 38 percent in 2002–2003. This meant that over 40 percent of the increase in corporation tax was collected from public enterprises (Table 4.7). This is partly due to the fact that public enterprises, unlike the private sector, do not undertake elaborate tax planning to minimize taxes.

Given that MAT was introduced to reduce the gap between the effective tax rates that companies face, it would be instructive to examine the variation in the tax rates as they exist today. Table 4.8 provides a classification of 50 major business houses in India in terms of their average effective tax rate.[15] The table clearly illustrates the wide spread in tax rates across different business houses. Interestingly, given that depreciation allowances were one important contributor to the divergence between book profit and income as per the Income Tax Act, even after correcting for depreciation, the variance continues to persist, reflecting the large impact of other tax

Table 4.7 Contribution of Public Sector Enterprises to Corporation Tax

Year	Tax Provision by Public Enterprises (Rs. Crore)	Total Collections (Rs. Crore)	Percent of Tax by Public Sector to Total
1990–1991	1229.3	5335	23.04
1991–1992	1674.11	7853	21.32
1992–1993	1804.37	8899	20.28
1993–1994	2109.93	10060	20.97
1994–1995	2581.46	13822	18.68
1995–1996	4186.66	16487	25.39
1996–1997	5192.51	18567	27.97
1997–1998	5634.11	20016	28.15
1998–1999	6499.00	24529	26.50
1999–2000	7706.25	30692	25.11
2000–2001	9313.62	35696	26.09
2001–2002	12254.32	36609	33.47
2002–2003	17429.95	46172	37.75

Source: Public Enterprises Survey, Government of India (various years).

Table 4.8 Distribution of Corporate Houses by Effective Tax Rate

Range	Corporate Tax Paid	Inclusive of Deferred Tax
0–3	J. K. Singhania Group, Essar (Ruia) Group, Williamson Magor Group, Arvind Mafatlal Group, Usha Rectifier Group	Usha Rectifier Group
3–6	Lalbhai Group, Gulabchand Doshi Group, HCL Group	
6–9	Videocon Group, Raunaq Singh Group, LNJ Bhilwara Group, Vardhman Group, Reliance Group [Ambani], Godrej Group, WIPRO Group, Dalmia Group	Lalbhai Group, Essar (Ruia) Group, Williamson Magor Group, Arvind Mafatlal Group
9–12	Goenka G.P. (Duncans) Group, Modi Bhupendra Kumar, Rasesh Mafatlal Group, Chidambaram M.A. Group, Hari Shankar Singhania Group, RPG Enterprises Group, Bangur B.D. Group, Om Prakash Jindal Group	WIPRO Group, Godrej Group, Rasesh Mafatlal Group, HCL Group, J.K. Singhania Group, Chidambaram M. Group, Modi Bhupendra Kumar
12–15	Vinod Doshi Group, Kirloskar Group, Ruchi Group	LNJ Bhilwara Group, Vinod Doshi Group, Kirloskar Group, Hari Shank Singhania Group
15–18	Piramal Ajay Group, DCM Group	Reliance Group [Ambani], Gulabchand Doshi Group
18–21	Shriram Industrial Enterprises Group, Ranbaxy Group, Nagarjuna Group, Mahindra & Mahindra Group, Vijaypat Singhania Group, Tata Group	Vardhman Group, DCM Group, Raun. Singh Group, Bangur B.D. Group
21–24	Lakshmi Group [Naidu G.V.], Larsen & Toubro Group	Vijaypat Singhania Group, Ranbaxy Group, Tata Group, RPG Enterprises Group, Piramal Ajay Group, Shriram Industrial Enterprises Group
24–27	Escorts Group, Bajaj Group, Murugappa Chettiar Group, T.V.S. Iyengar Group, Birla Group	Larsen & Toubro Group, Mahindra & Mahindra Group, Goenka G.P. (Duncans) Group, Bajaj Group
27–30	T.V.S. Iyengar Group, Birla Aditya Group, Kalyani Group, Firodia Group, MRF Group, Amalgamation Group, Finolex Group	Murugappa Chettiar Group, Dalmia Group
30–33	UB Group, Wadia (Bombay Dyeing) Group, Hero (Munjals) Group,	Finolex (Chhabria P.P.) Group, Birla Aditya Group, Ruchi Group, T.V.S. Iyengar Group, Kalyani (Bharat Forg Group
33–36		MRF Group, Hero (Munjals) Group, O Prakash Jindal Group, Wadia (Bomba Dyeing) Group, Amalgamation Grou
36–39		Lakshmi Group [Naidu G.V.], Firodia Group, Escorts Group, UB Group, Nagarjuna Group, Videocon Group

Source: Derived from the Prowess Database.

Note: Effective tax rate is the ratio of total corporate tax paid to book profits (profits before tax reported in profit and loss account). Revised accounting standards from 2001 require companies to set aside resources meet "deferred tax liabilities." Important among these liabilities is liability on account of accelerated deprec tion provisions of the Income Tax Act. The last column measures effective tax rate inclusive of deferred liabilities.

preferences. A similar exercise for a sectoral decomposition of economic activity brings to light a range of 4 to 38 percent. Given that these numbers pertain to a year when the MAT, too, was applicable, clearly the provision was not enough to ensure a narrow range. The budgetary process seeks to correct this observed feature through an increase in the rate for MAT in the budget for 2006–2007 to 10 percent. This appears to be a perverse solution to the perceived problem of leakages from the general tax regime and the resultant sustenance of zero-tax companies. The tax statutes seek to provide incentives on one hand and to neutralize or tone down the benefits of these incentives through the provisions of MAT. A simpler and more transparent alternative would be to reduce or eliminate incentives and eliminate the need for an additional levy.

UNION EXCISE DUTIES

The declining tax–GDP ratio of Union excise duties is a matter of concern, adding to the reduction in import duties. The reforms in Union excise duties, transforming this levy into ModVAT and then CenVAT, instead of improving the revenue productivity, have led to its decline over the years. The revenue from the tax as a ratio of GDP at 3.3 percent in 2004–2005 is significantly lower than the ratio in 1991–1992 (4.1 percent). A similar decline is witnessed, even if one considers the ratio of excise duty collections to GDP from the manufacturing sector.

That this decline is a cause for concern is apparent, given the overall context of declining reliance on customs duties as a source of revenue and an incomplete compensation by way of increases in the direct tax collections. The declining contribution from CenVAT to manufactured products is all the more intriguing in the wake of a fast-increasing corporation tax. Examination of the sectoral composition of the corporate income tax indicates that services-sector, power-generation, and primary-sector-based companies have recorded relatively faster growth, especially when compared with manufacturing units. In the event, the share of the manufacturing sector in corporate tax revenues declined from 60 to 39 percent. This, however, does not provide the whole answer. Even if one considers only the manufacturing sector, the ratio of CenVAT collections to payments of corporate income tax has not been stable. It is seen that the ratio increased steadily until 2000–2001 and declined thereafter. This behavioral trend is driven largely by the performance of corporate tax payments as a ratio of sales, which declined consistently until 2000–2001 and then recorded a reversal. One explanation for this decline could be found in the decline in interest rates and the corresponding increase in profits relative to sales from 2000–2001.

Another interesting feature of trends in CenVAT collections, as derived from the corporate sector database, is the general decline in the ratio of excise collections to sales. This ratio is computed alternatively for all manufacturing companies with positive profit and for companies with positive excise tax payments. In the case of companies with positive profit, the average rate of tax is lower and the rate of decline slower than that for companies with positive excise tax payments. This is a reflection of an increase in the extent of preferential treatments within the tax statutes. An expansion in the coverage or utilization of the preferential treatment would result in an expansion in sales without a corresponding expansion in the tax payments. While this could also be the result of an increase in share of exports in total value of output, correcting for this factor does not change the observed trends. The other set of factors that could induce such a result are the various categories of exemptions, like those for investment in depressed areas and for small-scale units.

Not only has the revenue productivity of CenVAT declined over the years, but even the composition shows an increase in revenue concentration, particularly toward commodities that serve as inputs into further production. Independently operating excise and sales tax systems and confining the tax to goods and to the manufacturing stage alone do not remove cascading. Also, final products in the manufacturing stage are not necessarily final consumer goods—goods transport vehicles being a prime example.

Decomposition of CenVAT collections, presented in Table 4.9, reveals some interesting features, with implications for both the efficiency and equity of the tax system. One of the most important features is the commodity concentration. Just five groups of commodities—petroleum products, chemicals, basic metals, transport vehicles, and electrical and electronic goods—together contribute 75 percent of total revenue collections from excise duty. Over the years, with diversification in manufacturing, the commodity concentration in excise duty is expected to decrease. Contrarily, the commodity concentration has only increased over the years with a single group, petroleum products, contributing to over 40 percent of the collections, with a more than three times increase in share over a 13-year period, while the value-added by this industry group has increased only marginally from 12 to 14 percent of GDP from the registered manu-

Table 4.9 Revenue from Union Excise Duties by Commodity Groups

	1990–1991	1995–1996	1998–1999	1999–2000	2000–2001	2001–2002	2002–2003	2003–2004
Food products	4.01	3.55	4.80	4.38	4.53	3.67	3.57	3.24
Tobacco products	8.29	8.07	7.95	6.74	6.74	6.57	5.90	5.58
Minerals and ores	8.38	8.68	7.18	6.66	6.24	5.99	5.76	6.24
Petroleum products	**13.93**	**12.39**	**22.46**	**29.56**	**32.91**	**38.32**	**40.37**	**40.99**
Chemicals	**11.15**	**14.42**	**11.14**	**9.79**	**10.17**	**9.86**	**9.31**	**8.86**
Plastics and articles thereof	2.50	4.04	4.21	3.66	2.28	2.38	2.39	2.52
Rubber products	4.93	4.62	2.90	2.65	2.16	1.96	1.79	1.27
Leather and wood products	0.56	0.43	0.23	0.20	0.20	0.17	0.15	0.15
Textiles and garments	10.78	8.54	6.25	5.20	4.84	4.68	4.62	3.73
Basic metals	**9.62**	**14.53**	**11.43**	**11.15**	**10.42**	**9.18**	**9.84**	**11.24**
Electrical and electronic goods/tools	**16.11**	**11.88**	**10.47**	**9.47**	**8.81**	**8.18**	**7.77**	**7.82**
Transport vehicles	**8.39**	**7.35**	**8.46**	**8.79**	**8.90**	**7.17**	**6.97**	**6.63**
Miscellaneous	1.35	1.51	2.51	1.76	1.81	1.88	1.57	1.73
Total	**100**	**100**	**100**	**100**	**100**	**100**	**100**	**100**

Source: Central Board of Excise and Customs, Ministry of Finance, Government of India.

facturing sector. This imposes a disproportionate tax burden on different sectors of the economy. Moreover, this type of commodity concentration does not allow for objective calibration of policies in regard to excise duties, as the Finance Ministry would not like to lose revenue from this lucrative source.

Another important consequence of this pattern of revenue collections is that an overwhelming proportion of the duties are collected from intermediate products, which are used in the production of goods or services that are not subject to excise. Besides petroleum products, which are used mainly in the transportation of goods and persons involved in or related to other manufacturing, the taxes on all goods serving as inputs to service providers, especially of services used as inputs to manufacturing activities, contribute to cascading and add to the production cost. Transport vehicles and related activities are an example. Such cascading is a significant source of inefficiency in the system and results in lack of transparency as well. It is difficult to speculate on the distribution of the tax burden in terms of different income classes, or on different manufacturing enterprises and on employment and incomes.

As is the case for the corporation tax, public sector enterprises pay a predominant proportion of CenVAT collections. The contribution of the public sector to total excise collections in 2002–2003 was about 42 percent (Table 4.10). It is also seen that the share fluctuates widely from year to year. The fluctuations are due mainly to the fluctuations in adminis-

Table 4.10 Contribution of PSEs to Excise Revenues of GOI

	Public Enterprises	Total Collections	Share of PSEs
1990–1991	9655.69	24514	39.39
1991–1992	9815.15	28110	34.92
1992–1993	12179.9	30832	39.50
1993–1994	12527.11	31697	39.52
1994–1995	16414.07	37347	43.95
1995–1996	17044.41	40187	42.41
1996–1997	22192.87	45008	49.31
1997–1998	21719.61	47962	45.29
1998–1999	23131.67	53246	43.44
1999–2000	32941.53	61902	53.22
2000–2001	20824.38	68526	30.39
2001–2002	31202.78	72555	43.01
2002–2003	34610.32	82310	42.05

Source: Public Enterprises Survey Various Issues, and Budget of GOI, various years.

Note: Tax Provision relates to the provision made for the corporate tax.

tered prices on items such as steel, coal, and petroleum products. In other words, the revenue from CenVAT is vulnerable to pricing and output decisions.

The most important, and in many ways the most far-reaching, reforms were those made for customs tariffs. Since 1991, imports subject to quantitative restrictions constituted 90 percent of total imports: these restrictions have been virtually eliminated today. The import weighted tariff rates have been reduced from 72 percent in 1990 to 15 percent at present. The peak rate of import duty also has been brought down from over 150 percent in 1991 to less than 20 percent at present (Virmani et al., 2004).

A major problem that emerges from the viewpoint of efficiency is the continuation of differentiated tax rates varying with the stage of production. The rates on raw materials and intermediate goods continue to be lower than those on consumer goods and capital goods. The import tariff reduction has continued to be guided by this "unprincipled principle" (Joshi and Little, 1996). Even the Kelkar Task Force on indirect taxes has suggested that the rate differentiation should be made on the basis of the stage of production. This approach retains the focus on greater protection for final-use industries, as compared to inputs and intermediate goods, and a continued reliance on the self-sufficiency model of development as against a comparative advantage model.

Table 4.11 presents customs collections by commodity group from 1990–1991 to 2003–2004. Interestingly, despite significant external liberalization, almost 60 percent of the duty is collected from just three commodity groups: namely, machinery (26.6 percent), petroleum products (21 percent), and chemicals (11 percent). Furthermore, the overwhelming proportion (over 75 percent) of the duty is collected from either machinery or basic inputs and intermediate goods. Thus, contrary to some fears, liberalization has not led to a massive inflow of consumer goods. By implication further reduction in duties and greater uniformity in the structure of duties would have beneficial effects on the economy. A detailed econometric study presented by Virmani et al. (2004) shows that a uniform reduction in tariffs has had favorable effects on production, exports, employment, and capital, and that these gains are different across different sectors.

The commodity group composition of import duties also shows a significant increase in the proportion of import duties collected from machinery

Table 4.11 Composition of Revenue from Customs Duties (percent)

	1990–1991	1995–1996	1996–1997	2000–2001	2001–2002	2002–2003	2003–2004
Food items	2.49	2.43	2.25	5.42	10.64	8.76	6.36
Tea/coffee	0.12	0.04	0.04	0.05	0.06	0.09	0.04
Beverages	0.08	0.13	0.07	0.09	0.22	0.16	0.10
Minerals and ores	1.38	0.74	0.52	1.34	1.55	1.80	1.74
Petroleum products	19.39	23.39	28.54	23.16	16.14	19.50	20.93
Chemicals	12.34	11.86	11.19	10.35	11.41	11.19	11.12
of which:							
Pharmaceutical products	0.06	0.07	0.05	0.21	0.30	0.44	0.29
Plastics	6.36	4.86	4.71	2.99	3.14	3.07	3.10
Rubber	1.38	1.32	1.48	1.39	1.40	1.30	1.33
Paper	1.04	0.65	0.74	0.70	0.71	0.69	0.89
Textiles	2.16	1.26	0.94	0.97	0.85	0.96	1.40
Cement products, etc.	0.20	0.19	0.14	0.19	0.21	0.23	0.26
Ceramics	0.58	0.52	0.45	0.69	0.78	0.75	0.98
Iron and steel	10.24	6.63	5.15	3.81	3.78	3.72	4.64
Other basic metals	4.28	4.95	4.38	2.12	2.30	2.17	2.50
Machinery	19.49	20.84	18.81	23.55	24.80	26.36	26.58
Transport equipment	3.29	4.04	4.69	3.94	3.96	3.37	4.14
Others	15.20	16.16	15.90	19.25	18.06	15.87	13.90
Total	**100**	**100**	**100**	**100**	**100**	**100**	**100**

Source: Central Board of Excise and Customs, Ministry of Finance, Government of India.

from 19.5 percent in 1990–1991 to 26.6 percent in 2003–2004. This has happened despite providing exemptions for the plant and machinery imported for several project imports. This implies that external liberalization is leading to adoption of more modern machinery and technology in the production process, which would have a favorable effect on productivity growth. The other item that has shown increased importance in revenue matters is food products. In contrast, revenue from iron and steel and other basic metals has shown a substantial decline over the years. This may be because these items have become more competitive, and, therefore, it is perhaps more attractive to buy them in the domestic market than to import them.

TOWARD FURTHER REFORMS IN THE TAX SYSTEM

In the last few years, reforming India's central tax system has received considerable attention. Several reports have comprehensively examined this system and made important recommendations for reform (India, 2001a, 2002, 2004). While there are differences related to some of the specific recommendations as compared to the TRC, broad agreement has been reached on the direction and thrust of reforms and on the emphasis placed on the reform of tax administration.

REFORM OF CENTRAL TAXES

The reforms with regard to the personal income tax will involve further simplification of the tax system, namely, withdrawal of tax exemptions and concessions given for specified activities, abolition of surcharge, and further simplification of the tax. As many transitional economies have found, there is considerable virtue in having a single tax rate with an exemption limit. The ability of an income tax system to bring about significant redistribution is limited, and it is increasingly being realized that equity should focus on increasing the incomes of the poor rather than on reducing the incomes of the rich. This objective is better achieved by expenditures on human development and not through the tax system (Bird and Zolt, 2005). Yet, moving toward a single tax rate may not be politically feasible at this juncture.

With regard to the corporation tax, broadening the tax base involves getting rid of tax preferences. In particular, the exemption for profits from exports, special economic and free trade zones, technology parks, area-based exemptions for backward area development, and infrastructure should be phased out. Similarly, the present rate of depreciation allowance, even after the reduction in 2005–2006, is quite generous and needs to be reduced to more realistic levels. There has been a great deal of flip-flop in regard to the taxation of dividends from one year to another. The most satisfactory solution in this regard is to partially integrate the tax with the personal income tax.

With regard to import duties, the reform will have to move in the direction of further reduction and unification of rates. Because most nonagricultural tariffs fall between 0 and 15 percent, a uniform tariff of 10 percent would considerably simplify and rationalize the systems (Acharya, 2005). Equally important is the need to get rid of the plethora of exemptions and concessional treatment to various categories, which include project imports. A minimum tariff of 5 percent on all exempted items would rationalize the duty structure and would increase revenue as well.

Wide-ranging exemptions are also a problem with excise duties. In particular, the exemptions given to small-scale industry have not only eroded the tax base but have inhibited the growth of firms into an economic scale. Similarly, various exemptions given to project imports have significantly eroded the tax base. Another important reform objective is to fully integrate the CenVAT with the taxation of services (India, 2001b).

EVOLVING A COORDINATED CONSUMPTION TAX SYSTEM

One of the most important reforms needed in an indirect tax system is the development of a coordinated consumption tax system for the country (Rao, 1998). This system is necessary to ensure fair distribution of the tax burden between different sectors and between goods and services. The reform should also improve the revenue productivity, minimize relative price distortions, and above all, ensure a common market in the country.

This effort involves coordinated calibration of reforms at central, state, and local levels. At the center, as mentioned above, the first step is to evolve a manufacturing stage VAT on goods and services. At the state level, converting the sales tax into VAT should be completed by allowing input tax credits not only for intrastate sales and purchases but also for interstate transactions. Also, appropriate mechanisms must be found to enable the states to levy the tax on services and to integrate it with the

VAT on goods, so as to arrive at a comprehensive VAT. An important problem in this regard is devising a system for taxation of services with an interstate coverage.

The local-level indirect tax reform relates to finding a suitable substitute for Octroi. Although most states in India have abolished Octroi, this process has made the local bodies dependent on the state government for revenues. In every country, property tax is a mainstay of local body finances; reform in this area should help in raising revenue productivity. Yet, this may not suffice. In this situation, the better option is to allow local bodies to piggyback on the VAT collections in urban local body jurisdictions. This will avoid cascading of the tax and minimize exportation of the tax burden by urban local bodies to nonresidents.

REFORM IN TAX ADMINISTRATION

In India, the poor state of tax administration has been a major reason for low levels of compliance and high compliance costs. This is due in part to the virtual absence of data on both direct and indirect taxes even at the central level. Not only does this lack of data hinder proper analysis of taxes needed to provide an adequate analytical background to calibrate changes in the tax structure, but it also makes proper enforcement of the tax difficult. Thus changes in the tax structure have had to be made in an ad hoc manner.

The consequence has been high compliance costs. The only estimate of compliance costs by Das-Gupta (2004a, 2004b) shows that in the case of the personal income tax, compliance cost is as high as 49 percent of the collections from the tax. In the case of the corporate tax, it is between 6 and 15 percent of the tax paid. Much of these costs arise from the legal costs of compliance. While these estimates should be taken with a note of caution, it is important to observe that the compliance cost of taxes in India is extremely high.

High compliance costs combined with a poor state information system have led to the continued interface of taxpayers with officials, negotiated payment of taxes, corruption and rent seeking, and low levels of tax compliance. An important indication of the poor information system is that even as the coverage of TDS was extended over the years, information was not assembled even to check whether those deducting the tax at source actually filed the returns. As the Comptroller and Auditor General of

India (CAG) report for 2003–2004 states, of the 0.63 million returns to be filed by TDS assessees, only 0.50 million were filed. Thus, more than 20 percent of the TDS assessees did not file returns. But even this is a vast improvement over the previous year when 80 percent of the TDS assessees did not file returns.

The recent initiatives on building the computerized information system in direct taxes follow from the recommendations of the KTF. The Central Board of Direct Taxes (CBDT) outsourced the function of issuing permanent account numbers (PAN). The Tax Information Network (TIN) has been established by the National Securities Depository Limited (NSDL). The initial phase has focused on ensuring that TDS assessees do in fact file the returns, as well as on matching and cross-checking the information from banking and financial institutions to ensure that the taxes paid according to the returns are credited into government accounts in the banks. The Online Tax Accounting System (OLTAS) was operationalized in July 2004 and helped expedite the number of refunds from 2.6 million in 2002–2003 to 5.6 million in 2003–2004. Not surprisingly, in the last four years, revenue from direct taxes increased at over 20 percent per year.

Similar initiatives have been taken in regard to indirect taxes as well. The customs e-commerce gateway (ICEGATE) and the Customs Electronic Data Interchange System (ICES) have helped to improve the information system and speed up the clearance processes. In 2003–2004, ICES handled about 4 million declarations in automated customs locations, which constituted about 75 percent of India's international trade. Progress has been made in building capacity in modern audit systems and computerized risk assessment with assistance from the Canadian International Development Agency (CIDA).

Another critical element in tax administration is the networking of the information from various sources. As mentioned earlier, to improve tax enforcement, systems must be developed in order to put together information received from various sources to quantify the possible tax implications in a judicially acceptable manner. In the first instance, the information networking should obtain data from various sources such as banks and financial institutions on various assessees. In the second, there must be a meaningful exchange of information between the direct and indirect tax administrations. In the third instance, it is necessary to exchange information between central and state taxes. Building a computerized information system will help to improve the enforcement of taxes.

NOTES

We would like to thank Professor Roger Gordon for detailed comments on the draft of the chapter.

1. Sections 32A and 32AB of the Income Tax Act include the provisions for investment allowances, while Section 32 provides the accelerated depreciation provisions.

2. The standard deduction was a provision maintained to neutralize the tax disadvantage that a salaried taxpayer faced. While a self-employed taxpayer is entitled to deduct all his expenses toward earning the income as costs, there is no such provision for the salaried. The standard deduction was meant to address this concern.

3. Under this requirement, a contribution to the savings plan is deductible from gross taxable income and the income from a savings plan is also exempt from the tax. However, the withdrawal of savings and the benefits from it in the form of interest and dividends are subject to tax. This is also known as consumption taxation of savings.

4. The change in 1997–1998 was introduced for the stated purpose of encouraging plough back of profits by companies in place of distribution of dividends. However, since a 10 percent tax on dividends and higher taxes in interest income was perceived to be an anomaly, the rate was increased to 20 percent in 2001–2002. In 2002–2003, the income was to be taxed in the hands of the recipients in order to reduce the inequities built into a uniform tax. There were withholding provisions of 10 percent—recipients in higher tax brackets could claim credit for this amount. It should be mentioned that some withholding provisions were always in place whenever the tax was payable by the recipient. However, these were at the rates equivalent to the lowest income tax slab prevalent at the time.

5. The tax credit in subsequent years is available for amounts over and above the MAT payable in that year. In other words, in every financial year, any given firm is expected to pay at least the minimum alternate tax.

6. This was discontinued in the 2006–2007 budget.

7. The budget for 2006–2007 expands the scope further to include an additional 15 categories of services.

8. There are two separate levies on sale of goods—a CenVAT levied and collected by the central government and a state VAT levied and collected by the state governments. As discussed above, the CenVAT applies only on manufacture of goods and allows for tax credit to flow between this tax and service tax. In the states, the levy applies on the sale of goods alone.

9. Whether reimbursement of medical expenses or contributions to pension funds should be considered "preferences" is a debatable issue. In the context of India, the extent of deductions on these counts is limited and prescribed by the Income Tax Act. For instance, all reimbursements of medical expenses up to Rs. 15,000 per annum per employee are deductible from taxable income, but for expenses beyond this limit, the rest is considered part of taxable income. This therefore does not provide a rational basis for treatment of medical expenses. Furthermore, this option is available only to salaried employees and not to self-employed individuals. In the case of contributions to pension funds too, the limit is Rs. 10,000. Contributions beyond this level are from tax-paid incomes.

10. "Exempt-exempt-exempt" refers to a form of treatment whereby incomes, if saved, are not subject to a tax; income on these savings (i.e., interest or dividends), when it accrues, is not taxed; nor is income taxed when it is withdrawn from savings and consumed.

11. The act defines fringe benefits to mean any privilege, service, facility, or amenity that is directly or indirectly provided by an employer to an employee by reason of his or her employment, or any reimbursement made by an employer directly or indirectly for any purpose, or any free or concessional travel ticket for private journeys, or any contribution by an employer toward an approved superannuation fund.

12. While in principle duty drawback for exports would not be considered an incentive, when the form of the scheme does not maintain a clear link between the extent of duty suffered by the exported good and the duty drawback offered, the scheme takes on the form of a tax preference. In India, drawback rates are specified by law on the basis of industry averages of inputs used, and not on the basis of invoices for taxes paid.

13. A similar system is already in place in India for supporting the tracking of interstate sales for taxation under the central sales tax act. This system requires that the importer provide documentary evidence of being a taxpayer in the importing state in order to avail the lower rate of tax. An alternative mechanism could be one whereby the importer declares up front to the tax department the details of the consignment intended for import from another state and the exporting state uses this information to provide the exporting dealer with zero-rating.

14. Effective tax rates are derived by applying the tax structure to reference income levels. Given the limited sample size, such an exercise would not be empirically sound and hence is not reported.

15. A business house has been used in Prowess to include all companies where one entity has a majority share in equity holding.

REFERENCES

Acharya, S. (2005, May 14). "Thirty Years of Tax Reform in India." *Economic and Political Weekly*, 40, pp. 2061–69. Reprinted in S. Acharya, *Essays on Macroeconomic Policy and Growth in India*. New Delhi: Oxford University Press, 2006.

Bagchi, A., and Nayak, P. (1994). "A Survey of Public Finance and the Planning Process: The Indian Experience." In *Tax Policy and Planning in Developing Countries*, A. Bagchi and N. Stern, eds. Delhi: Oxford University Press.

Bagchi, A., Rao, R. K., and Sen, B. (2005). "Raising the Tax Ratio by Reining in the 'Tax Breaks': An Agenda for Action." TRU Working Paper No. 2, NIPFP, New Delhi. www.nipfp.org.in/working_paper/wp06_nipfp_tr_042.pdf.

Bhalla, S. (2005). "Tax Rates, Tax Compliance, and Tax Revenue in India 1988–2004." www.oxusresearch.com/downloads/ce070704.pdf.

Bird, R. (1993). "Federal Provincial Taxation in Turbulent Times." John F. Graham Memorial Lecture Series. *Canadian Public Administration*, p. xxxvi.

Bird, R., and Zolt, E. (2005). "Redistribution via Taxation: The Limited Role of the Personal Income Tax in Developing Countries." *International Studies Program Working Paper Series, at AYSPS* (Andrew Young School of Policy Studies). GSU paper 0507. International Studies Program, AYSPS, Georgia State University.

Centre for Monitoring the Indian Economy (CMIE). "Prowess Database." Mumbai, India.

Chelliah, R. (1986). "Change in the Tax Structure: A Case Study of India." Paper Presented at the 42nd Congress of International Institute of Public Finance, Athens, Greece.

Das-Gupta, A. (2002). "Central Tax and Administration Reform in the 1990s: An Assessment." In *Development, Poverty and Fiscal Policy: Decentralisation of Institutions,* M. G. Rao, ed. New Delhi: Oxford India Paperbacks, Oxford University Press.

———. (2004a, March). "The Compliance Cost of the Personal Income Tax in India, 2000–2001: Preliminary Estimates." *NIPFP Working Paper No. 9.* New Delhi: NIPFP.

———. (2004b, March). "The Income Tax Compliance Cost of Corporations in India, 2000–2001." *NIPFP Working Paper No. 8.* New Delhi: NIPFP.

Das-Gupta, A., and Mookherjee, D. (1997). "Design and Enforcement of Personal Income Tax in India." In *Public Finance, Policy Issues for India,* S. Mundle, ed. New Delhi: Oxford University Press.

India. (1971). *Direct Taxes Enquiry Committee.* New Delhi: Ministry of Finance, Government of India.

———. (1977). *Report of the Indirect Taxation Enquiry Committee.* New Delhi: Ministry of Finance, Government of India.

———. (1991). *Tax Reform Committee, Interim Report.* New Delhi: Ministry of Finance, Government of India.

———. (2001a, May). "Report of the Advisory Group on Tax Policy and Tax Administration for the Tenth Plan." New Delhi: Planning Commission, Government of India. http://planningcommission.nic.in/aboutus/committee/wrkgrp/tptarpt.pdf.

———. (2001b). *Report of the Expert Group on Taxation of Services.* New Delhi: Ministry of Finance, Government of India.

———. (2002a, December). *Report of the Taskforce on Direct Taxes.* New Delhi: Ministry of Finance, Government of India. http://finmin.nic.in/kelkar/final_dt.htm.

———. (2002b, December). *Report of the Taskforce on Indirect Taxes.* New Delhi: Ministry of Finance, Government of India. http://finmin.nic.in/kelkar/final_idt.htm.

———. (2004). *Report of the Task Force on Implementation of the Fiscal Responsibility and Budget Management Act.* New Delhi: Ministry of Finance, Government of India. http://finmin.nic.in/downloads/reports/frbm/start.htm.

———. (2005). *Report of the Comptroller and Auditor General (Direct Taxes).* New Delhi: Government of India.

Joshi, Vijay, and Little, I.M.D. (1996). *India's Economic Reforms 1991–2001.* New Delhi: Oxford University Press.

Karnataka. (1996). *Report of the Committee of State Finance Ministers on Stamp Duty Reform.* New Delhi: NIPFP.

———. (2001). *First Report of the Tax Reforms Commission.* Finance Department, Government of Karnataka.

Rao, G. M. (1998, July 18–24/25–31). "Reforms in Tax Devolution and Evolving a Co-ordinated Tax System." *Economic and Political Weekly,* 33, pp. 1971–76.

———. (2000). "Tax Reform in India: Achievements and Challenges." *Asia-Pacific Development Journal,* 7(2).

Rao, R. K. (2005). "Reforming the State Tax System: Transition to VAT." Paper prepared for the Policy Research Network, sponsored by the Asian Development Bank.

TECS. (2004). "Impact Evaluation Study of North East Industrial Policy 1997." Tata Economic Consultancy Services, Mumbai, India.

Virmani, Arvind, et al. 2004. "Impact of Tariff Reforms on Indian Industry: Assessment Based on a Multi-sector Econometric Model." *ICRIER Working Paper No. 135.*

CHAPTER 5

History of Russian VAT

Sergei Koulayev

On December 6, 1991, Russia adopted a value-added tax (VAT). The new tax system, which was meant to replace preexisting turnover and sales taxes, became effective as of January 1, 1992. Thus, fiscal year 1992 was the first year in Russian history when the VAT was collected. In this chapter, we present the history of legislation, revenue performance, and administration of the Russian VAT during the fiscal years of 1992–2005. Today, the VAT is one of Russia's major taxes, bringing in about one-third of total tax revenue, only second to revenue generated by the enterprise-profit tax. The history of its collection reveals problems whose importance goes beyond the VAT itself.

The direct predecessor of the VAT was the turnover tax,[1] one of the main sources of tax revenues in the Soviet system. Knowledge of this tax system is necessary to understanding some peculiar features of Russia's VAT: as we shall see, the Soviet-style approach to taxation had a substantial effect on the early stage of development. In the Soviet Union, the turnover tax was raised at the retail level, but only on the goods whose retail price was higher than the wholesale price. Such goods included durable goods, luxury products, alcohol, and tobacco. For goods such as foodstuffs and a wide array of consumer goods, which were sold for prices below their wholesale prices, the turnover "tax" became a subsidy. The tax could be raised either as a percentage of projected turnover or per physical unit sold. Effectively, there existed hundreds of tax rates, as every enterprise negotiated with its ministry a rate that would achieve an acceptable level of profitability. Thus, the turnover tax was not a "tax" in the usual meaning of the word; rather, it was more of an accounting device used to level the profitability of enterprises across industries.

In 1991, many retail prices were set free. The proceeds from the turn-over tax began to fall drastically—from 12.6 percent of GDP in 1985 to 6.3 percent of GDP. Indeed, as the amount of tax per unit of a good was fixed, while prices went up, the share of the tax in the final price began to fall. Consequently, revenues from the turnover tax increased more slowly than the turnover itself. For example, in 1991, the nominal value of turnover went up by 70 percent, while proceeds from the turnover tax increased by only 15 percent. At the same time, amounts of subsidies started to increase to the degree that wholesale prices were still kept be-low the market level. The successful implementation of the turnover tax—in the form it was practiced in the Soviet Union—required strict administrative controls over wholesale and retail prices, which were no longer possible.

Facing a revenue crisis that arose at the end of the 1980s, the Soviet government was forced to reform the old tax system to make it more com-patible with a market system. After some discussion, a decision was made to rely on a VAT. The method for collecting the VAT was similar to that implemented to collect the turnover tax, which made the transition easier. As the decision had to be made quickly, all tax legislation was enacted within two months, which did not leave much time for analysis and preparation.

In this chapter, our aim is to give a broad overview of the legislative and administrative developments affecting the Russian VAT from 1992 to 2006, the 14 years it took to create a modern, functioning VAT system. Although further improvements were made after 2006, we do not present them in such detail. Rather, the reader may consult Table 5.A.1, which summarizes the Russian VAT as of 2009. The material is organized in the following way.

In the first section, we briefly report changes in legislation on the VAT, in chronological order, for every year from 1991 to 2005. This sec-tion can serve as a useful reference point, especially with respect to the major VAT reforms undertaken in 2000–2002. It can also be used as an illustration of how difficult and lengthy the political process of tax re-form can be, as it can take years to implement seemingly obvious and necessary changes.

In the next section, we discuss several aspects of the Russian VAT, as it existed before the beginning of 2006. First, we describe developments in methods of accounting for VAT credits and liabilities for various categories of economic agents and different types of transactions. We then discuss these methods as applied to Russian economic reality. Second, we examine the varying treatment of trade with the Commonwealth of Independent States (CIS)[2] and non-CIS countries, and possible reasons for adopting such treatment and whose interest it served. Of special importance is the subsection on VAT exemptions and preferences, which for many years constituted a large problem in the operation of this tax. We present the evolution of exemptions, as they appeared in response to economic difficulties and disappeared in response to backlashes in tax revenues. The first two sections necessarily overlap, but their goals are different: the first section seeks to give the reader an idea of the timing of reforms, whereas the second section provides a unified view of reforms by examining key aspects of VAT.

Finally, the last section discusses problems associated with administration of VAT. First, we provide a general overview of the situation with tax enforcement, which is the most problematic part of tax administration in Russia. We then elaborate on sensitive topics of VAT administration such as the management of tax returns (such as rebates on exports and treatment of negative liability), and the fight against evasion practices involving "fly-by-night" firms, manipulations with invoices, and accounting records.

A BRIEF HISTORY OF LEGISLATION ON VAT

In Russia, the VAT has a relatively short history, having been instituted only in 1992. This makes it feasible to track its development on a yearly basis, through an examination of legislation, administration, and revenue performance. It is possible to distinguish three subperiods: first, the period of introduction of VAT into the taxation system, covering 1992–1995, characterized by frequent adjustments to law and practice; second, the period of "stagnation" from 1996–1999, a period of failed attempts to reform VAT, most likely due to political constraints, as there was no lack of understanding of the necessity of such reforms, both by the national government and by Western experts; third, the period of active reforms, starting by adoption of the Tax Code (Part I in 1999 and Part II in 2000), when the Russian VAT was moving quickly toward modern standards, practically reaching them at the beginning of 2006.

EARLY DAYS: 1992–1995

1992

The initial law, enacted on December 6, 1991, introduced the VAT at a rate of 28 percent, which was relatively high by the standards of Western European countries, where rates varied from 6 to 10 percent in 1992. Taxable persons included all economically active agents whose yearly income from economic activity (production, services, etc.) exceeded 100,000 (later, 500,000) rubles. The cash method of accounting for both tax liabilities and tax credits has been established, with an exception made for some types of enterprises that could choose between cash and the accrual method for their liabilities.

On February 3, 1992,[3] a lower rate of 15 percent was introduced for foodstuffs. This rate became effective as of September 1992.

On May 22, 1992,[4] enterprises were allowed to claim tax credits only on inputs for which they had actually paid. New exemptions were introduced, such as construction of housing, enterprises with more than 50 percent disabled employees, and part of output of agricultural enterprises realized to pay wages. The timing of tax payments was dependent on the monthly revenues of an enterprise: payments were required every four months for those below 100,000 rubles[5] and monthly for those above this figure. Also, enterprises with revenues above 300,000 rubles had to make advance tax payments every two months, roughly equaling one-third of the previous month's tax payments.

Tax rates were changed soon again, on July 16, 1992,[6] when the base rate was reduced to 20 percent, and the lower rate to 10 percent, effective January 1, 1993. In 1992–1995, the Russian economy experienced three-digit rates of inflation that disrupted the economy. Fighting inflation became the primary goal of economic policy. To this end, the government lowered the tax rate from 28 to 20 percent, effective January 1, 1993, hoping that this would have an anti-inflationary effect. This was not the case, however, due to the downward rigidity of prices and high inflationary expectations.

Under the same law of July 16, 1992,[7] credits were allowed for VAT paid on capital goods and intangibles, in equal portions over two years, but only if they were put into production in the reporting period. Also, in response to high inflation, the government increased the size of advance payments required of enterprises with monthly revenues exceeding 300,000 rubles: the size of advance payments was determined by the amount of the previous month's calculated taxes multiplied by 2.5.

The law of December 22, 1992,[8] effective January 1, 1993, increased the tax base by including sales of collateral as well as receipts for all kinds of "financial assistance" or other "special" transfers from customers. Under the same law, imports were made taxable (during 1992, imports were not taxable). A few exempt import categories were introduced: food and agricultural products, equipment for R&D, and medical equipment.

During the year, tax revenues grew rapidly: the share of VAT in consolidated budget revenues increased from 25.4 percent in January to 43 percent in December, and constituted 40 percent for the whole year. The positive dynamics of VAT during 1992 could be explained by frequent changes made to the law. For example, additional revenues created by the amendment that included "financial assistance" from customers into the tax base amounted to 23.5 percent of October revenues. Another source of revenues was the increase in advance payments made by larger enterprises. Also important was the creation of a clearing house by the Central Bank, which netted out the mutual debts of enterprises, resulting in a marked increase in sales. This episode signaled the role of nonpayments in tax collection.

1993

On January 29, 1993,[9] by the instruction of the State Tax Service (or the Ministry of Taxation, as it is called in Russia), the advance payments made by larger enterprises (whose revenues exceed 300,000 rubles) were replaced by payments made every two months on the basis of realized turnover. Soon, the threshold was increased to 500,000 rubles.

In 1993, the Russian VAT became closer to the theoretical standard as credits were allowed for VAT paid on capital inputs, but with a motivation that inputs were allowed for credit only after they were put into production (i.e., accounted as costs of production). Credits were to be paid off (or counted toward VAT liabilities) during two years, in equal portions. An important order, signed by the president on December 22, 1993,[10] mandated that beginning in 1994, 25 percent of the collected VAT would be allocated to the budgets of local governments. This order lasted until 1999 when the percentage was changed to 15 percent. Finally, in 2001, fiscal federalism in the VAT was abandoned, and 100 percent of VAT revenues accrued to the federal budget.

The beginning of the year still showed high rates of tax collection, partly because the higher rate of 1992 (28 percent) was still de facto effective due to the Ministry of Taxation's delays in instructions, and also due to the inclusion of imports in the tax base. However, revenues fell monotonically later in the year. In addition to the lower VAT rate, factors that contributed to this decline were the proliferation of exemptions and the spread of evasion practices: taxpayers learned about the new tax and figured the ways to avoid it. Since then, VAT performance remained at approximately the same level, if measured by its share in GDP.

1994

On January 1, 1994, a special tax of 3 percent was introduced, effectively increasing the tax rate to 23 percent (and 13 percent, correspondingly). On January 17, 1994,[11] by order of the Ministry of Taxation, all entrepreneurs who worked on an individual basis (that is, without forming a legal entity) became exempt from the VAT. This order remained in effect until 2000 (inclusive) and also reduced the period for crediting capital and intangible inputs from two years to six months.

The tax base was further broadened to include all transfers received from other enterprises. With this change, the VAT effectively became a turnover tax because it broke the link between the VAT liability and the instance of sales of goods and services. For example, there were episodes when the VAT was levied on agricultural enterprises on the amount of budget subsidy they received. The immediate reason behind this ruling was an attempt to fight evasion. Firms were using lower prices to reduce their tax liabilities and side payments to compensate for reduced revenues. Another form of evasion was through the use of loans (discussed later in this chapter, in the section "The Nature of the Russian VAT"). The less obvious reason, however, was that the mind-set of tax collectors and the method of administration had changed little since the Soviet era, when the turnover tax was the main tax in effect. This kind of inertia even led to discussions of a possible return to the turnover tax,[12] and although the VAT remained in place, it retained its hybrid form until the reform of 2000–2002. As a consequence, there has been a dramatic increase in the use of cash in transactions, which put them into a zone unreachable by tax collectors.

On January 24, 1994,[13] thresholds for monthly and bi-monthly tax payments were increased to 1 million and 3 million rubles, respectively (see above for details).

On August 10, 1994,[14] by order (ukaz) of the president, the method of calculating VAT in the case of negative value-added was established. In particular, it was maintained that negative tax liability that arose from selling goods below their cost was not to be reimbursed from the budget. In December[15] of the same year, rules for determining prices for such transactions were further clarified. The law was effective from January 1, 1995 until 1999, when the first part of the new Tax Code was introduced.

1995

The year 1995 was characterized by attempts, made by Parliament and the president, to adjust the Russian VAT to Western standards, due to pressure from the International Monetary Fund (IMF). Specifically, there followed a declaration[16] to move to an invoice method of accounting for VAT and to a delivery (accrual) method for the timing of VAT liability—which, however, remained only on paper. There followed a removal of exemption on construction of housing and a significant reduction of food products subject to lower rate. Another important contribution made during this year was the introduction of a single tax for small enterprises.

On February 23, 1995, a special tax of 3 percent was introduced and it applied to small enterprises. It was subsequently reduced to 1.5 percent and eliminated in 1996.[17]

On April, 25, 1995,[18] the construction of housing was no longer exempt from the VAT. By the same law, the range of food products allowable for the 10 percent rate was reduced significantly.

On December 29, 1995,[19] a simplified method of taxation for small enterprises (comprised of 15 employees or less) was established. The multitude of taxes (including the VAT) levied at the federal and local levels were replaced by a single tax, paid on the basis of a year's sales.

STAGNATION: 1996–1999

1996

In 1996, the special tax of 3 percent was eliminated, and the schedule of VAT rates returned to 0 percent, 10 percent, and 20 percent.

In order to be able to receive IMF credits, the Russian government was required to further reform the VAT. These steps were spelled out, as in the previous year, in a joint declaration[20] made by the government and the Central Bank, which expressed the intention for widespread use of an invoice method of VAT accounting across industries and services.

This declaration was supported by a presidential order, signed on May 8, 1996.[21] This order stated that effective January 1, 1997, every taxable person, for every taxable transaction engaged in with his or her customers and suppliers, was required to fill in duplicate invoices. A government order[22] signed the same day further clarified the accounting of these invoices. To be sure, invoices were used in taxation before, in the Soviet era, for collection of the turnover tax. The innovation of the 1996 law was the introduction of specifically VAT invoices, with clear rules of their format and use. However, as seen from the language of the government order, these invoices were introduced to double-check for correct tax filing and did not completely replace the old (accounts-based) methods of accounting.[23] Further reform of the VAT was achieved on April 1, 1996,[24] when capital inputs and intangibles were finally allowed for credit immediately after they appeared on the balance of the enterprise and not after they were actually used in production, as was the case before.

1997

By the law of April 28, 1997,[25] an exemption on imports of technological equipment and public transport vehicles was removed. In reality, however, these items were not taxed in 1997 or 1998 (due to a special law issued in the summer of 1998 that extended the exemption for the rest of the year).

At the end of the year, on December 29, 1997,[26] stricter rules for claiming rebates on exports were established. The main purpose of this legislation was to eliminate a popular method of avoiding VAT by making fake exports (see below). These rules stated that effective January 1, 1998, rebates could be claimed only if documentary proof of actual exporting activity had been provided and only after it had been verified by tax authorities.

1998

In early 1998, the government issued an order[27] that attempted to deal with invoice fraud, which had gained popularity since 1997, when (partial) invoice-based accounting for VAT was introduced. In particular, the order declared illegal the exchange of blank invoice forms between enterprises. In August 1998, Russia was hit by an economic crisis. As interest rates on government debt skyrocketed, foreign investors began to withdraw. When the Central Bank's reserves were almost depleted, the government defaulted on internal debt and on a restructuring plan on external debt. The ruble depreciated drastically, from 6 to 26 rubles for a dollar in a couple of weeks. Despite the crisis, reform on taxation continued. On July 31, 1998, the government enacted a law that introduced Part I of the Tax Code. However, disagreement between the government and Parliament on certain aspects of reform prevented Part I from bringing about any significant change to the nature of the VAT. Rather, Part I mainly provided a general clarification of tax administration.

Along the same lines, on August 11, 1998, the Ministry of Taxation strengthened the requirements of documentary proof for every export transaction of aluminum, in response to the widespread practice of falsified export operations in this industry.

Because of the economic crisis, 1998 saw exceptionally low revenues from the VAT and other taxes: 5.7 percent of GDP in total for the whole year. As the crisis unfolded in August and September, tax revenues dropped to 3.8 percent of GDP. However, the end of the year showed signs of a turnaround, as revenues reached a level of 9 percent of GDP in December.

1999

The highest priority of the new government, headed by Evgeny Primakov, who took office after the economic crisis of 1998, was the implementation of comprehensive tax reform and the unification of legislation through adoption of a tax code. Thus in 1999, Part II of the Tax Code was debated in Parliament.

In addition to these discussions, several changes were made to the VAT in response to the economic crisis. For instance, production and distribution of cinemas were included in the list of articles exempt from VAT. In April 1999, the share of the federal budget funded by VAT revenues was increased from 75 to 85 percent. At the end of May 1999,[28] a special economic zone (a tax-free zone) was created in Magadan, effective until 2005.

TOWARD A MODERN VAT: 2000–2005

The transformation of the Russian VAT into its internationally adopted version began in 2000. Amendments to the VAT had been passed prior to 2000, but they had a sporadic character that indicated the absence of any well-specified plan that would involve the coordinated efforts of both government and Parliament (Duma). It is difficult to judge now why it took so long to arrive at a consensus, especially on such an important matter as the VAT—a tax that generates a large portion of budget revenues, the efficient operation of which can benefit all members of society. One possible reason for the delay in reform was dissension within the Duma, whose members could not agree on the form tax reform should take. In any case, it would be unfair to say that government lacked the will for reform. In fact, the government introduced proposals of tax reforms described in this section to the Duma as far back as 1996. In addition, active discussion of reforms took place among economists, taxpayers, the government, and foreign advisers as early as 1995. In the following, we first present the main changes made to the VAT, as they appeared in the initial version of Chapter 21 of Part II of the Tax Code that was introduced by the law of August 5, 2000, and, second, we point to key changes that occurred after the law was enacted, between 2002 and 2005.

Tax Reform of 2000–2002

The main package[29] of reforms, in the form of the second part of the new Tax Code (the first part was signed in July 1998, effective January 1, 1999), came into force on January 1, 2001. Perhaps the most important advancement of Chapter 21 of the Tax Code was the unification and codification of legislation on VAT. Chapter 21 required that any changes to the VAT had to be introduced via federal law—that is, through the parliamentary process—and thus made the tax clearer and more predictable for taxpayers. A description of other significant reforms follows below. We discuss some of these changes later, in the section "The Nature of the Russian VAT."

Entrepreneurs working on an individual basis (that is, without forming a legal entity) again became taxable persons under the VAT (they were exempt from VAT by the law of January 17, 1994),[30] as well as all other legal persons conducting economic activity. At the same time, all taxpayers with revenues not exceeding 1 million rubles per quarter of the year (about US $30,000) were exempt. This requirement was intended to improve the effectiveness of tax administration by allowing tax inspectors to focus on more important taxpayers, as well as to reduce the tax burden on small businesses. The voluntary registration of taxpayers had not yet been introduced, however.

On July 1, 2001,[31] the destination method was adopted for treating trade with CIS countries, not including, however, sales of oil and natural gas (these have been included since 2005; see below). Before that, all imports from CIS countries were treated as if they were produced domestically (origin method). Transition to the destination method had become possible owing to improvements in customs controls on the borders between members of CIS.

Some changes had also been made in the administration of export tax rebates, in an attempt to fight tax evasion through falsified exports. According to the ruling of July 1, 2001, the decision to give a tax rebate was to be made by local tax inspectors, if the amount of export did not exceed 5 million rubles per month, or if the exporter was a "traditional" exporter, that is, engaged in exporting on a regular basis. Otherwise, if an export operation was too large or an irregular one, then the decision would be delegated to a higher-level department within the Ministry of Taxation. In any case, the decision had to be made within two months.

The legal status of the zero-rating of exports was also improved. The new Tax Code formally defined the notion of a 0 percent rate, established a list of documents needed to claim a tax rebate, and defined the rights and responsibilities of both taxpayers and tax collectors. These changes allowed taxpayers to seek protection in the courts if they believed that tax authorities had acted incorrectly. Previously, the administration of export rebates had been governed by a series of orders issued by the State Tax Service itself, which gave plenty of room for refusals or deferrals of tax rebates on exports. As a result of the new legislation, the volume of rebates paid to exporters as well as the rebates owed to them increased.

Since 2001, all VAT revenues have accrued to the federal budget. Exemptions and preferences have undergone a major revision. In 2000, the list of food products and goods for children that were subject to a lower tax rate of 10 percent was revisited and reduced. Some tax-free zones, such as Baikonur, have been eliminated, or their preferential treatment has been reduced (since 2004, only two free economic zones exist: in Kaliningrad and Magadan). In 2001, the most important innovation was the removal of exemptions on printed products (books, newspapers, etc.) and medical products[32] (except those socially most important). Beginning on January 1, 2002, these products, both imported and domestic, were subject to a tax rate of 10 percent. This led to some increase in prices for these products in January 2002 by a few percentage points. At the end of 2002,[33] the 10 percent rate on these products was increased to 18 percent, which has been effective since 2005. This does not mean, however, that the list of exemptions had come into complete concordance with international practices. For example, firms where most employees are disabled were still exempt, as well as public transportation and some other activities.

The VAT paid on capital inputs was allowed for immediate credit. This finally equalized the tax treatment of industries with different capital intensity of production. However, inputs for capital construction were to be credited only when the construction was finished and the object was put on the balance. Also, since 2001, negative tax liability can be reimbursed directly from the budget, as an alternative to carry-forward provisions. However, conversations with businesspeople and tax practitioners reveal that, in practice, the government remains reluctant to make cash reimbursements (an informal discount is 30 percent of one's credits). For normally functioning enterprises, however, if inflation is not high, it does not make a large difference whether or not a tax return is received in cash or as a reduction of future liabilities. Special circumstances that occur when negative liability is generated by selling below cost have also disappeared with the removal of the accounting notion of "cost" from legislation on VAT. This was a step toward disentangling VAT taxation and firm accounting procedures—a process that is ongoing.

Regarding VAT invoices, a significant number of improvements and clarifications have been introduced in their use for various economic activities,[34] relative to the original law of July 29, 1996. However, the mixed nature of accounting for VAT liability has essentially remained: while invoices were required from all taxpayers, they were not sufficient for rebates, and they had to be complemented by bookkeeping records. This requirement was mainly explained by the fears of fraudulent rebate claims based on falsified invoices.

2003–2004

In line with a general policy of reducing the tax burden, the base tax rate was changed in 2003,[35] effective January 1, 2004, from 20 percent to 18 percent (while the lower tax rate of 10 percent was kept in place).

In August 2004,[36] the taxation of trade in oil and natural gas between CIS countries was put on a destination basis in order to eliminate the exception initially created in Chapter 21. Russia was one of the last countries to adopt this method and did so mostly as a result of pressure from other partners, since the original method was more beneficial from the point of tax collection. By estimates of the Ministry of Finance, the change in the method of taxation of oil and gas alone would cost the federal budget more than $1.2 billion for 2005.

2005

A large reform package[37] was enacted in July 2005, effective January 2006. In particular, the accrual method of accounting for VAT was finally introduced. According to the law, the moment of liability arises on the earlier of two dates: the date on which the goods are delivered (services) and the date on which payment (partial payment) is made. The reimbursement of VAT credits was no longer conditioned on whether or not payment was made to the supplier. In other words, the system has finally moved to the accrual method of accounting. This brings the new VAT law much closer to the international standards. One of the remaining major differences, however, was that invoices were still not sufficient for calculating tax credits and liabilities, and had to be supplemented by accounting records.

The same law corrected a much debated aspect of the original version of Chapter 21 of Part II of the Tax Code, which was adopted in August 2000. According to the new version, VAT paid for capital construction is to be reimbursed only when the building (or other construction) is finished and put on the balance. This was a remnant of the differential treatment of capital inputs inherited in the 1990s. Since January 2006, construction has been treated equally with all other types of inputs.

An important advancement was made in the management of export rebates. Beginning in 2007, VAT credits on exports have been administered with the same timing and documentary requirements as credits on domestic sales. The period allocated to tax authorities for validity checks has been reduced to two months from the date of submission of a tax declaration (or a customs declaration in the case of exports), and no more than one month is allowed for processing claims by the Treasury (if the claims are found to be valid).

In the foregoing, we have presented only a few of the many reforms carried out after adoption of the Tax Code; the list is far from being comprehensive. Rather, we have focused on what we believe were the more drastic changes that made the Russian VAT closer to best practices and, hopefully, more efficient. A more detailed discussion of these changes from the perspective of the nature of Russian VAT can be found in the next section. The current characteristics of VAT (as of 2009) are summarized in Table 5.A.1.

THE NATURE OF THE RUSSIAN VAT

On the surface, the principle behind a VAT is very simple. By definition, the amount of VAT owed to the budget is the difference between the tax received from customers and the tax paid to suppliers. However, the exact implementation of this rule in Russia was very different from its implementation in developed countries. The principal deviations can be organized into the following categories: first, the way VAT liabilities are calculated and VAT credits are reimbursed for different types of transactions and economic agents; second, the type of information that is used to calculate VAT (e.g., invoice forms, accounting records, declarations, etc.); third, the way international trade is taxed (origin versus destination method, or a combination of both); and finally, the set of exemptions and preferences, which themselves can be grouped into standard (those that are more widespread across countries) and nonstandard ones. Most of the deviations have been eliminated through the reform process undertaken from 2000 to 2005, but one should distinguish between formal and actual differences. In the next section, we start with perhaps what was the most problematic part of the Russian VAT—the way VAT liabilities are calculated and VAT credits are given for different types of inputs.

HYBRID METHOD OF ACCOUNTING FOR VAT CREDITS AND LIABILITIES

From the beginning until the year 2006, the Russian VAT was asymmetric in its treatment of VAT credits and liabilities. In this section, we discuss the anomalies of calculating VAT credits and liabilities that made the Russian VAT different from the standard version. There are two main types of anomalies: first, the unequal approach to crediting different types of inputs (capital, inventories, construction, etc.); and second, the use of a cash method of VAT accounting, which makes tax transfers both to and from government conditional on actual payment for the taxed transaction. While unequal treatment of different inputs is obviously distortionary and inefficient (although it did not prevent it from surviving until 1999–2000), arguments can be made both pro and contra the cash method in the context of Russia's economic reality of that time.

VAT Liabilities

From 1992 until the beginning of 2006, the cash method of accounting for VAT liability was predominantly used. According to this method, VAT liability, which is based on the payments received from customers, arises only when the actual payment for sold goods and services is received. Beginning in 1994, taxpayers were given a choice between the cash and accrual (delivery) method for calculating VAT liabilities (where VAT liability arises on the day of delivery), but almost all taxpayers preferred the cash method because it allowed them to defer payment of the tax and, more importantly, because the determination of VAT credits was based only on the cash method. (We discuss the advantages and disadvantages of the cash method in more detail below.)

The sales of final output (wholesale and retail) of enterprises are taxed differently from the sales of inputs. The tax base was the difference between sales and the amount paid for supplies, that is, markup. In 1995,[38] the taxation of markup was eliminated for wholesale enterprises (for them, the amount of tax owed was the difference between VAT paid and VAT received), while retail enterprises (including restaurants) were still being taxed on markups, VAT inclusive. Since 2001, markups have been calculated without the inclusion of VAT, which placed the taxation of retail sales on the common ground with everything else. Such a differential approach[39] has resulted in the problem that in practice, it was often difficult to distinguish between production and distribution activities, which allows businesses to optimize their taxes by shifting (or misclassifying) their operations to the least-taxed activity. Essentially, the result is the same as with the existence of exemptions and multiple rates: loss of revenue and distortion of economic decisions.

In response to evasion practices, a law enacted on December 22, 1992, provided that the tax base must include not only payments made specifically for purchased goods and services, but also other payments (transfers) received from the customer as a barter or as a "donation." Through subsequent decrees and orders, the Ministry of Taxation has developed this provision to respond to new practices of hiding inter-enterprise payments. One such method of evasion that firms undertook was to decrease the price of supplies and then make a side payment to the supplier, in the form of "financial assistance." Implementation of this rule brought with it both practical and legal difficulties. On the practical side, it required tracking of various payments made to enterprises and their subsidiaries. On the legal side, it was difficult to judge what payment should be included in the tax base from the view of principles of VAT outlined by law. Adoption of the full accrual method in January 2006 relieved tax authorities of some of these difficulties, but the problem of side payments used to avoid taxation remains. In particular, according to the current version of VAT as spelled out by Chapter 21 of the Tax Code, advance payments received from customers (and paid to suppliers) constitute a tax base, even though goods are not yet delivered and services are not performed. An exception, which can be viewed as a form of tax support, is made for goods whose production cycle exceeds six months (mostly manufacturing, construction, etc.).

VAT Credits

According to the law of December 16, 1991, only supplies put into production were allowed for credit. For example, inputs coming into inventories were not creditable, and only those leaving inventories for production were. Such an approach came from Soviet accounting practices, where production costs were understood in physical terms (i.e., as inputs used in production) rather than in financial terms (i.e., as inputs purchased and to be used in the future).[40] After a few months of uncertainty, the law of July 16, 1992,[41] stated explicitly that a cash method should be used for VAT credits (as well as for VAT liabilities, as stated above). Along the same lines, VAT on inputs that were purchased for promissory notes can be credited only when notes are actually paid off. This created an additional incentive for (eligible) firms to choose the cash method for VAT liabilities, as the tax base was the difference between taxes received from customers and taxes paid to suppliers.

Among inputs, special treatment was given to capital goods and intangibles. In the initial version of the law, capital goods and intangibles were not eligible for credit at all. Later, the law of July 16, 1992[42] (effective January 1, 1993) allowed the tax paid for these items to be credited in equal parts during the two years after the items were put into production. Later, the two-year period was reduced to six months and completely eliminated as of April 1, 1996.[43] In fact, this correction turned out to be ineffective because high inflation and uncertainty about the actual receipt of credit eroded the real value of the tax credit, and no adjustments were made in that respect. Only with the adoption of Part II of the Tax Code in 2000 was the link between the purchase of inputs and the production process abandoned.

When VAT credits and liabilities were calculated by the cash method, the amount of tax owed to the government was the difference between VAT actually received from customers and VAT actually paid to suppliers (until 2001, this applied only to inputs put into the production in the current period). This difference often turned out to be negative. In theory, the situation when VAT liabilities are less than VAT credits does not constitute a problem: the direction of payment should be from the budget to the taxpayer. In practice, however, the state had always been reluctant to do so. In Russia, until 2006, as in many developing countries, excess credits on inputs would be carried forward to count against future tax liabilities. The effect was the same as with inputs that were purchased but not put into production, because such carry-forward provision makes holding capital inputs taxable for some time, which increases the effective tax rate on capital-intensive goods.

A special case of negative tax liability arises due to sales below cost. Since 1995,[44] tax provisions have explicitly stated that such liability should not be credited, as the manipulation of the price of sales was an important channel for evasion. This is yet another example of an attempt to fight evasion by altering the nature of the tax rather than by solving the problem directly. Only in 1999, with the adoption of Part I of the Tax Code, was negative liability due to below-cost sales no longer a problem, at least theoretically. In practice, tax authorities were still willing to account for it against future liabilities instead of paying directly from the budget. A more detailed discussion of tax returns can be found in the section "Administration of VAT."

Cash Versus Accrual Method: Discussion

Most countries that levy a VAT have favored the accrual method over the cash method as the choice of accounting. In Russia, poor tax administration and delays in payments created a significant trade-off between the two methods, which was resolved in favor of the cash method (in fact, a hybrid method, as explained above). Based on theory and the experience of other countries, a strong case can be made for establishing a symmetric accrual method as a compulsory method of accounting for VAT.[45] What follows below are conventional arguments in favor of the invoice method, as well as drawbacks of the Russian version of the cash method.

The first and perhaps most important argument in favor of the accrual method is the simplicity of calculating taxes. This method, in Russian practice sometimes called the "delivery method," determines the taxable event—that is, the consumption of goods and services—more precisely than the cash method because the timing of payments usually is not related to the timing of consumption. This leads to the more timely arrival of tax revenues to the budget, which is an important consideration during inflation.

Second, the cash method makes it possible to defer the date of VAT liability by accumulating fictitious nonpayments—usually, by making sales through fly-by-night firms that avoid taxation. The invoice method makes this accumulation of nonpayments meaningless. Moreover, firms would like to receive payment as soon as possible, in order to be able to pay VAT owed to the government.

Third, the accrual method is simpler to administer, as it only requires establishing the fact of delivery. The cash method complicates matters by requiring firms (or auditors) to track the different payments and to tie them to particular transactions. Many firms employ various schemes to obfuscate such tracking or to hide payments from the view of tax inspectors. Under the accrual method, every taxpayer can be treated as a separate entity for audit purposes, for there is no need to track payments to upstream or downstream partners.

Fourth, the requirement of the Russian version of the cash method that creditable inputs be put into production is questionable because it distorts the tax base and economic decisions. On the one hand, the cash method creates a link between the timing of VAT liabilities of supplies to the timing of production decisions. On the other hand, it makes holding inventories more costly, which hurts, for example, retail enterprises. As mentioned above, this requirement was abandoned in 2000.

Finally, the cash method version adopted in 1992 created an additional burden for the taxpayer because it required, in principle, full inventory accounting for every reporting period depending on the size of the enterprise. This accounting requirement was even more burdensome for taxpayers if different types of inputs were subject to different tax rates or if the tax rates changed over time. In such cases, a method of moving average VAT was used to tax outgoing inventories,[46] which further distorted the tax base and made spot checks by tax authorities more problematic.

Despite its shortcomings, the adopted method of accounting for VAT credits had practical advantages during the economic turmoil of the 1990s, which was marked by corrupt and poorly administered tax collection, massive tax evasion, and mutual nonpayments among enterprises. Here are some of these advantages.

First, the combination of cash and accounting method on VAT credits protects the budget from the most harmful form of tax evasion, which occurs when fake invoices are produced to overstate claims on VAT credit.[47] During the 1990s, when the tax administration and enforcement were still in development, and corruption among tax inspectors had yet to be eliminated, it was important that such protection work automatically. The validity of this argument, however, has been questioned by the experience of other CIS countries, which adopted the invoice method much earlier than Russia but did not suffer from massive evasion of VAT through false invoices. Also, similarly to fake invoices, fake cash receipts can be produced[48] at low cost. Therefore, it seems this advantage was more perceived than real.

Second, an enterprise operating in an environment of mutual nonpayments often will not be able to pay taxes before it receives payments for its sales. In this case, the strict enforcement of the accrual method is simply not feasible.

Third, there was a historical reason for the initial adoption of the cash method: Soviet accounting methods based the notion of financial income on the actual transfer of cash rather than the right to receive it.

Transition to the Accrual Method
Considerable economic and political difficulties are associated with a transition to the accrual method. On one hand, it entails a steep increase in tax liabilities for enterprises that are subsidizing the rest of the economy— especially those in the energy sector—as these enterprises have the largest arrears owed to them by their customers. At the same time, it hurts the most cash-strapped enterprises, as these enterprises are often in arrears to their suppliers. On the other hand, moving to the accrual method is costly, for it introduces a completely novel method of accounting for VAT. This would require additional training of personnel, development and testing of new forms and protocols, education of taxpayers, and so on. More importantly, because it is accompanied by a shift to the use of invoices, it requires an effective system of checking the validity of VAT claims, as fake invoices can easily be produced.

A law signed in July 2005 introduced the accrual/invoice method of accounting, effective January 2006, and provided for transition conditions intended to deal with the problems of greater tax liabilities and fake invoices. During the two-year transition period, enterprises using the cash method of accounting for VAT liabilities were forced to make an inventory of outstanding debt for unpaid but received supplies and credits for products unpaid by customers but delivered to them, until December 31, 2005. The difference would constitute the tax base for VAT owed to the budget, effective as of January 1, 2006. This amount was to be paid off during a two-year period, from January 2006 until January 2008, by the cash method. VAT owed to the budget for a given transaction was to be paid as soon as the relevant payment was received from the customer. If during two years, a firm failed to pay off this amount, it would be charged in the first tax period of 2008. Enterprises using the accrual method of accounting for VAT liabilities should perform the checks of debits and credits in a similar fashion and are entitled to receive VAT credits owed to them during the first half of 2006, in equal portions (more precisely, these credits are counted toward VAT liabilities that a firm generated during 2006). These transition clauses appear to be very lenient especially to enterprises whose customers do not pay regularly. Essentially, the law provides these enterprises with a two-year delay for tax liabilities accumulated up to December 31, 2005, at the expense of the state budget, in the hopes that the transition to the accrual method will be smooth.

The problem of fake invoices is more fundamental, as it is directly related to the quality of tax enforcement. Current estimates of tax evasion in Russia show that the effectiveness of the current system of tax administration does not allow for complete reliance on invoice forms in determining taxes. Therefore, even though by law a properly filled invoice together with tax declaration constitute a basis for claiming a tax rebate, the tax authorities often conduct additional checks, using accounting records and payment receipts to verify the validity of the claim.

TREATING INTERNATIONAL TRADE

A significant share of Russia's international trade involves country members of the Commonwealth of Independent States (former Soviet republics), which results in a consistently large and positive balance of trade. Despite the fact that these countries are independent states, the long history of economic interdependence created customs borders that are not as strictly enforced as those vis-à-vis the rest of the world. Perhaps more importantly, the shift to the destination method required coordination of CIS countries as well as resolution of some of the tolling. For example, it was not uncommon for an input from a CIS country to be imported into Russia, used in production, and then sent back to the original firm without a sale.[49] These considerations can explain why from 1992 until 2001, the origin principle governed the taxation of trade within the CIS and the destination principle governed the taxation of trade with nonmember countries.

Under the destination principle, which is the one most widely adopted around the world, exports leave the country without tax surcharges because tax rebates are given to exporters when their goods cross the border.

In other words, the importing country has full control over the tax burden that its consumers face because imported and domestic goods have the same VAT in their prices. This can be seen as a form of tax support for national exports, but in Russia, this effect was muted owing to the Ministry of Taxation's reluctance to pay off export rebates. The more a rebate is delayed, the less its value for the firm, especially during a period of inflation. It is immediately clear that the ability of customs officials to check that goods have actually crossed the border is the crucial factor in operation of the destination principle. When customs controls are weak, as they have been between Russia and CIS, falsified exports are possible when a good receives a rebate but never leaves the country.

In contrast to the destination method, exports are taxed under the origin method, while imports are not; thus, imports from different countries will have a different VAT in their prices.[50] This does not mean that the origin method is free from problems of evasion that occur when border controls are weak—as soon as illegal exports cross the border, they can be sold in the country of destination on a tax-free basis. This kind of evasion, however, is not as harmful as falsified exports, as it only reduces tax revenues, while the falsified exports lead to direct monetary losses from the budget.

In addition to its prevention of some forms of tax evasion, the origin method also provides benefits with respect to tax revenues: a large positive trade balance means that a country collects more taxes from foreign consumers than from domestic consumers who are paying the price of imports. At the same time, the structure of imports, most of which are agricultural goods, make the destination principle less attractive, as these imports would be subject to a lower 10 percent tax rate. Most likely, this was why Russia was so reluctant to put its trade with CIS on a destination basis, while other country members of CIS had agreed on this policy much earlier.[51]

Part II of the Tax Code of 2000 defined the notion of and the rules of application for zero-rated[52] products and services. Such products and services included exports (except oil and natural gas exports to members of CIS), international transportation, space projects, and certain sales of precious metals to governments and banks. Since January 1, 2002, trade with CIS countries was put on a destination basis as well. According to the projected budget for 2002, this change would have reduced the tax base by about 0.6 percent.

Treatment of trade with CIS countries was further aligned with the destination principle in August 2004,[53] when oil and natural gas exports were included in zero-rated products and services under Part II.

EXEMPTIONS AND MULTIPLE RATES

Since its inception, the VAT has been seen not only as a revenue-generating device, but also as an important instrument of social policy. The VAT was used to stimulate economic activity and to support socially disadvantaged groups by giving exemptions or lower (possibly, zero) rates to certain kinds of activities and by exempting certain categories of economic agents.

Attempts to estimate revenue losses due to VAT preferences often lead to results that cannot be compared to losses incurred by other countries, because there is no universally accepted list of activities to be exempted. The Russian approach to VAT preferences is expansive in that it categorizes a number of activities that are not normally subject to VAT as tax expenses, such as exports, holding of financial instruments, educational services, banking operations, insurance, and nongovernment pension funds. This approach gives rise to inflated, unrealistic estimates of tax losses. Another controversial aspect of such calculations is that they are often based on the assumption that the tax base would not change if certain preferences were eliminated. Finally, when comparing figures of revenue losses as a percentage of GDP, one should control for tax-raising ability: a figure of 1 percent of GDP in a country that collects 80 percent of the theoretical VAT is completely different from 1 percent GDP in a country that is able to raise only 50 percent of theoretically possible VAT revenues. Nevertheless, it may be of interest to trace the dynamics of revenue losses, while keeping in mind that the figures can be only a rough reflection of the reality. For this purpose, we have made some calculations—see Tables 5.A.2 and 5.A.3. The law of December 6, 1991, introduced a number of VAT exemptions.[54] Some of the exceptions—such as financial services, education, health care, public transportation, and folk arts—were quite common among countries that levied a VAT. They were aimed at social and economic goals, such as the promotion of research, education, and cooperation with foreign firms. Others were created in response to specific circumstances of the time period (such as stays in sanatoria, which were historically part of the social benefits provided to workers in the Soviet era), and subsequently were eliminated as the Russian VAT was modernized.

The list of exempt or lower-rated products or activities has changed from year to year, in response to economic fluctuations. Currently, the following categories are exempt:

a. Some socially important medical products and services
b. City transportation
c. Apartment rentals
d. Educational services provided by noncommercial organizations
e. International transportation as well as related services
f. Banking operations, insurance, financial operations (stocks, mutual fund shares, etc.)
g. Other transactions not considered to be part of the realization of goods and services

From these categories, one can distinguish a number of motivations for such preferences: support for lower income people and the disabled; public health; the promotion of research and development; education and culture; and the provision of housing.

Support for Lower Income People and the Disabled
It was recognized from the beginning that the transition from social planning to a market system would have a large negative impact on the most economically vulnerable groups of population, such as lower income workers, pensioners, and the disabled. As a result, support of these groups has been a focal point of VAT since its inception. Such support appeared in the form of lower tax rates for food and goods for children, exemptions for individual entrepreneurs, and exemptions for public transportation.

Food and Products for Children. On February 3, 1992, a lower rate of 15 percent was introduced for food products, as well as for certain goods for children. This rate was subsequently lowered to 10 percent[55] and remains in place today. This measure proved to be one of the largest revenue losers, however. Its projected cost[56] to the budget was 0.21 percent of GDP in 1993 and 1.47 percent of GDP in 1994. The list of products subject to the 10 percent rate has changed numerous times at the government's discretion in response to economic fluctuations and budget shortages. For example, in 1993, imports of the products listed were declared exempt but in 1995 were subject to a 10 percent rate,[57] in an attempt to correct for poor revenue performance in 1994.[58] Relative success came only in 1998 with the elimination[59] of a lower rate on certain food products and goods for children (both imported and domestically produced), which was supposed to generate 0.34 percent of GDP in additional tax revenues. Among these food products, only bread, other bakery products, milk, milk products (except ice cream), and specialized food for children and for diabetics were left under the lower rate. The list of goods for children had also been reduced, leaving only goods for babies and school supplies. In reaction to the economic crisis, however, many preferences were reintroduced at the end of the year (which was reflected in 1999 figures). As Table 5.A.3 shows, the year 1998 was one of the best performing years in terms of minimizing tax losses. Thereafter, the list continued to change at the discretion of the government until the reform of 2000–2002, when the list became fixed by law; it has remained unchanged since then.

Individual Entrepreneurs and the Disabled. In the context of unemployment and wage nonpayments, small-scale entrepreneurship, such as the sale of home-produced fruits and vegetables or the resale of manufacturing goods and textile bought from abroad, has always been an important means of subsistence. To promote individual entrepreneurship, while saving on costs of administering VAT generated from these small taxpayers, the government exempted these taxpayers. In particular, in 1992–1994, individual entrepreneurs who did not form a legal entity (that is, a firm) were exempt from VAT, given that their revenues did not exceed a certain limit. In 1995,[60] in an effort to simplify taxation of small entrepreneurs, the revenue restriction was removed. Moreover, for all organizations with less than 15 employees, the government replaced VAT and other taxes with a single tax.

Exemptions from VAT based on legal definitions and head counts, rather than on economic activity, proved to be very inefficient, as they created opportunities for tax evasion. Consequently, these exemptions were removed by the Tax Code of 2000, which stated that for an entrepreneurship to be eligible for exemption from taxpayer duties, its quarterly revenues could not exceed 1 million rubles. In 2005, this limit was raised to 2 million rubles.

In addition to aiding individual entrepreneurs, the VAT was used to support the troubled agricultural sector. Beginning in 1992, the output of agricultural enterprises allocated for wages was exempt from the VAT. Agricultural enterprises were also given special treatment in terms of granting tax credit for purchased capital inputs. Whereas capital inputs in other industries were to be reimbursed during a two-year period (later changed to six months—see discussion in the section "The Nature of the Russian VAT"), agricultural enterprises could claim these credits as soon as capital purchases were entered into accounting. The Tax Code, adopted on August 5, 2000, maintained these preferences and provided a more precise definition of agricultural enterprise, which today can be defined as a firm for whom 70 percent of revenues comes from the sale of agricultural products. Finally, the law[61] of August 20, 2004, in an attempt to revitalize the market for land, made the sale of land exempt from VAT.

The Russian VAT has also been used to support and provide services for the disabled. Inadequate government support for the disabled population, together with the absence of a health insurance system, makes the case for special tax treatment. Since there is usually little market demand for the labor of the disabled, the government attempted to stimulate demand by exempting products produced by such labor. These are usually enterprises that produce simple manufacturing goods, such as electric outlets and tools, using labor-intensive technologies. In 1992, tax reforms provided an exemption for enterprises that fulfill a 50 percent hiring quota of disabled persons. In 1993, this preference was augmented by the exemption of production and imports of equipment for the disabled.

This exemption turned into a popular channel for evasion, in which highly profitable capital-intensive firms hired a sufficient number of disabled persons to become tax exempt. In 1996, a restriction was added, which stipulated that trading, broker, and other intermediary companies that fulfilled the 50 percent hiring quota were no longer exempt, unless those companies were owned by associations of disabled persons. In 1997, companies that consisted of disabled persons but traded natural resources were also excluded from the list, as the government tried to prevent oil companies from using this method of evasion. Despite all the criticisms, and contrary to the exemption of small entrepreneurs, the new Tax Code of 2000 had left the exemption for disabled persons in place. The only change was that the hiring quota for disabled persons was raised from 50 percent to 80 percent. In 2002, revenue losses due to this exemption were estimated at 0.01 percent of GDP—a modest number compared to revenue losses suffered from exemptions on medical services or transportation.

Public Transportation. Public transportation, provided by both public and private entities, was declared exempt with the introduction of VAT in 1991 and remains exempt. In fact, transportation provided by the government is a consistently unprofitable activity even in such cities as Moscow; thus, if the principles of VAT are applied, such preferences should not generate revenue losses. Most of the revenue losses arise from the exemption of private sector activities, and these appear to be very large. In 2002, for example, revenue losses were estimated to be 0.14 percent of GDP.

Public Health

The system of public health services inherited from the Soviet Union was considered to be obsolete by many, even before the Russian economy became a market economy. Although the coverage was wide and prices were affordable, the quality of services was generally poor, with modern medical technologies being adapted quite slowly. With the transition to a market economy, the situation only became worse, as tax revenues plummeted and the government was no longer able to support the system as it had previously. Plans were made to reform the system to allow for private health providers and insurers. These plans were not implemented, however, and until now, the health insurance industry is still in its infancy. Nevertheless, despite its inability to implement structural changes, the government was resolved to make health services (especially medications) more affordable through the provision of tax preferences. The law of May 22, 1992, exempted paid medical services, production and sales (as well as imports) of drugs and medical equipment, and, as a reminder of the Soviet era, stays in sanatoria. Beginning in May of 1997, government purchases of various types of medical and safety equipment from abroad were declared exempt.[62]

In 2002,[63] the exemption of all drugs and medical equipment was replaced with a tax rate of 10 percent. Together with the removal of the exemption on printed products, this measure was supposed to bring an additional 0.3 percent of revenues. Initially, according to the law of January 2, 2000, this removal was not complete because it kept exempt a narrow list of "socially important" items, perhaps as a display of reverence to social problems. In December 2001,[64] however, even this list was reduced, leaving exempt certain medical equipment. Medical services remained exempt, however, and in 2002, private medical practices were included as well. The wording of "stays in sanatoria" has also changed: today, only services provided by sanatoria located in Russia are exempt, and they are subject to strict documental requirements (basically, only state-subsidized vacations are eligible). This effectively withdrew most of the domestic market for recreation from coverage.

Promoting Research and Development

Beginning in 1992, research and development activities, as well as cooperation with foreign firms, were given tax preferences. In particular, the law of December 1991 declared exempt patents, licenses, and copyrights. Also, R&D operations financed by the budget (and later, R&D funded by state-created research funds) were exempt, as well as R&D activities in universities. Interestingly, in 1993, the wording of tax laws that regulated exemptions of patents and licenses changed substantially: "patents and licenses associated with industrial objects, except intermediary services in this domain."

The laws that regulated imports associated with R&D were a different story. In 1993, imports of equipment for research and development were declared exempt. Later, in 1996, this exemption was significantly expanded: not only was R&D equipment exempt, but also any "merchandise imported within contracts of joint venture with foreign enterprises" (Federal Law N 25-FZ, from April 1, 1996). Indeed, this was a generous way to support research cooperation: the removal of this exemption in 2001 generated an additional inflow of revenues in the subsequent year of approximately 0.06 percent of GDP. No change was made in subsequent years until 2000, when old R&D-related exemptions were removed effective 2001. Today, R&D efforts financed by the government and various research funds, such as those similar to the National Research Foundation and research conducted by universities, are exempt. Thus, VAT preferences for R&D now have a more modest goal: tax relief for a given set of institutions rather than the stimulation of R&D activity in the economy as a whole. As we have seen in the case of public health, making medical services more affordable is ineffective when these services simply do not exist in an adequate quantity and quality. Similarly, in the case of R&D, one cannot hope to revive innovation in the economy by giving innovators tax relief when there is no demand for innovation on the other end.

Education and Culture

Numerous exemptions have been allocated to services in the domain of education and culture. In the initial version of the VAT law, enacted in December 1991, the wording regarding these categories was particularly vague: exempted categories included educational services provided by schools, universities, and other educational establishments; payments for use of sports facilities by children; services provided by "establishments of culture and art," religious activities and entertainment events (such as rock concerts), and movies. At the end of 1995, "culture-related" exemptions were massively extended to include all kinds of mass-media products, printed products (except advertising), as well as related transportation services.[65] These categories have become a major source of revenue loss. In 1999, in line with the general policy of supporting national cinematography, the creation and distribution of movies classified as "national cinema"[66] (movies whose production is approved by state officials and is partially financed by government) were declared exempt. The law of January 2000 clarified the notion of educational services as only those provided by licensed noncommercial enterprises,[67] and only those stated in their license. Thus, consultant services and sales of educational material (books), as well as rental of office space[68] are not exempt. The same law also provided for a deadline for exemptions of printed products (and medical services), which were to expire as of 2002. In 2002, the exemptions were replaced with a tax rate of 10 percent, which was changed to the common rate of 18 percent in 2005.

Supply of Housing

Housing shortages had always been a major social problem in the Soviet era. In order to receive an apartment from the state, people often had to wait for years at a time. After the demise of social planning, however, market forces did not ameliorate the situation. On one hand, people could not afford to buy an apartment, as an affordable mortgage was (and continues to be at this time) nonexistent. On the other hand, investors have shown little interest in this domain (although the situation has changed dramatically in recent years). In a naïve attempt to stimulate construction of housing, the government declared construction exempt from VAT on May 22, 1992.[69] This preference was expected to reduce the cost of construction by 7 to 10 percent. In practice, however, it did not make housing more affordable or investment more attractive, and it quickly became one of the "leaders" in revenue losses. Revenue losses from the construction exemption accounted for 0.10 percent of GDP in 1993 and 0.85 percent in 1994. On May 1, 1995, the exemption on construction of housing was replaced with a tax rate of 10 percent.[70] Nevertheless, budget losses from this preference remained high: in 1996, they were expected to amount to 0.32 percent of GDP.

As a result of these losses, the reform of 2000–2002 (Chapter 21 of the Tax Code) removed the exemption for construction of housing by governments of all levels, leaving only housing for military personnel. The size of the eliminated exemption was estimated to be 0.2 percent of the tax base. Also, housing rentals[71] continued to be exempt. Although the construction of housing is no longer exempt, sales of housing are exempt according to the law of August 2004.[72] The same law also made sales of land exempt in an effort to facilitate the market for land in Russia. The gradual removal of preferences on construction is a reflection of the inefficiency of this policy.

Discussion

Whether the implementation of a lower tax rate for socially important activities indeed achieved the desired outcome is hard to determine. For example, large revenue losses due to a lower tax rate on foodstuffs could be interpreted as a way of subsidizing the costs borne by the general population. However, the extent to which these subsidies have reached the part of the population who need them the most is unclear. Also, lower-income people tend to buy food products in markets from local sellers, who are generally exempt from VAT due to their small size (since 1995). If this is the case, then higher-income people who made purchases in stores benefited the most from these subsidies.

While the benefits of having a zero or lower tax rate are uncertain, the disadvantages are clear: losses in tax revenues (see estimates for 2002 in Table 5.A.4) and additional complexities in the enforcement and collection of VAT. The latter concern is not to be underestimated, the reasons for which will be described below.

First, the use of multiple tax rates and exemptions introduces two forms of distortions into economic activity. On one side of the equation, activities taxed at a zero or lower rate are naturally stimulated, as their profitability increases. If these are socially important activities, and their positive impact is thought to be greater than the loss of tax revenues, then it is a desirable outcome and the goal is achieved. One the other side of the equation, however, such activities can become the focal point of tax evasion, as taxable entities try to hide their sales under the umbrella of these activities or misclassify their businesses. In this way, what was intended to be a welfare-enhancing instrument becomes a major cause of revenue loss.

Second, tax-exempt products and products taxed at lower rates are costly in terms of both administration and revenue. Take, for example, a tax reform undertaken in 2000–2002, which taxed previously exempt products, such as drugs and print and medical equipment, at a rate of 10 percent. This created the need to reimburse from the federal budget the negative difference between VAT received from sales of these products and VAT paid to suppliers, whose output was taxed at a rate of 20 percent.

Third, the implementation of these privileges is problematic. Because legislation usually provides only a vague wording of exemptions, tax authorities may either interpret the law too narrowly, in which case their effect is minimized, or too broadly, in which case the distortionary effect is likely to outweigh the positive impact. At the same time, because taxpayers tend to present their activities as falling into a tax-exempt category, the tax authorities must check the validity of these claims. As the number of exemptions and goods subject to lower rate increases, the probability that false claims will go undetected also increases, given the limited resources of tax inspectors.

Despite these difficulties, Russia cannot abandon tax relief for the arts, the disabled, lower income people, and innovation. Still, many commentators have argued that offering lower or zero rates of the VAT is a poor way to provide support. These objections are serious, and we have discussed some of them. Direct support of socially beneficial activities seems to be much more effective, in terms of both produced results and cost to the budget. However, in a situation marked by poor institutional capacity to organize such support, by corruption at all levels of the bureaucracy, and by a tight government budget that already is in deep arrears to state workers, soldiers, and pensioners, the automatic support given by tax preferences becomes more appealing. This, for example, can explain the long life of the notorious exemption on enterprises that employ the disabled. Despite all fair criticisms of this method of providing support to the disabled, it survived numerous tax reforms that removed many other socially beneficial exemptions (such as medical products and construction of housing). Indeed, even if, as we argued above, costs are high and most benefits are not received by the disabled, the existence of these enterprises provides jobs for the disabled, jobs that market forces would fail to create without the exemption.

ADMINISTRATION OF VAT

The development of tax administration in Russia can be separated into two stages: the period before 1999 and the period after. Before 1999, the progress in tax administration had been very slow. On one hand, proper enforcement of tax law was often infeasible,[73] for a variety of reasons including economic conditions (mutual nonpayments, barter, lack of liquidity), inability to cope with widespread avoidance (corruption, incompetence, and lack of resources among tax collectors are responsible), and the political weakness of the government, as tax liabilities of large enterprises were determined through a bargaining process between enterprises and authorities rather than on the basis of law. On the other hand, the law[74] itself existed in the form of various legislation acts, president's orders, Ministry of Taxation letters, and the like—many of which contradicted each other and which frequently changed. This allowed for different interpretations of tax liability and resulted in underpayment on the part of taxpayers and overcharging on the part of tax authorities. This failure to develop a proper tax administration culminated in a deep fiscal crisis, with the state unable to perform its social functions, and later the debt crisis of August 1998. The government attempted to fill the gap in the budget by giving almost unlimited power[75] to tax authorities, as opposed to taxpayers, by imposing high tax rates and high penalties for nonpayments.

The European, in its February 9–12, 1998 issue, describes one instance of the workings of the tax police:

> Two heavily armed men in leather jackets and helmets ran up the stairs of the building and pushed open the door of a Moscow trading company. "Nobody move"—they shout. They point guns at the terrified employees and demand to know where the safe is. They empty it and remove from office everything that looks valuable. This isn't a visit from the mafia but a call from Moscow tax police.[76]

However, the attempt to resolve the problem with force did not succeed. The unbalanced powers of tax collectors created corruption,[77] while high tax rates disadvantaged both firms operating in the formal sector and small firms with little bargaining power. In contrast, the largest enterprises continued to be the largest nonpayers.[78] The fact that emergency measures could not improve the situation was understood early enough, probably in 1996, but, despite this realization and pressures from the IMF, the constraints of political process and subsequent economic crisis delayed reforms until 1999.

After two years of debate in Parliament, beginning on January 1, 1999, Part 1 of the new Tax Code came into force,[79] whereby the tax legislation finally took a unified form. It was also a completely new code of tax administration, in which the powers and responsibilities of tax authorities were clarified and strengthened. Although by itself this did not resolve many of the problems of tax collection, progress was made in several directions.

Most importantly, steps were taken to restore a balance of power between tax authorities and taxpayers. At least theoretically, tax authorities now had to follow established procedures in performing their actions, especially those of enforcement; taxpayers now were better informed of their rights and, more importantly, were able to seek protection in courts. This improvement reduced the risk of conducting business and improved tax compliance.[80]

Also, for the first time, the new code defined such basic notions as taxation subject, tax agent, and tax declaration, and introduced the concept of a unique taxpayer identification number. Principles of determination of "market price" for purposes of taxation were also established, which reduced the amount of discretion on the part of tax authorities and the amount of uncertainty on the part of a participant of the transaction.

Legislation improvements were accompanied by a reduction in the number of different taxes, the simplification of the tax regime for small enterprises, and a reduction of tax rates. To keep tax revenues on the same level, lower tax rates required better tax collection; therefore, beginning in 2000, the government tightened the tax discipline.[81] In some sense, today we see a reversion to the pre-1999 era, but this time, improvements are happening not through changes to the tax code itself but through the addition of detailed instructions that clarify administrative procedures, as outlined by the law.[82] The court system has played an increasingly important role in the administration of taxes: tax authorities are more actively using the courts to enforce payment of taxes or fines for past nonpayments, as well as to resolve conflicts that arise from application of tax law. At the same time, since 2003, enforcement actions have been performed by a general enforcement agency, the Ministry of Internal Affairs. Previously, the Ministry of Taxation had its own division, the tax police, for enforcing tax collection (the tax police was abolished in July 2003). Also, by the order of the president, in March 2004, the power to amend tax laws or procedures shifted from the Ministry of Taxation to the Ministry of Finance.

Although the aforementioned steps are great improvements in making tax collection in Russia more uniform and equitable, the court proceedings of the early 2000s, including the case against the Yukos oil company and others, reveal that businesses still face a great deal of uncertainty with respect to their tax liabilities. The Yukos case has showed how the government can put pressure on a private company through exaggerated tax claims. The amount of "calculated" tax liabilities was so large that the company was eventually liquidated, with its assets captured by a state-backed oil company. Powers exercised by tax authorities are constantly increasing, yet this is not offset by better formulated and more user-friendly powers of the taxpayers. Tax administration today in Russia is an actively changing field, but detailed discussion of its problems is outside the scope of this chapter. Let us now turn to problems of administration that are specific to VAT. The two most acute problems are probably the administration of returns of VAT credits and the fight against various methods of tax evasion.

TAX RETURNS

The administration of tax returns is perhaps the most problematic issue related to administration of the VAT in Russia. Generally, tax authorities have been reluctant to pay VAT credits generated by business activities, whether export operations or an activity within the country. Since rebates can be paid off only when approval of the tax authority is received, the tax authority has the power to delay payment, either in an attempt to extract rents, or because of inefficient bureaucratic procedures governing the verification of the legality of a rebate claim. One way or another, firms, especially exporters, must wait several months and spend a significant amount of human resources in order to receive rebates. Most nonexporting firms prefer not to go to such lengths and settle for the use of rebates to pay their future tax liabilities. Difficulties with receiving rebates create economic distortions because it disadvantages firms with negative tax liabilities (such as exporters), firms that incurred large investments in the current period, or newly created firms.

Attempts are made to optimize the existing system of validity checks, mainly through differentiating reputable taxpayers (those that have regular operations and have established a history of timely tax payments) from the rest. At the same time, the discretionary nature of decision making may provide an incentive for cooperation between corrupt officials and firms. For example, the Yukos case demonstrated that the company under investigation had registered several fake firms in tax-preferential zones of

Russia (where the tax rate was either zero or low) and conducted the bulk of its sales of gas through these firms. Meanwhile, these firms did not pursue any business activities in these regions, and their directors were employees of Yukos in Moscow. During the years of their operations, they successfully claimed and received VAT rebates worth millions of dollars.

FLY-BY-NIGHT FIRMS

Fly-by-night firms (fake firms, or *odnodnevki*) are created specifically for the purposes of evading taxes.[83] The name "fly-by-night" points to the temporary nature of these firms: once the action is over, the firm disappears. Some of these firms are short-lived, while others may exist for a longer period of time and implement a number of evasion exercises. Since tax fraud is a criminal offense in Russia (and other countries), the primary reason for creating a separate legal entity is to protect the beneficiaries of tax evasion from prosecution. Usually, these firms are registered to people who have no relation to the matter—for example, a homeless person who was paid to become a director of the firm—or to nonexisting people, using information taken from lost passports. At the same time, wholly different people control the flows of resources, and it is generally difficult to prove the relation of these people to the illegal activities being undertaken. In other words, for such a firm to operate effectively, some tricks are necessary at the registration process, such as falsified documents about persons, location of the firm, or capitalization. Through a number of contractual transactions, such a firm accumulates a large amount of tax liabilities as a VAT taxpayer and then disappears without paying it, while the corresponding amounts of VAT credits are left in the hands of the related beneficiaries. Here are a couple of examples of typical schemes used in Russia, all involving a sort of collusion with one or both sides of the transaction, and sometimes with government officials.

One example is that of a company selling imported goods on the domestic market. First, through an agreement between customs officials and the importing company, the customs value of imported goods is lowered (by changing the classification, for example), which in its turn lowers the amount of the VAT owed to budget. Second, imported goods are sold at lower prices to a fly-by-night firm, which then resells the goods to the actual seller (either directly or through an intermediary) at much higher wholesale prices. This accumulates most of the added value in the fly-by-night firm. Third, goods are sold and the VAT is paid by the beneficiary

company, while the fake firm liquidates without paying taxes. The exporting firm employs this exact scheme; it exploits the fact that giving the tax
rebate to an exporter cannot be conditioned on whether the company that
procures the exported goods (usually, a fly-by-night firm) has actually
paid its incoming VAT. The difference here is that the cooperation of customs officials is not required.

Another popular scheme involves the sale of services by fly-by-night
firms to a beneficiary company at a very high price.[84] The nature of this
transaction makes it difficult to check the real value of the services, which
include consulting, marketing, and advertising services. In fact, Russian
legislation allows the VAT to be paid to the seller of services separately
from the payment for the services themselves, so the actual payment for
services becomes redundant. The fly-by-night firm liquidates and returns
the received VAT to the beneficiary company, in the form of bonds, for
example.

The actual beneficiaries of these schemes are legal enterprises that wish
to avoid direct involvement with evasion activities. These enterprises are
not involved in the creation of fly-by-night firms, but rather use readily
available solutions. The specificity of the Russian market for tax minimi-
zation schemes is such that these services are supplied by banks, created
specifically for such illegal purposes by some financial company. The head
company deals with the creation and liquidation of fly-by-night firms,
makes contact with potential clients, and uses its subordinate banks to
conduct transactions. If detected, the bank, and not the client company,
bears the greatest amount of risk because it is difficult to prove that the
client company actually knew about illegal intentions of the fly-by-night
firm. In this view, the Central Bank's recent reform, which raised capital
requirements and thus led many small banks to cease to exist, should have
contributed significantly to the fight against fly-by-night firms.

Another noticeable feature of VAT-related schemes is the manipulation
of the transaction price.[85] At first glance, such a possibility calls for the
development of formal procedures to determine the fair market price, but
in the context of a bureaucratic culture of a developing country like Russia,
these procedures may be actually quite harmful as they give tax authorities
discretion to interfere with market mechanisms and thereby create rents. It
is more advisable to make these procedures applicable through the courts
rather than through tax inspectors.

Tax authorities do not remain idle in this respect; on the contrary, the
number of liquidated firms and the amount of imposed penalties have

grown, and regular checks and special operations have been undertaken. Thus, the continuing popularity of fly-by-night firms can be explained only by the inability of tax authorities to fight this phenomenon.

Failures can occur at the registration stage, the detection stage, or the prosecution stage. It seems that the registration stage is the most important stage when failures should be minimized. As we noted earlier, the possibility of registering a firm by providing false information is key to the operation of fly-by-night firms, as it affords protection from prosecution. A new law,[86] effective July 2002, which regulated registration of new firms, did much to combat such fraudulent registration. The new law simplified the process of registration through the principle of one window and, perhaps most importantly, consolidated the registration of firms as legal entities and as taxpayers to fall under the purview of one organization, the Ministry of Taxation. Previously, it was not uncommon that a firm would register with the state but fail to register as a taxpayer. It was also hoped that shifting the firm registration process to the tax authority would also solve the problem of fly-by-night firms. However, the law did not specify procedures for verifying this information, nor did it establish the necessary time frame for doing so. The law also did not impose any specific punishment for providing false information at the registration stage, but rather relied on general rules promulgated by administrative and criminal codes. Possible reforms of the law are being debated at this time, and hopefully improvements will be made in the near future. Even with the current legislation, however, progress can be made by improving the coordination between tax authorities, enforcement agencies (e.g., the militia), and passport registration bureaus. Government officials hope that creation of a database of lost passports—a project launched in 2006—will facilitate the collaboration. Today, informational exchange between tax authorities and militia is limited because each entity uses different programming products; this allows for registration with incorrect information or documents, such as a person's lost passport.

If a firm has been successful in registering with false information, it will continue with its plan of tax evasion. The question then becomes whether or not these actions will be detected. In addition to the database of lost passports, the government plans to create a database of VAT invoices, which will allow it to compare invoices of sellers and buyers and to identify potential cases of fraud. Although this may be a good idea in theory, in practice the administrative costs of comparing 14 billion invoices every year in Russia would be prohibitive, especially considering the tax authority's already limited resources. The characteristics of the firms themselves could also be used to identify potential fly-by-night firms: those with a small capital but large transactions, where the founder is usually a single physical person, and those that do not report taxes regularly. The task now is to incorporate this filter into legal procedures, which would allow tax authorities to narrow their focus on a group of selected firms.

When the illegal actions of a fly-by-night firm are detected, tax authorities submit the case to the court, demanding liquidation of the firm and prosecution of the participants. Such cases are never simple, however, because there is usually only indirect evidence of the involvement of the actual players rather than the nominal ones (i.e., those whose names appear in registration documents) and even less evidence as to illegal intent. Court practices for handling these kinds of cases have yet to be developed, both in terms of the court's literacy on the subject of taxation and in terms of the creation of precedents for decisions based on indirect evidence.

Economic intuition suggests that a firm will undertake an illegal activity only if the expected benefits of doing so are greater than the expected costs, which are determined by the likelihood of detection and possible losses in that case. As our discussion has shown, the probability of detection remains low, and there still is much room for improvement in this area. Such efforts themselves would not be effective unless accompanied by stricter punishment standards, both by increasing the amount of fines and by providing for personal liability, including criminal liability, for managers involved in tax avoidance schemes.

FALSIFIED EXPORT OPERATIONS

From the beginning, Russia adopted a destination method of treating trade with non-CIS countries. As the system of receiving export rebates gradually improved, firms had greater incentive to shape their sales in the form of exports to exempt them from the VAT, which could be accomplished through several methods. For instance, firms could export the goods, re-import them into the country, and then sell them on black markets. Alternatively, firms could sell the goods domestically and hope to receive a rebate on the claimed exports before it was detected that the goods had never left the country. Close cooperation between tax and customs authorities is needed to counteract such fraudulent activity. In terms of legislation, the legislature should introduce a measure stating that export rebates will be granted only after the goods cross the border and the transaction is recorded by customs authorities. Since July 1, 2001, the power to grant tax rebates has been held by local tax inspectors if the amount of the export does not exceed 5 million rubles a month or if the exporter is a traditional one, that is, performs such business on a regular basis. If an export operation is larger than 5 million rubles per month or is an irregular transaction, then the decision is delegated to a higher-level department in the Ministry of Taxation.

FAKE INVOICES

According to Ministry of Finance calculations, the amount of claimed VAT rebates in 2002 was 78.6 percent of VAT owed to the budget. This figure rose to 81.5 percent in 2003 and reached 85 percent in 2004. Many believe that large portions of these claims are generated from fake invoices. Firms can either produce a completely fake invoice[87] (which is more likely to be detected because invoices are registered documents and are identified by unique numbers) or purchase an invoice from another firm that actually purchased inputs but cannot claim credit on them, because the Ministry of Taxation is reluctant to grant such credits. For example, this could be a firm that has negative liability on VAT or a firm whose output is exempt, such as an exporter, and who finds it difficult to receive a tax credit. Thus, a black market for false invoices exists, and the value of an invoice is exactly the sum of the VAT calculated for it.

FALSE ACCOUNTING RECORDS

The Russian VAT is especially vulnerable to falsification of accounting records. Deviations in accounting records are more difficult to detect than is production of fake invoices. Since this kind of evasion can be fought only by conducting periodic checks, tax laws must set clear standards for the registration and accounting of invoices, in order to reduce the costs of such checks and improve their efficiency. The difficulties that hamper an accounting-based system of VAT could also be resolved by transitioning to an invoice-based system of VAT, which makes the checking process more automated: it is sufficient to compare amounts stated in invoices to the actual amount of tax paid.

APPENDIX

Table 5.A.1 Characteristics of Russian VAT as of 2009 *(Chapter 21 of Part II of the Tax Code)*

Date introduced	1992
Base rate	18%
Discounted rate	10%: agricultural products, foodstuffs, products for children, periodicals, books, a list of medical products
Threshold, scope	Tax period is three months. The threshold is then two million rubles of turnover for the last three months (except for: firms and/or individual entrepreneurs selling excises or involved in import operations)
	Excluded are foreign companies related to Winter Olympic games of 2014 in Sochi
Exempted transactions and agents	Renting out space to foreign companies registered in Russia
	A relatively short list of "important" medical devices, equipment for disabled, glasses, orthopedic products
	A relatively short list of private medical services, related to diagnostic, transportation, giving birth, care for the elderly
	Transportation, except taxi
	Housing—sales and rental
	Culture and entertainment (including cinema, but only movies approved by the government), sport events
	Recreation services
	Patents and licensing of intellectual property
	Creation of technological innovations
	Religious organizations
	Production and services by disabled
	Sales to foreign companies involved in the organization of Winter Olympic games
Zero-rating	Export operations and free-trade zones, related transportation services
	Passenger transportation outside the country
	Products and services related to activity in outer space
	Products and services for foreign diplomats, missions, etc.
	Russian-built ships
Burden of proof to claim zero-rating	Necessary documents to claim rebates on export:
	Copy of the contract
	A notification from the bank confirming the receipt of payment for the goods sold (services procured)
	Customs declaration
	Copy of transportation documents with a stamp of customer border control
	The time frame of 180 days
	These documents are submitted together with tax declaration
Determination of taxable event	Accrual method. The taxable event occurs at the earliest of the dates:
	(1) Receipt of payment
	(2) Delivery of the good or service, or the transfer of property rights

(continued)

Table 5.A.1   *(continued)*

	Advance payments, partial payments are included in the tax base, except when the production cycle exceeds six months. In that case, the taxpayer has the right to determine the taxable event as the date of delivery (finishing the construction, etc.).
	Barter, transfers of property, and bequests are included in the tax base at market prices.
Treatment of VAT credits	VAT paid on inputs for production of goods and services, subject to VAT taxation, is to be deducted from VAT liabilities. For capital goods, this happens only after they are put on the balances.
	VAT paid on inputs allocated to the production of exempt goods and services, and also VAT paid by enterprises that are not VAT taxpayers, can be included in the cost of production (deduced from the profit tax).
Negative VAT liability	If VAT credits exceed VAT liabilities in some tax period, the difference is to be reimbursed from the budget.
	After they receive the tax declarations, tax inspectors can check the validity of such claims, and if the result is positive, the decision to reimburse has to be made within seven days, and money must be returned within five days from such decision.
	If at the time of such claim the taxpayer is overdue on his or her payment of taxes or fines to the budget, then the negative VAT liability is contributed to the overdue items.
	The time frame for filing the tax declaration that claims such reimbursement is three years.
VAT invoices	VAT invoices, together with tax declaration, are the basis for claiming a deduction of VAT credits from VAT liabilities.
	The seller has to issue an invoice emphasizing the amount of tax, to the buyer, within five days of the transaction (delivery or payment).
	There is no such requirement for retail transactions; it is enough if the receipt contains the amount of tax.
Treatment of trade revenues	Destination principle.

Table 5.A.2   Projected Revenue Losses by VAT, 1993–1994 and 2000–2003 *(as a percentage of GDP)*

	1993	1994	2000	2001	2002	2003
Exemptions	0.61	1.62	0.97	0.86	0.81	0.80
10% rate	0.24	4.13	0.38	0.44	0.54	0.45
Total (% of GDP)	0.85	5.75	1.35	1.29	1.35	1.24

Source: Appendix to federal budget for various years; author's calculations; GDP data from Ministry of Finance.

Table 5.A.3 Actual Revenue Losses by VAT, 1997–2003

	1997	1998	1999	2000	2001	2002	2003
Exemptions	1.68	1.42	1.9	2.14	1.2	1.39	1.17
10% rate	0.42	0.27	0.27	0.27	0.42	0.42	0.4
Total (% of GDP)	2.1	1.69	2.17	2.41	1.63	1.81	1.57
Total (% of VAT)	28.44	28.38	36.5	38.5	23.6	26.1	23.7

Source: Ministry of Taxation; Ministry of Finance; calculations by Institute of Economies in Transition (IET).

Table 5.A.4 Planned Revenue Losses Due to Exemptions and 10 Percent Rate, by Type of Exemption, 2002 *(as a percentage of GDP)*

Total Revenue	10.3
Selected exemptions	1.22
Public health	0.43
Transportation	0.14
Education and culture	0.25
Research and development	0.13
Rental of housing	0.26
Invalids	0.01
10% rate	1.04

Source: Ministry of Finance; author's calculations.

NOTES

This chapter was written while the author was a graduate student of economics at Columbia University. I thank Roger Gordon, as well as an anonymous referee, for helpful comments. Special thanks to Ilya Trunin of the Institute of Economies in Transition in Moscow (www.iet.ru), whose writings on Russia's VAT (in Russian) have helped me a great deal in preparing this material.

1. For a more detailed discussion of turnover and sales taxes, see Summers and Sunley, IMF Working Paper, 1995.

2. The Commonwealth of Independent States is a supranational body formed after the breakup of the Soviet Union; it consists of former republics whose aim is cooperation in both economic and political spheres.

3. Ruling of Presidium of VS RF and Ministry of Economy and Finance RF No. 2264-1 of 2.3.1992, "O social'noj zaschite naseleniya i ob uporyadochenii regulirovaniya cenoobrazovaniya na otdel'nye vidy produkcii."

4. Law of Russian Federation, "O vnesenii izmenenij i dopolnenij v Zakon RSFSR 'O naloge na dobavlennuyu stoimost,'" No. 2813-1 of 5.22.1992.

5. At that time, this amount was equivalent to US $500. This figure is not quite reliable, however, since the exchange rate was volatile (MICEX).

6. Law of Russian Federation, "O vnesenii izmenenij i dopolnenij v nalogovuyu sistemu Rossii," No. 3317-1 of 7.16.1992.

7. Law of Russian Federation, "O vnesenii izmenenij i dopolnenij v nalogovuyu sistemu Rossii," No. 3317-1 of 7.16.1992.

8. Law of Russian Federation, "O vnesenii izmenenij i dopolnenij v otdel"nye zakony Rossijskoj Federacii o nalogah," No. 4178-1 of 12.22.1992.

9. Letter of State Tax Service No. B3-4-05/70H and Ministry of Finance No. 04-03-02 of 1.29.1993, "O poryadke ischisleniya i uplaty naloga na dobavlennuyu stoimost."

10. Ukaz of President RF No. 2268 of 12.22.1993, "O formirovanii respublikanskogo byudzheta Rossijskoj Federacii i vzaimootnosheniyah s byudzhetami sub'ektov Rossijskoj Federacii v 1994 godu."

11. Letter of State Tax Service No. VG-4-16/5n of 1.17.94, "O poryadke primeneniya Ukaza Prezident," RF No. 2207 of 12.22.1993, "O nekotoryh izmeneniyah v nalogooblozhenii i vo vzaimootnosheniyah byudzhetov razlichnyh urovnej."

12. L. Lykov, "Nalogovaya politika: effektivnost' rychagov i stimulov," *Voprosy ekonomiki,* 1994.

13. Telegram of STS RF No. VZ-4-05/10n, Minfina RF No. 9 of 1.24.1994, "O poryadke vneseniya NDS v byudzhet."

14. Ukaz of President of RF No. 1677 of 8.10.1994, "Ob utochnenii dejstvuyuschego poryadka vzimaniya naloga na pribyl' i NDS."

15. Federal Law No. 57-FZ of 12.6.1994, "O vnesenii izmenenij i dopolnenij v zakon Rossijskoj Federacii 'O naloge na dobavlennuyu stoimost.'"

16. Government order No. 334 of 4.15.1995, "Ob utverzhdenii zayavleniya Pravitel"stva Rossijskoj Federacii i Central"nogo Banka Rossijskoj Federacii ob ekonomicheskoj politike v 1995 godu i merah po ego realizacii."

17. Federal Law No. 25-FZ of 2.23.1995, "O special'nom naloge s predpriyatij, uchrezhdenij i organizacij dlya finansovoj podderzhki vazhnejshih otraslej narodnogo hozyajstva RF i obespecheniya ustojchivoj raboty predpriyatij etih otraslej."

18. Federal Law No. 63-FZ of 4.25.1995, "O vnesenii izmenenij i dopolnenij v zakon Rossijskoj Federacii 'O naloge na dobavlennuyu stoimost.'"

19. Federal Law No. 222-FZ of 12.29.1995, "Ob uproschennoj sisteme nalogooblozheniya, ucheta i otchetnosti dlya subektov malogo predprinimatel'stva."

20. Statement of Government of RF and Central Bank of RF of 2.22.1996, "O srednesrochnoj strategii i ekonomicheskoj politike na 1996 god."

21. Ukaz of Prezident RF No. 685 of 5.8.1996, "Ob osnovnyh napravleniyah nalogovoj reformy v Rossijskoj Federacii i merah po ukrepleniyu nalogovoj i platezhnoj discipliny."

22. Government order No. 914 of 7.29.1996, "Ob utverzhdenii poryadka vedeniya zhurnalov ucheta schetov-faktur pri raschetah po nalogu na dobavlennuyu stoimost."

23. Specifically, forms 868 and 868a—invoices of the old style.

24. Federal Law No. 25-FZ of 4.1.1996, "O vnesenii izmenenij i dopolnenij v zakon Rossijskoj Federacii 'O naloge na dobavlennuyu stoimost.'"

25. Federal Law No. 73-FZ of 4.28.1997.

26. Order of STS RF No. AP-3-03/252 of 12.29.1997, "O vnesenii izmenenij i dopolnenij v instrukciyu Gosnalogsluzhby Rossii," No. 39 of 10.11.95, "O poryadke ischisleniya i uplaty naloga na dobavlennuyu stoimost."

27. Government order No. 108 of 2.2.1998, "O vnesenii izmenenij i dopolnenij v postanovlenie Pravitel'stva Rossijskoj Federacii," No. 914 of 7.29.1992, "Ob utverzhdenii poryadka vedeniya zhurnalov ucheta schetov-faktur pri raschetah po nalogu na dobavlennuyu stoimost."

28. Federal Law No. 104-FZ of 5.31.1999.

29. Federal Law No. 36-FZ of 1.2.2000, "O vnesenii izmenenij v zakon Rossijskoj Federacii 'O naloge na dobavlennuyu stoimost,'" Federal Law No. 118-FZ of 8.5.2000.

30. Letter of STS No. VG-4-16/5n of 1.17.1994, "O poryadke primeneniya Ukaza Prezidenta RF," No. 2207 of 12.22.1993, "O nekotoryh izmeneniyah v nalogooblozhenii i vo vzaimootnosheniyah byudzhetov razlichnyh urovnej."

31. Letter of STS No. VG-6-03.502 of 6.29.2001.

32. Federal Law No. 179-FZ of 12.28.2001.

33. Federal Law No. 195-FZ of 12.31.2002.

34. Federal Law No. 117-FZ of 8.5.2000, Government order No. 914 of 12.2.2000.

35. Federal Law No. 117-FZ of 7.7.2003.

36. Federal Law No. 102-FZ of 8.18.2004.

37. Federal Law No. 119-FZ of 7.22.2005.

38. Federal Law No. 63-FZ of 4.25.1995.

39. Summers and Sunley, IMF Working Paper, 1995, p. 22.

40. For further discussion, see Summers and Sunley, IMF Working Paper, 1995, p. 13n.4.

41. Law of Russian Federation, "O vnesenii izmenenij i dopolnenij v nalogovuyu sistemu Rossii," No. 3317-1 of 7.16.1992. See also Law of Russian Federation, "O vnesenii izmenenij i dopolnenij v Federal Law RSFSR 'O naloge na dobavlennuyu stoimost,'" No. 2813-1 of 5.22.1992.

42. Law of Russian Federation, "O vnesenii izmenenij i dopolnenij v nalogovuyu sistemu Rossii," No. 3317-1 of 7.16.1992.

43. Federal Law No. 25-FZ of 4.1.1996, "O vnesenii izmenenij i dopolnenij v zakon Rossijskoj Federacii 'O naloge na dobavlennuyu stoimost.'"

44. Ukaz Prezidenta RF No. 1677 of 8.10.1994, "Ob utochnenii dejstvuyuschego poryadka vzimaniya naloga na pribyl," i NDS.

45. A. Tait, "Value Added Tax: International Practice and Problems," IMF 1988; H. H. Zee, in *Value-Added Tax: Tax Policy Handbook,* P. Shome (ed.). IMF, 1995.

46. For details, see "VAT instruction 1" on December 9, 1991.

47. This form of evasion is most harmful psychologically. From the purely rational point of view, however, underpayment of VAT to the budget is no less harmful than overpayment of VAT credit.

48. I thank an anonymous referee for pointing this out.

49. I thank an anonymous referee for pointing this out.

50. Potentially, the origin method creates incentives for tax competition between countries, but this has not been realized in practice.

51. The other country-members of CIS include Azerbaijan, Armenia, Belarus, Georgia, Kyrgyzstan, Moldavia, Tadzhikistan, and the Ukraine.

52. See paragraph 1 of Article 164 of the Tax Code.

53. Federal Law No. 102-FZ of 8.18.2004.

54. For further discussion on initially introduced exemptions, see Summers and Sunley, IMF Working Paper, 1995.

55. Federal Law No. 3317-1 of 7.16.1992.

56. The projected cost is calculated by dividing planned losses by actual GDP of that year.

57. Federal Law No. 63-FZ of 4.25.1995, "O vnesenii izmenenij i dopolnenij v Zakon Rossijskoj Federacii 'O naloge na dobavlennuyu stoimost.'"

58. In general, 1994 was a record year in terms of revenue losses, which increased sevenfold over the previous year (see Table 5.A.2).

59. Government order No. 787 of 7.17.1998, "O prodovol'stvennyh tovarah, po kotorym primenyaetsya stavka naloga na dobavlennuyu stoimost," v razmere 10 procentov.

60. Federal Law No. 222-FZ of 12.29.1995, "Ob uproschennoj sisteme nalogooblozheniya, ucheta i otchetnosti dlya sub'ektov malogo predprinimatel'stva."

61. Federal Law No. 109-FZ of 8.20.2004.

62. Federal Law No. 73-FZ of 4.28.1997, "O vnesenii izmenenij v Zakon RF 'O naloge na dobavlennuyu stoimost.'"

63. Federal Law No. 36-FZ of 1.2.2000.

64. Federal Law No. 179-FZ of 12.28.2001.

65. Federal Law No. 188-FZ of 11.30.1995.

66. Federal Law No. 10-FZ of 1.6.1999.

67. Federal Law No. 117-FZ of 8.5.2000 (with later modifications).

68. In fact, this is an important source of revenue for state colleges and institutes.

69. Law of Russian Federation, "O vnesenii izmenenij i dopolnenij v Zakon RSFSR 'O naloge na dobavlennuyu stoimost,'" No. 2813-1 of 5.22.1992.

70. Federal Law No. 63-FZ of 4.25.1995, "O vnesenii izmenenij i dopolnenij v Zakon Rossijskoj Federacii 'O naloge na dobavlennuyu stoimost.'"

71. This preference has existed since 1992, partially because it was not feasible to enforce it. Only recently has the market of apartment rentals begun to emerge from the shadow economy.

72. Federal Law No. 109-FZ of 8.20.2004.

73. See M. Ponomareva and E. Zhurvskaya, "Federal Tax Arrears in Russia," *Economics of Transition*, 12, 2004.

74. Tax administration in particular was regulated by two main laws (as well as numerous letters and instructions from the tax ministry): Law of Russian Federation, "O gosudarstvennoj nalogovoj sluzhbe RSFSR" No. 943-1 of 3.21.1991g and Law of Russian Federation, "Ob osnovah nalogovoj sistemy v Rossijskoj Federacii" No. 2118-1 of 12.27.1991.

75. These powers included the creation of the Temporary Emergency Committee in 1996 by the order of the president. For many, this committee was reminiscent of a commission with the same name that existed in the 1920s. It was abolished in 1999.

76. F. Gregory and G. Brooke, "Policing Economic Transition and Increasing Revenue: A Case Study of Federal Tax Police Service of the Russian Federation 1992–1998," *Europe-Asia Studies*, 52, no. 3, 2000.

77. To fight corruption, the law of 1994 stated that up to 25 percent of collected penalties could be diverted to the material benefits of tax collectors. This measure

greatly stimulated the collection of penalties but not of taxes. Only in 2001 was the measure abolished as ineffective.

78. The Large Taxpayer Unit was created in 1998.

79. For a more detailed discussion of novelties and problems of new tax code from the point of view of the tax administration, see A. Zolotareva, "Nekotorye problemy nalogovogo administrirovania," IET, 2000.

80. When interviewed as to why they were avoiding paying taxes, many business-men referred to the predatory behavior of tax collectors (for example, the notorious tax police) as well as uncertainty about claims on their tax liability. Making tax en-forcement more civilized, as well as lowering and clarifying tax liabilities, improved the image of tax collection activity, transforming it from an external threat to sur-vival of business to a social service.

81. For example, the estimated amount of uncollected taxes at the end of 1994 was as high as 2.4 percent of GDP. This number gives an idea about the level of tax dis-cipline in the 1990s.

82. Federal Law No. 154-FZ of 7.9.1999, "O vnesenii izmenenij i dopolnenij v chast' pervuyu Nalogovogo kodeksa Rossijskoj Federacii."

83. For a more detailed discussion of fly-by-night firms, see D. Treisman (1999), "Russia's Tax Crisis: Explaining Falling Revenues in a Transitional Economy," *Eco-nomics and Politics*, 11.

84. Instead of buying directly from a fly-by-night firm, the purchase can also be made through an affiliated firm whose output is exempt from VAT. This is an espe-cially popular tactic among exporters who do not want to have a direct connection with illegal firms.

85. In some instances, even without the help of fly-by-night firms, parties may be able to reduce the total amount of tax liabilities arising from a transaction by ma-nipulating the terms of agreement and by using side payments. For example, a seller can charge artificially low prices in order to reduce his tax liability. In return, a buyer will give the seller fake credit (a financial transaction, usually not subject to VAT) that will never be paid back. The buyer will have an interest to do so if he has nega-tive liability on taxes that he finds unlikely to be paid by the government or if he is exempt from VAT.

86. Federal Law No. 129-FZ of 8.8.2001, "O gosudarstvennoj registracii yuri-dicheskih lits."

87. For a review of best practices in this area, see: K. S. Jap, "The Value-added Tax Law in Force," *Bulletin for International Fiscal Documentation*, International Bureau of Fiscal Documentation (Amsterdam), 40, July 1986.

CHAPTER 6

Tax Reform in Kenya: Policy and Administrative Issues

Nada O. Eissa and William Jack

Kenya's tax system has undergone almost continual reform over the last 20 years. On the policy side, rate schedules have been rationalized and simplified, a new value-added tax has been introduced, and external tariffs have been brought in line with those of neighboring countries in East Africa. At the same time, administrative and institutional reforms have taken place. Most notable among these reforms was the creation of the semiautonomous Kenya Revenue Authority (KRA) in 1995, which centralized the administration of tax collection.

Kenya has the trappings of a modern tax system, including, for example, a credit-invoice VAT, a Pay As You Earn (PAYE) individual income tax with graduated but arguably moderate rates, and a set of excise taxes focused on the usual suspects (alcohol, cigarettes, gasoline, etc.). However, with up to 70 percent of GDP produced and possibly as much as 75 percent of labor employed in the informal sector, the ability of the tax system to raise sufficient revenue with minimal distortions is severely circumscribed. In such an environment, raising around one-fifth of GDP in tax revenue is likely to impose very large distortionary costs on the economy. Continued reform of both the policy instruments and the administrative and enforcement capacity of the tax system is therefore imperative.

This chapter provides a broad overview of the Kenyan tax system, the reforms that have occurred over the past two decades, and the administrative structures that are in place. To properly assess the distortionary costs of the current tax system, we undertake microeconometric analysis of the effects of the tax reforms pursued by the government, using individual-level tax return data when available. We discuss the proposed methodology for this subsequent research in the concluding section.

TAX REFORM IN KENYA

From independence in 1963 until the early 1980s, public spending in Kenya was financed through a somewhat uncoordinated set of taxes and fees inherited from British rule and supplemented by foreign aid inflows.

The oil shock in the early 1970s led to the country's first significant fiscal crisis, in response to which some relatively minor tax reforms were undertaken. Sales taxes were introduced as a means of generating extra revenue, and trade taxes were used in an attempt to reduce the ballooning balance-of-payments deficit. One motivation for the relatively heavy reliance on good-specific sales and excise taxes was the belief that the government could "get the prices right," especially through its use of trade taxes in the pursuit of, first, import-substitution policies and then export-led growth strategies.

Personal, and to a lesser extent corporate, income taxes were seen as serving primarily redistributive roles in the 1970s.[1] During the period 1974 through 1985, the tax rates on both personal and corporate income were high.[2] Marginal personal income tax rates ranged from 10 percent on the first shilling to a top rate of 65 percent. The tax rate applied to the income of domestic corporations was 45 percent in 1974, while foreign corporations faced a rate of 52 percent. Analysts have observed (e.g., Karingi et al., 2004a) that little personal income tax was collected in the top brackets of the tax schedule. This could have been due to low labor productivity— few people could hope to earn incomes high enough to put them in the top bracket. But it is likely that both the absolute size of the top personal income tax rate, and the fact that it was 20 percentage points higher than the corporate tax rate, contributed to the lack of reported income by taxpayers at the top end.

In the early 1980s, growing budget deficits began to loom. Following the second oil price shock, and fueled by uncontrolled public spending, the budget deficit ballooned to average over 6 percent of GDP between 1986 and 1993.[3] Perhaps in anticipation of these developments, in 1986 the Kenyan government approved the Tax Modernization Programme (TMP) aimed at broadening the tax base, and in 1987 it adopted the Budget Rationalization Programme intended to place controls on public spending.

The primary aim of the TMP was to raise the revenue-to-GDP ratio from 22 percent in 1986 to 24 percent by the mid-1990s, although this target was increased to 28 percent in 1992 (Muriithi and Moyi, 2003). These targets have so far proved elusive (see below). The intent of the reform was, in some respects, similar to that of the Tax Reform Act of 1986 in the United States—the revenue increase was to come about through lower tax rates, broader tax bases, and closed loopholes.[4] Whether Kenya was on the wrong side of the Laffer curve before the TMP began is unclear, although the high marginal income tax rates suggest it could have been.

On the other hand, broadening the tax base and closing loopholes would require bringing more individuals and businesses into the tax system, itself a challenge given the administrative weakness of the existing tax system. The main organizational change aimed at strengthening administrative capacity was the incorporation of the Kenya Revenue Authority in 1995.

The KRA centralized tax collection activities, which had previously been undertaken by departments in the Ministry of Finance (Muriithi and Moyi, 2003). Over the last 10 years, the KRA has adopted internal management reforms aimed at combating corruption among revenue officers and improving taxpayer services.

A number of East African countries have created tax collection authorities over the last decade. These institutions are semiautonomous from government and act under the supervision of a board of directors that includes bureaucrats, possibly a senior representative from the Ministry of Finance, and representatives from the private sector. They are meant to have a certain degree of financial and operational independence, for example, to allow more flexible employment practices than exist in the public service, and as a means of providing insulation from unwarranted political influence and corruption. In the end, however, they rely on discretionary funding from the Ministry of Finance, so their independence from the government is not complete. Of course, the formulation of tax policy is rarely (and should not be) the responsibility of the revenue administration but remains a ministry, and government, prerogative.

THE STRUCTURE OF TAX REVENUES

Tax revenues grew as a proportion of GDP from around 10 percent in the 1960s to about 20 percent by the early 1980s (Karingi et al., 2004b). In the years immediately following the introduction of the TMP revenues gradually increased, reaching 24.6 percent of GDP in 1995–1996, after which they stabilized at around 23 percent until the end of the decade (KRA, 2005a Annual Revenue Performance Report). In 1999–2000 revenues fell below 20 percent of GDP, and this decline continued until they reached a low of 17.8 percent of GDP in 2001–2002. Subsequently, there was a slow increase to 20 percent of GDP in 2004–2005. This evolution is illustrated in Figure 6.1.

The share of GDP currently collected in taxes is larger than that in many other sub-Saharan African countries. Kenya had a per capita GDP of about $360 in 2000 (in current dollars), and many people eked out a paltry and miserable existence on less than a dollar a day (and continue to do so). The poverty rate by this standard was 22.8 percent in 2000, and 58.3 percent of the population lived on less than $2 a day.[5] Raising around 20 percent of GDP in taxes is either impressive or dangerous, depending on the distortionary costs and the productivity and efficiency of public spending.

The share of the economy that is either informal or untaxable for other reasons is likely large. For example, Table 6.1 shows the evolution of the sectoral decomposition of output since independence. These data do not translate precisely into measures of easily taxed output, but the fact that agriculture currently contributes 25 percent and other services 47 percent suggests that a large share of output is produced in the informal sector.[6]

Table 6.2 provides a more direct measure of the share of output produced in the informal sector, which by 2002 employed nearly three-quarters of the

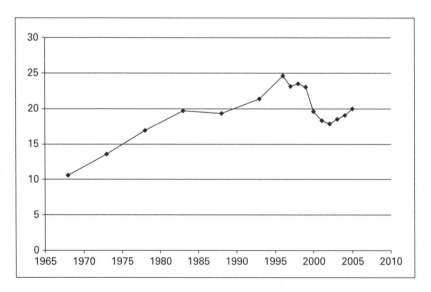

Figure 6.1   Tax Revenue, 1968–2005 (as a Percentage of GDP).

Source: Karingi et al. (2004a) and KRA (2005).

Note: Figures for 1968–1993 are four-year averages.

Table 6.1   Distribution of GDP by Sector

	1964–1973	1974–1979	1980–1989	1990–1995	1996–2000
Agriculture	36.6	33.2	29.8	26.2	24.5
Manufacturing	10.0	11.8	12.8	13.6	13.3
Public Services	14.7	15.3	15.0	15.7	14.8
Other Services	38.7	39.7	42.4	44.5	47.4

Source: Karingi et al. (2004a, p. 15).

Table 6.2   Recorded Employment, 1996–2002 *(in thousands)*

	Formal Sector		Informal Sector (percent of total)	Total
	Wage Employees	Self-employed and Family Workers		
1996	1619	63	2644 (61.1)	4326
1997	1647	64	2987 (63.6)	4698
1998	1678	65	3353 (65.8)	5097
1999	1689	65	3739 (68.1)	5493
2000	1695	65	4151 (70.2)	5912
2001	1677	65	4624 (72.6)	6367
2002	1700	65	5086 (74.2)	6852

Source: Karingi et al. (2004a, p.18).

workforce. Of course, labor productivity in this sector is likely to be low. Nonetheless, getting 20 percent of GDP out of the rest of the economy suggests relatively high tax burdens and distortions thereon.

The broad structure of tax revenues has changed to some extent. Income taxes (including taxes on both corporate and personal incomes) accounted for about a third of revenues from the late 1970s to the late 1990s, although the share was as high as 44 percent in the early 1970s. Reliance on import duties has fallen as the result of a move away from protectionist tariff policies and the integration of East African economies. They accounted for about one-quarter of revenues immediately before the TMP but had reached only 15 percent by the early and mid-1990s. Excise taxes, primarily levied on alcohol, tobacco, and petroleum products, offset some of this change rising from 10 to 16 percent of revenues over the same period. Finally, VAT revenues accounted for 25 percent of taxes by 2001, down from 36 percent in the early 1990s when the tax was first introduced. Falling VAT rates during this period can account for some of this shift, but evasion and moves into tax-exempt activities could also be at work, as well as improvements in corporate income and PAYE tax collections. Before the introduction of VAT, the sales tax (which the VAT replaced) had contributed between a quarter and a third of revenues from the mid-1970s to the late 1980s.

A more detailed view of recent developments is shown in Figure 6.2, which shows the evolution of the structure of tax revenues since 1995, when the KRA was established. A clear feature is the increase in the relative importance of PAYE income tax withheld at source, offset by a reduction in the share accounted for by corporate tax revenues. Indeed, in 1995–1996 corporate tax revenues were 1.8 times PAYE taxes, but by 2004–2005, the ratio was only 60 percent. It is tempting to attribute this change to a convergence of the top personal income tax rate and the corporate tax rate, although one might expect to see such a relationship between corporate tax revenues and personal income taxes paid by higher-income individuals who are less likely to be in the PAYE group. However, the fact that the share of revenue from the two taxes (PAYE and CIT) combined did not change significantly over this period suggests that some of this kind of income shifting might have taken place.

Figure 6.2 also makes clear that import duties have fallen in relative importance over the 10-year period to 2005. Withholding tax revenues (on interest, dividends, and certain other sources of nonwage income) have

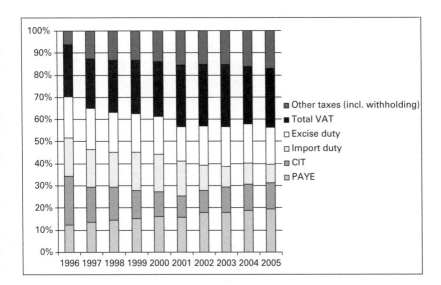

Figure 6.2   Structure of Revenues, 1996–2005.

Source: Tables 7 and 23, KRA 2005b, Statistical Bulletin.

been steady at between 4 and 5 percent of total taxes, but other taxes increased from about 3 percent in 1995–1996 to over 12 percent in 2008.

SPECIFIC POLICY REFORM MEASURES

In this section we discuss the features of the major tax instruments that are currently employed and how they have evolved over time.

VAT

In 1989, the government passed legislation to introduce a credit-invoice value-added tax, which became effective on January 1, 1990. At this time, the concept of tax policy simplicity had not firmly taken root in Kenya: the VAT was introduced with a standard rate of 17 percent, but with 14 other rates (the highest being 210 percent) that made the VAT appear more like a differentiated commodity tax regime. This multiplicity of rates was particularly difficult to rationalize in light of the fact that excise taxes on specific classes of goods were maintained during (and indeed after) the transition and implementation of the VAT.

The high and wide range of rates is thought to have led to widespread misclassification and other methods of tax evasion. In response to these concerns, the number of VAT rates was quickly reduced to four by 1993–1994, when the top rate was set at 40 percent. Since then, the rates have been lowered further, and currently there is just a single standard rate of 16 percent, with some sales zero-rated and others exempt. (See Table 6.3.)

All businesses with annual turnover greater than KSh 3 million are supposed to register as VAT taxpayers and submit monthly returns.[7] In addition, certain traders and members of certain professions are required to register independently of their turnover, but this requirement is not well enforced.[8] The number of businesses registered for VAT is currently about 54,000, up from 36,000 two years ago. However, only about 30,000 VAT returns were received each month in 2004–2005, suggesting that many firms are dormant (have fallen below the threshold but have failed to deregister, which itself can be a costly process) or noncompliant. The large, and possibly inefficient, increase in the number of registered firms is thought to be due to a number of issues, including the requirement that any firm seeking a contract with a government agency must be VAT-registered (even if it falls below the threshold, and even if it ends up not winning a contract), and the so-called "VAT withholding" regime, dis-

Table 6.3 VAT Rates in Kenya, 1989–2006

Year	Number of VAT Rates	Standard Rate	Highest Rate
1989–1990	15	17	210
1990–1991	9	18	150
1991–1992	8	18	100
1992–1993	6	18	50
1993–1994	4	18	40
1994–1995	4	18	30
1995–1996	4	15	25
1996–1997	3	15	15
1997–1998	3	17	17
1998–1999	4	16	16
1999–2000	4	15	15
2000–2001	4	18	18
2001–2002	4	18	18
2002–2003	4	18	18
2003–2004	3	16	16
2005–2006	1	16	16

Source: Karingi et al. (2004b), KRA.

cussed below. This distribution of VAT payers and collections is shown in Table 6.A.1 in the Appendix.

In most VAT systems, the seller of a product is required to remit a tax on sales. In practice, the system can be implemented in a number of ways. First, the seller might base the calculation of tax payable on an explicit accounting of value added. Alternatively, the seller assesses VAT on gross sales but claims a credit for VAT already paid on inputs. Under both of these systems, only the net amount of VAT is sent to the tax collection agency. Alternatively, the seller may be required to write a check for the VAT assessed on gross sales and claim a refund for the VAT paid on inputs.

In Kenya, the responsibility for paying the VAT on certain sales rests not only with the seller but also with the buyer, a system referred to as VAT withholding.[9] VAT withholding was first introduced in late 2003 and applied to government agencies that purchased goods and services subject to the VAT. There was a concern that the government, through these agencies, was paying VAT-inclusive prices to suppliers, who were not necessarily remitting the revenue to the KRA. Subsequently, other purchasers were brought into the withholding regime, and in 2004–2005 there were about 2000 so-called VAT withholding agents—purchasers who were required to withhold VAT. In that year, about 40 percent of VAT revenue was collected from these agents.

One concern with withholding is that it can provide too strong an incentive for firms to register for the VAT. Suppliers who fall below the turnover threshold but who sell to withholding agents are induced to register in search of refunds on inputs, clogging up the system.

The effect of withholding (see the Appendix for an illustrative example) is to put some businesses, in particular importers of oil, in a more or less permanent net credit position, in which they seek VAT refunds from the KRA each month. This, however, has led to compliance problems, as those subject to withholding rationally expect delays in receiving refund checks. The mentality of the KRA, given its focus on tax collection, is one of revenue maximization, and refund payment is low on its list of priorities. This policy is of course self-defeating if compliance falls enough. One view among tax administrators is that the VAT-withholding system has complicated tax collection and created perverse incentives for tax collectors. The implication is that direct improvements in enforcement (on which the withholding system was first focused)—for example, through the auditing of suppliers to government agencies—are preferable.

The government is currently considering the introduction of a presumptive tax, referred to as a Unified Tax System (UTS).[10] The intention of this policy is to target untaxed business income by bringing into the tax net those businesses that neither pay income tax nor are part of the VAT system. Included in the latter group are businesses that are currently required to register as VAT payers but choose (illegally) not to and those that have annual turnover less than the existing registration threshold (KSh 3 million). In principle, any business that is not required to register for VAT, and does not choose to do so, should be covered by the presumptive tax. That is, the VAT/income tax system and the presumptive tax system are intended to be mutually exclusive, although some businesses can choose the regime in which to operate.

It is proposed that the tax, which is yet to be introduced, will be related to gross turnover; where such information is not available, it will be lump-sum. The proposal is that the lump-sum liabilities will be differentiated geographically and by sector. This two-dimensional stratification, along with the turnover component, is likely to add a degree of complexity to what is supposed to be an administratively simple tax.

For those businesses that currently fall under the VAT threshold, there may be some incentive to register under the presumptive tax regime, depending on penalties for noncompliance and the "benefits of formality." One would expect little participation response, however, from those that currently have turnovers above the KSh 3 million VAT threshold but choose (illegally) not to register. Indeed, some fear that the presumptive tax could induce informality—in this case defined as deregistration for VAT—as it legitimizes opting out of the VAT system.

PERSONAL INCOME TAX

Individuals pay taxes on earned income at graduated rates. By administrative necessity, the personal income tax has traditionally been levied only on formal sector workers. Until 2003, most payers of the personal income tax did not file a return but simply had tax withheld at source. Some believe that the requirement to lodge a return has increased compliance costs and administrative costs significantly, while having little impact on revenues.[11]

For example, currently about 600,000 individuals submit an annual income tax return, but only 10,000 to 20,000 businesses (that should) withhold PAYE taxes. If many individuals had other sources of taxable income, individual returns might be necessary. However, only about 2,000 individuals submit returns with nonwage income that adds to taxable income. It is likely, although there are no data to confirm this suspicion, that many high-income individuals simply evade tax payments through nonreporting and choice of compensation strategy. Thus, though not much revenue is collected from the personal income tax in excess of PAYE taxes, there could be a considerable amount of potential tax revenue from these sources. However, focusing on high-income, and politically well-connected, individuals is particularly sensitive in Kenya.

In the late 1980s, the personal income tax was levied at eight different marginal rates ranging from 10 to 65 percent. The top rate was reduced to 45 percent in 1990, 35 percent in 1996, and 30 percent in 2000, where it remains today. The current rates are 10, 15, 20, 25, and 30 percent.

Each taxpayer is eligible for a (nonrefundable) credit known as personal relief, which amounts to a little more than the amount of tax that would be payable in the first tax bracket.[12] Thus, in practice, the tax schedule is equivalent to one with a uniform exemption followed by rates ranging from 15 to 30 percent. Karingi et al. (2004b; Table 6) have estimated the maximum income an individual could earn before paying any personal income tax for the years 1995 through 2003. They find that this maximum income increased from 2.3 times to 4.1 times the national per capita income over this period.

Until recently, there were two forms of relief, or credit: a personal relief and a larger family relief. Unmarried individuals could claim the personal relief, and married men could claim the large family relief. Married men were required to pay tax on their combined household income. Although KRA income tax forms are currently divided into "self" and "wife," the incomes of each are now taxed independently and each receives a single personal relief or exemption.[13]

Self-employment and partnership income is taxed under the same tax schedule as wage income. Nonwage incomes, in the form of dividends, interest, and certain other incomes, including royalties and management, professional, and commission fees, are subject to a final withholding tax at source.[14] These taxes are effectively separate and at specific rates from the income tax. Given this arrangement, there seems little reason to require wage earners (most of whom have only a limited amount of interest or dividend income) to file formal returns.

Capital gains are exempt from the personal income tax in Kenya. Although there are arguments against the taxation of capital gains, it appears that the dominant reason for the exemption in this case is that one of the primary stores of wealth (and sources of capital gains) is real estate, the ownership of which is concentrated in the hands of the political elite.

Pension contributions up to 30 percent of pensionable salary are deductible against gross income, and a credit of 15 percent of the cost of life insurance premiums and education policies for family members (capped at KSh 36,000 each) is also available.[15] Mortgage interest payments up to KSh 100,000 (KSh 150,000 effective January 1, 2006) are also deductible.

During the period of reform, some attempts have been made to introduce a presumptive tax in lieu of the income tax to reach the informal sector, in particular agriculture. It is widely believed that these efforts have generally failed (Karingi et al., 2004a). Whether the presumptive tax in lieu of the income tax and as a supplement to the VAT will meet with greater success is yet to be seen.

About 40,000 firms are currently registered as corporate income tax payers.[16] Tax rates on domestic firms have fallen from 45 percent in the mid-1970s to 30 percent currently. (Tax rates imposed on foreign-owned corporations were 52 percent, but have fallen over the last 30 years to 32.5 percent today.)

Corporations that are located in export processing zones (EPZs), which are found in Nairobi and Mombasa, and can show that they produce for export are granted a generous 10-year corporate tax holiday.[17] Firms outside the EPZs can deduct 20 percent of the costs of investment in (new or second-hand) plant and equipment up front (equivalent to a 6 percent investment tax credit) and then amortize the remaining cost of the investment following specified depreciation formulae. Certain investments, such as hotel construction and some agricultural investment, are given favorable treatment.

EXCISE TAXES

Excise taxes are levied on (imported) oil products, as well as consumption of beer and spirits, cigarettes, matches, and tobacco. Before the TMP, excise taxes had been levied at specific rates, but moderate to high inflation induced a change to an ad valorem basis. Later, in the 1980s, the tax regimes were selectively switched back to specific charges in the face of undervaluation by traders.

Prior to 1990, taxes on cigarettes had provided more than half of non-oil excise tax revenues, and beer about one-quarter. However, coincident with the introduction of the VAT, the specific tax on beer was replaced with a 100 percent tax rate, and these shares were effectively reversed (Kiringai et al., 2002).

ADMINISTRATIVE STRUCTURE AND REFORMS

In this section, we discuss a number of administrative features of the Kenyan tax system, including the internal organization of the Kenya Revenue Authority, the auditing and refund processes, and penalty provisions. We end the section with a brief description of a tax amnesty that was adopted in 2004.

ORGANIZATION OF THE KRA

Tax collection responsibilities are divided between two main departments in the Kenya Revenue Authority: the Domestic Tax Department (DTD) and the Customs and Excise Department (CED). The DTD covers personal and corporate income taxes, the withholding tax, the VAT on domestically produced goods, and some other small taxes. Until mid-2005, the CED was responsible for all excise tax collection (on both domestically produced goods and imports), all trade taxes, and VAT collected on imports. On July 1, 2005, responsibility for domestic excises was shifted to the DTD.

The Authority has 17 so-called stations, or regional branches. Four of these stations are in the capital Nairobi (Nairobi North, South, East, and West) and two are in Mombasa, the main port. Although the responsibilities of the Nairobi stations are geographically determined, all four offices are located in the same building as the central KRA administration.[18] One of the 17 stations is the Large Taxpayer Office, whose clients are not geographically determined (see below). In addition to the stations, a number of much smaller "satellites" provide a limited range of services, including taxpayer registration, tax forms, and payment facilities with an additional nine satellite offices.

In 1997–1998, the KRA created a Large Taxpayer Office (LTO) to specifically monitor and provide services to taxpayers that contribute the bulk of revenues. Fully 70 percent of taxes are remitted by around 500 taxpayers, although of course the incidence of these taxes, which include, for example, PAYE, VAT, and custom and excise taxes, is much broader.

The primary eligibility criterion for treatment as a large taxpayer subject to LTO control is annual turnover of KSh 1 billion (about US $15 million). In addition, firms in certain lines of business, including banks, financial institutions, and finance companies, are subject to inclusion in the LTO regardless of turnover. Finally, government agencies and certain parastatals are also included. Currently, approximately 300 companies are subject to LTO treatment, and these contribute roughly 60 percent of revenue. A number of companies that meet the threshold are not included (for reasons unknown to the authors), and it is believed that doubling the number of taxpayers covered by the LTO would mean this office collected about 70 percent of revenues.

One internal problem with using a Large Taxpayer Office to focus auditing and taxpayer services on high-yield clients is that revenues from these companies are no longer collected through the relevant branch office, or station. The transfer of responsibility to the LTO meets some resistance from said stations, as they often lose a large fraction of their collections. While in principle this should have no impact on incentives or performance—any explicit or implicit incentive schemes for regional branches should be easily corrected for the loss of identifiable large revenue earners—the expectation is that loss of such clients portends general loss of prestige and influence for the station.

The auditing strategy of the LTO is to audit about one-third of firms subject to its control each year. The coverage rate for medium-sized taxpayers is much lower, but a target of about 10 percent is thought to be appropriate.

AUDITING

In principle, the tax system is moving in the direction of self-assessment, whereby individuals and firms calculate their tax liability directly and submit returns and payments. Administrative assessment, on the other hand, requires that each taxpayer's liability is calculated by a revenue official, using data supplied by the taxpayer. In practice, there is a continuum of systems between these two, distinguished by the probability of being audited. Auditing activities have recently been streamlined with the merger of the Income and VAT departments under the DTD. This consolidation has allowed joint audits of VAT and income taxes, including PAYE taxes that are the responsibility of the employer (who is often a VAT payer).[19] In 2004–2005, a total of 2,000 audits were undertaken, raising KSh 5.5 billion (KRA, 2005b). To improve compliance among taxpayers, the KRA has developed an audit handbook and is engaged in continuing taxpayer education activities.

The KRA, the Treasury, and KIPPRA[20] recently fielded a survey to assess tax compliance issues in Kenya. Preliminary results show that 74 percent and 72 percent of respondents had been subject to a VAT and (corporate) income tax audit, respectively. Roughly one-third and one-quarter of respondents reported being audited annually for VAT and income tax purposes. These audit rates appear high, but as participation in the survey was voluntary, they may well be overestimates of actual audit rates.

TAX REFUNDS

It is revealing that while most taxpayers surveyed reported being satisfied with the procedures for tax registration and payment, they also assessed the procedures for appeals, exemptions, remissions, and refunds as "very poor" and "unfair" (Tax Compliance Study). Typically, at least 60 days elapse before a refund is processed, and this delay can be as long as 120 days. The DTD processes all refunds, including those for VAT collected on imports.[21] (The CED processes all refunds of import excises and duties.)

All requests for refunds (e.g., for excess VAT paid) must be audited,[22] which may delay compensation and certainly adds to the cost of receiving compensation for overpayment of net taxes. A further impediment to the speedy refund of excess payments is that such transfers are treated under the budget as expenditures, not as negative revenues. This distinction is important in practice (although of course not in theory) because it means

Parliament must pass an appropriation bill with funds earmarked for re-funding. This leads to backlogs, which are intermittently cleared, only to start growing again immediately. In addition, there appears to be a dis-agreement between the KRA and the Treasury over the size of refunds re-quired, which again leads to delays. Refund policy should clearly be much more automatic, unless there are serious concerns over fraud that would be determined on a basis of risk assessment.

PENALTIES AND INTEREST

Penalties for non- or underpayment of taxes are defined by law, and interest of 2 percent per month is charged on tax arrears, calculated starting from the date the tax was due. While it is standard practice to punish noncompliance starting on the date the tax was due, long delays between the submission of a return and auditing tend to increase interest payments by those who are found to have underpaid. The relatively high (2 percent) monthly interest rate provides the KRA with little financial incentive to speed up auditing.[23]

Some observers have identified a legislative source of inflexibility in the penalty system. In particular, penalties for nonpayment of VAT, income tax, and customs and excise taxes are defined under three separate laws, which are difficult to coordinate and to adjust as changing circumstances require. Proposed legislation would integrate the penalty provisions and leave them to be implemented through regulations.

Eighty percent of respondents to the survey above claimed that penal-ties and interest were too high, but this is not surprising. Two things that are not clear from the survey are (1) whether the penalties and interest are imposed consistently, or whether tax payments are negotiated with reve-nue officials on a case-by-case basis, and (2) what effects these sanctions have on compliance and the choice to enter the formal sector.

The physical process of paying any bill in Kenya, where the postal sys-tem is notoriously unreliable, is costly and protracted, often requiring a personal visit to a far-away office. Accordingly, the KRA has attempted to facilitate easier payment of taxes. It has opened a cash-receiving center for income tax payments in a regional center (Eldoret) and has expanded the number of points at which annual income tax returns can be collected and submitted. However, the process remains exceedingly labor intensive. Even with high unemployment and a low shadow wage, the congestion costs imposed by the mechanisms for interacting with the KRA must surely be large.

Table 6.4 2004 Tax Amnesty Results

	Revenue (KSh billion)	Number of Applicants
Income tax	2.98	2,258
Customs and excise	0.32	450
VAT	1.50	865
Total	**4.80**	

Source: KRA, 2005, Statistical Bulletin.

The situation is somewhat better for customs duties and VAT collections. Taxpayers are now required to pay self-assessed taxes directly to a bank, although this can simply push the problem on to the banking sector, which itself is not highly automated.

TAX AMNESTY

On June 10, 2004, the minister of finance announced a tax amnesty that permitted individuals, firms, and other corporate bodies to pay previously undeclared taxes or duties by the end of the calendar year without penalties or interest. The KRA reports the results of this exercise, as shown in Table 6.4. In the table, income tax payments reflect primarily corporate income tax proceeds. It is somewhat difficult to interpret the figures, as the KRA did not report the baseline or counterfactual against which the estimates were calculated. Perhaps more importantly, it is not evident what the dynamic effects of this amnesty will be on future incentives to pay tax in full and on time.

CONCLUSIONS AND DIRECTIONS OF FUTURE RESEARCH

The fixed costs of running a modern tax collection system, coupled with the informal nature of much economic activity, make it difficult to raise public funds in poor countries. Questions of how to efficiently raise more revenue, and how to reduce the administrative and distortionary costs of raising existing revenue, are two sides of the same coin. Our descriptive summary of the Kenyan tax system above suggests a number of avenues of future research that might yield insights into these questions.

With the recent introduction of mandatory filing of personal income tax returns, the Kenya Revenue Authority is amassing a large amount of micro data that could be used to assess the incentive effects of taxes on labor supply and taxable income more generally. We see two separate avenues of research in this vein. First, we consider focusing on employees who traditionally did not file a return (and had PAYE taxes withheld). For these individuals, the change in filing requirement has effectively reduced the opportunity cost of claiming certain deductions, since previously, any filing costs were avoided by not making such claims.

Second, an analysis of the behavior of high-income taxpayers is desirable. Such individuals, to the extent they have had nonwage income, have been required to file individual tax returns since the inception of the KRA in 1995. We envision using the reductions in tax rates over this period—the top marginal rate fell from 37.5 percent to 30 percent between 1995 and 2000—to estimate the responsiveness of taxable income to those rates and the associated distortionary costs.[24] Given the possibility of income shifting—from corporate to personal income—the responsiveness of corporate tax payments would need to be incorporated into this analysis.

Other studies would likely require survey data in addition to information from tax returns. For example, understanding the effects of the presumptive tax, if one is introduced, would necessarily involve collection of data on the nature and extent of informality. Nor are the normative impacts of the policy clear-cut. A revenue-maximizing tax collector sees the benefits of reducing informality, but not necessarily the compliance costs imposed. More fundamentally, while entry into the formal sector is often assumed to benefit businesses by improving their access to credit and other financial markets, the extent to which (a) this is true, and (b) informal credit markets are crowded out, can only be assessed empirically.

We have said relatively little in this chapter about the distributional impact of the tax system in Kenya. Due to the large proportion of individuals in the informal sector, as well as the personal relief (exemption) in the personal income tax schedule, the instruments that impose the highest direct costs on the poor are no doubt excise taxes and the VAT (despite zero-rating and exemption of some products under the latter). Quantification of the burden requires more precise information on household consumption patterns by income category, as well as assumptions or evidence about the incidence of these taxes. We suggest, however, that an important distributional concern is not so much how much tax is paid by the poor (or more generally, what the effect of the tax system is on their welfare), but how little tax is paid by the rich, owing to tax avoidance, tax evasion, or direct manipulation of the tax laws and regulations by the elite.

APPENDIX
VAT WITHHOLDING

Consider an importer who purchases oil for KSh 100. Ignoring excise and import duties, he pays VAT of KSh 16 for a total cost of KSh 116. The shipping agent remits a check for KSh 16 to the KRA. Suppose the importer's value-added is KSh 25. Under a typical credit-invoice VAT, he would sell the oil to a retailer for KSh 145, including KSh 20 (= 16% of KSh 125). He would either remit a check for KSh 20 to the KRA and seek a refund of 16, or simply remit a check for the net amount, KSh 4. This is shown in the top panel of Figure 6.A.1.

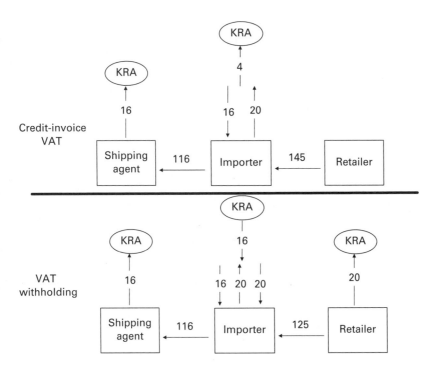

Figure 6.A.1   Credit-invoice VAT Versus VAT Withholding.

Table 6.A.1 Distribution of VAT Taxpayers, 2004–2005

Annual Turnover (KSh million)	Number of Taxpayers	Cum. %	Total Turnover (KSh million)	Average Turnover (KSh million)	Total VAT (KSh million)	Average VAT Paid (KSh million)	Cum. % VAT Paid
250	501	0.9	533,923	1,066	18,375	36.7	61.9
100–250	709	2.2	106,775	151	2,980	4.2	72.0
50–100	840	3.8	58,823	70	1,918	2.3	78.4
10–50	3,690	10.6	80,681	22	3,057	0.8	88.7
5–10	2,343	15.0	16,702	7	827	0.3	91.5
3–5	1,942	18.6	7,521	4	407	0.2	92.9
<3	43,934	100.0	8,954	0.2	2,112	0.1	100.0
	53,959		813,379	15.1	29,676	0.5	

Source: KRA presentation, IMF-sponsored workshop on tax administration, Kenya School of Monetary Studies, Nairobi, November 29, 2005.

Under VAT withholding, the importer again purchases the oil for KSh 116 but now sells to the retailer for only KSh 125. The shipping agent remits a check for KSh 16 as before, but now the *retailer* pays VAT of KSh 20 (= 16% of KSh 125) on its purchase. In practice, the importer is liable for VAT of KSh 20, but receives a credit for KSh 20 paid by the retailer, as well as a credit of KSh 16 already paid on inputs. Thus the importer has an excess credit of KSh 16, which he must claim as a refund. This is shown in Figure 6.A.1.

NOTES

Prepared for the Initiative for Policy Dialogue Tax Task Force. Thanks to Roger Gordon, Dickson Khainga, Jonah Ogaro, Andrew Okello, and Alice Owuor for providing information.

1. The theory of optimal taxation (Diamond and Mirrlees, 1971a, b; Mirrlees, 1971), including the choice between direct and indirect taxation (Atkinson and Stiglitz, 1976), was of course in its infancy in this period.

2. There is a tendency in Kenya to lump discussion of personal and corporate income taxes into a single income tax category. We will try to avoid this practice in this chapter.

3. If we are to believe that one-half to three-quarters of GDP is produced in the informal sector, then estimates of output and any other quantities as a share thereof need to be interpreted with caution. However, as we do not have specific information on the way in which GDP is calculated, it is difficult to tell in which direction there is likely to be a bias, if any.

4. TRA86 was intended to be revenue neutral, compared with the intention of raising revenue in Kenya.

5. Per capita income had risen to $480 in current dollars by 2004. These data are from the World Bank.

6. Some agriculture output comes from large tea, coffee, and pineapple plantations, which are relatively easily taxed.

7. The government may change the filing requirements of smaller businesses, which would file bi-monthly instead.

8. Even though it is not enforced, many VAT taxpayers do have turnover less than the standard threshold, thereby bloating the system that the VAT registers.

9. This terminology is consistent with the requirement that the purchaser of labor services be required to pay tax on wages paid under the more familiar income tax withholding.

10. There is currently in place a presumptive tax on agriculture, which is a 2 percent tax on gross proceeds from sales to agricultural traders (middlemen), available to those who opt out of the personal income tax regime. Compliance is very limited, and tax collections are virtually zero.

11. Individuals submit paper personal income tax returns, which the KRA stores in hard copy. On the other hand, the KRA stores electronic copies of PAYE returns

by employers, but there is no cross-link between employers' and individuals' returns. In particular, the employer returns have no means of identifying which employees have had PAYE tax remitted on their behalf. There is some evidence that the PAYE tax is being withheld by employers but not remitted to the KRA, a simple case of theft.

12. In 2004 the relief was KSh 12,672, while the bottom tax rate of 10 percent applied to the first KSh 116,160 of income.

13. Married women have the option of filing separately.

14. The withholding rates are 15 percent on gross interest earnings, 5 percent on qualified dividends, and 10 percent on ordinary dividends.

15. It is believed that the requirement that all wage earners submit a personal income tax return could have led to a loss in revenue to the extent that individuals who were previously unaware of the deductibility of certain expenses began to take advantage of these preferences. Of course, the reduction in revenue (if any) does not mean that the welfare impact of this change in behavior was negative.

16. It is perhaps striking that there are about twice as many firms registered for CIT as there are paying PAYE taxes. One possible explanation for this disproportion is that many companies are created for reasons other than hiring employees, perhaps simply as investment holding companies, or as parent companies that own subsidiaries that in turn hire the employees.

17. There are about 70 firms in the EPZs. They are of course required to withhold and remit PAYE taxes during this period.

18. The building that houses these offices, the Times Tower, was constructed specifically for the KRA. It is the tallest building in East Africa and has no tenants other than the KRA.

19. Prior to the merger, the Income Tax Department was organized on a functional basis, with separate offices for each department—for example, taxpayer services, auditing. However, multiple tasks in the VAT Department were carried out by all individuals, with little functional delineation. The newly merged department has adopted a functional organizational structure.

20. Kenya Institute for Public Policy Research and Analysis.

21. Refund claims that are certified by accredited accountants are, according to KRA policy, supposedly fast tracked. This effectively outsources part of the verification process from the KRA at the taxpayer's expense—a kind of price discrimination across taxpayers. This policy is unique to Kenya.

22. Similarly, businesses are required to submit corporate tax returns accompanied by a set of audited accounts.

23. Except to the extent that a shilling in the hand is worth more than 1.02^m in the m-month-old bush.

24. In a recent paper, Auriol and Warlters (2005) use a CGE model to compute the marginal cost of public funds for a (large) number of African countries. Our micro-level approach would be complementary to their macro simulation methods.

REFERENCES

Atkinson, A., and Stiglitz, J. (1976). "The Design of Tax Structure: Direct versus Indirect Taxation." *Journal of Public Economics*, 6, pp. 55–75.

Auriol, E., and Warlters, M. (2005). "The Marginal Cost of Public Funds in Africa." IDEI Working Papers 371. Toulouse: Institut d'Économie Industrielle (IDEI).

Diamond, P., and Mirrlees, J. (1971a). "Optimal Taxation and Public Production I: Production Efficiency." *American Economic Review*, 61, pp. 8–27.

———. (1971b). "Optimal Taxation and Public Production II: Tax Rules." *American Economic Review*, 61, pp. 261–278.

Karingi, S., Pamba, E., and Nyakang'o, E. (2004a). "Tax Reform Experience in Kenya." Tax Policy Unit. Nairobi, Kenya: KIPPRA.

Karingi, S., Wanjala, A., Kamau, A., Nyakang'o, E., Mwangi, A., Muhoro, M., and Nyamunga, J. (2004b). "Fiscal Architecture and Revenue Capacity in Kenya." KIPPRA Discussion Paper DP/45/2004. Nairobi, Kenya: KIPPRA (Kenya Institute for Public Policy Research and Analysis).

Kenya Revenue Authority. (2005a). "Annual Revenue Performance Report FY 2004/05." Nairobi, Kenya: KRA.

———. (2005b). "Statistical Bulletin (July 2004–June 2005)." Nairobi, Kenya: KRA.

KIPPRA. (2005). "Tax Compliance Study." Draft report.

Kiringai, J., Ndung'u, N., and Karingi, S. (2002). "Tobacco Excise Tax in Kenya: An Appraisal." KIPPRA Discussion Paper DP/21/2002. Nairobi, Kenya: KIPPRA.

Mirrlees, J. (1971). "An Exploration in the Theory of Optimum Income Taxation." *Review of Economic Studies*, 38, pp. 175–208.

Muriithi, M., and Moyi, E. (2003). "Tax Reforms and Revenue Mobilization in Kenya." AERC Research Paper 131. Nairobi, Kenya: African Economic Research Consortium (AERC).

CHAPTER 7

Korea's Tax System: A Growth-Oriented Choice

Joosung Jun

Korea's tax system does not much resemble systems found in developed countries. The tax bases are narrow, and the overall tax burden is relatively low. Tax revenue as a fraction of GDP has increased steadily over the past decades, but at around 20 percent it is still among the lowest in the Organisation for Economic Co-operation and Development (OECD; Table 7.1).[1] Including social security contributions, Korea's tax burden amounted to 25.3 percent of GDP in 2003, about two-thirds of the OECD average of 36.3 percent. Three decades ago, the gap was even wider, with Korea collecting only half of the revenue that OECD countries did as a percentage of GDP.[2] The tax burden rose noticeably in the late 1970s, reflecting the introduction of a broad-based VAT in 1977. The 1997 financial crisis triggered a wide array of changes in tax policy and economic structure, and thus had a significant impact on tax revenue.

The personal income tax, a dominant source of revenue among rich countries, is of relatively minor importance in Korea. As shown in Table 7.2, taxes on individual income accounted for only 11.5 percent of total tax revenues in 1980 and have increased very modestly to 12.7 percent in 2003. Taxes on corporate income have instead grown to be a more important source of revenue over the same period, collecting 15.3 percent of total revenue in 2003.[3] Taxes on consumption are by far the dominant source of revenue, at 34.4 percent in 2003, although their share has been on a declining trend. More than half of consumption tax revenues come from the VAT, with the rest contributed by a variety of excise taxes. In contrast to the situation in developed countries, property taxes raise a significant share of tax revenue, at 12.8 percent in 2003.[4] In the early 1980s, customs duties were as important as individual income taxes, but their revenue share has steadily declined in reflection of trade liberalization. Social security contributions have increased markedly, with a strong jump in the late 1990s as noted in Table 7.1, although their share is still small compared to the cases in most developed countries.

The tax level and structure are influenced by the nation's tax policy objectives, economic structure, and enforcement capacity. In the early stages of economic development, growth objectives were a dominant force shaping the tax system in Korea. Various tax incentives were provided to the export and other targeted industries, particularly in the heavy and chemical sectors, while there were generous savings incentives at the personal level. In addition, highly leveraged manufacturing firms were able to make substantial tax savings through interest deductions.[5] They also benefited from low effective taxation of capital gains that facilitated their investment financing with retained earnings.[6] Such tax preferences are still in place, although their nature and extent have been modified in accordance with changes in economic structure and policy objectives.

Raising revenue to finance infrastructure and education has been an integral part of Korea's growth strategies.[7] Due to enforcement problems with the self-employed and with smaller firms, however, the income and consumption tax bases are very narrow. Personal income tax collected was less than revenue from tariffs until the mid-1980s, and most of the corporate and value-added taxes have been paid by a limited number of large corporations. Until recently, the revenue contribution of the VAT, which is the most broad-based tax, seldom exceeded 4 percent of GDP.[8]

Table 7.1 Tax Revenue in Selected OECD Countries *(as a percentage of GDP[1])*

	1975	1980	1985	1990	1995	2000	2003	1975–2003 Change
Korea	14.9	17.1	16.1	17.9	18.1	19.6	20.4	5.5
	(15.1)	(17.2)	(16.4)	(18.9)	(19.4)	(23.6)	(25.3)	(10.2)
OECD total[3]	23.5	24.5	25.7	26.7	26.5	27.9	26.8	3.3
	(30.3)	(32.0)	(33.5)	(34.8)	(35.7)	(37.1)	(36.3)	(6.0)
United States	20.3	20.6	19.1	20.5	20.9	23.0	18.8	−1.5
	(25.6)	(26.4)	(25.6)	(27.3)	(27.9)	(29.9)	(25.6)	(0.0)
Sweden	33.8	33.6	36.2	38.7	35.1	39.1	35.8	2.0
	(42.0)	(47.3)	(48.2)	(53.2)	(48.5)	(53.9)	(50.6)	(8.6)
Mexico	–	13.9	15.0	15.0	13.9	15.4	15.8	1.9[2]
	–	(16.2)	(17.0)	(17.3)	(16.7)	(18.5)	(19.0)	(2.8)

Source: OECD (2005), *Revenue Statistics 1965–2004.*

1. Figures in parentheses are with social security contributions included.
2. For Mexico, the change for 1980–2003 is reported.
3. Unweighted averages.

To compensate for this revenue shortfall, the Korean government made extensive use of earmarked taxes, which appeared to arouse less resistance from taxpayers. Its lack of enforcement capacity also led the government to impose flat-rate withholding taxes on most capital incomes and to tax property transactions more heavily than property holdings.[9] About two-thirds of property-related revenue comes from transaction taxes (Table 7.2), which face less resistance from the taxpayer than holding taxes. Also noticeable has been the wide use of surtaxes, levied on top of other taxes payable. Such "hidden taxes" amounted to about 8 percent of total revenue in 2003.[10]

Overall, the Korean tax system has not evolved along the lines found in developed countries. Efficiency and equity have been emphasized as the guiding principles in most tax debates, but actual tax policy has focused more on specific policy objectives: promoting savings, investment, and R&D, as well as securing sufficient revenue to finance public infrastructure and education. Korea's tax policy has thus been highly growth-oriented.

Table 7.2   Tax Revenue by Type of Tax, 1980 and 2003

	1980		2003	
	% of GDP	% of Total	% of GDP	% of Total
Total tax revenue	**17.2**	**100.0**	**25.3**	**100.0**
Individual income	**2.0**	**11.5**	**3.2**	**12.7**
Personal income tax	1.7	9.9	2.9	11.3
Surtax on personal income tax	0.3	1.6	0.3	1.3
Corporate income	**1.9**	**11.0**	**3.9**	**15.3**
Corporate income tax	1.3	7.3	3.5	14.0
Surtax on corporate income tax	0.7	3.8	0.3	1.4
Consumption	**8.0**	**46.6**	**8.7**	**34.4**
Value-added tax	3.8	22.0	4.6	18.2
Excise taxes	3.9	22.4	3.3	13.0
Surtax on excise taxes	0.4	2.2	0.8	3.3
Property	**1.5**	**8.9**	**3.2**	**12.8**
Taxes on transactions	0.8	4.4	2.0	7.8
Surtax on transaction taxes	0.0	0.0	0.2	0.9
Taxes on wealth holding	0.8	4.4	0.9	3.4
Surtax on wealth taxes	0.0	0.0	0.2	0.6
Customs duties	**2.6**	**11.4**	**1.0**	**3.9**
Customs duties	2.0	11.4	0.9	3.7
Surtax on customs duties	0.6	3.8	0.0	0.2
Social security and payroll	**0.3**	**1.6**	**5.0**	**19.8**
Other	**0.9**	**5.2**	**0.3**	**1.2**

Source: National Tax Service (1981, 2004), *Statistical Yearbook of National Tax*; OECD (2005), *Revenue Statistics 1965–2004*; and author's calculations.

Note: See Table 7.A.1 in Appendix for a detailed description of individual tax items.

At the same time, the tax structure appears to have been influenced by various enforcement problems. It is argued in this chapter that many of the tax incentives provided might have served not so much the purpose of promoting targeted activities as keeping taxpayers from disappearing into the informal sector. Generous nontax compensations have also been available for heavily taxed large corporations. To the extent that these preferences have supported tax base protection by mitigating evasion pressures, the revenue and efficiency costs associated with them in most discussions of Korean tax policy have been overstated.

In a word, tax design in Korea has reflected its own unique policy objectives and economic structure, which differ significantly from those in other countries. Unless these underlying factors change, more conventional tax policies observed among developed countries should be considered with caution.

This chapter provides a critical review of Korea's tax system, summarizing its key statutory features and emphasizing the ways in which enforcement problems as well as policy objectives influence tax design. We begin by describing the basic structure of the tax system. The following section then examines the implications of growth objectives and tax enforcement for tax design. We next consider the impact of the 1997 financial crisis on the nation's economic structure and policy objectives and the resulting changes in the tax revenue structure. The final section concludes by summarizing key challenges facing the system.

THE BASIC STRUCTURE

The Korean tax system is highly complex, as illustrated in Table 7.3,[11] with taxes being collected at both the national and local level. National taxes consist of three groups: internal taxes, three officially earmarked taxes,[12] and customs duties. As of 2003, the personal and corporate income taxes and the VAT accounted for about half of total tax revenue, or 70 percent of national taxes.[13] Although only 22.4 percent of tax revenue was collected at the local level, local governments accounted for more than half of total government spending,[14] implying significant grants and transfers from the central government.[15] Property-related taxes account for more than half of local tax revenues; the resident tax, the local education tax, and the tobacco consumption tax ranked as the other most important items.[16] Social security taxes are levied at the rate of 4.5 percent on both employers and employees and on the self-employed at lower rates.

Table 7.3   Tax Structure of Korea, 2003

	Billions of Won	% of GDP	% of Total	
Total taxes	**147,797**	**20.5**	**100.0**	–
National taxes	**114,664**	**15.9**	**77.6**	**100.0**
Internal taxes[1]	92,231	12.8	62.4	80.4
Personal income tax	20,787	2.9	14.1	18.1
Corporate income tax	25,633	3.6	17.3	22.4
Value-added tax	33,447	4.6	22.6	29.2
Special excise tax[1]	4,733	0.7	3.2	4.1
Liquor tax[2]	2,726	0.4	1.8	2.4
Security transaction tax	1,607	0.2	1.1	1.4
Inheritance and gift taxes	1,315	0.2	0.9	1.1
Other[3]	1,983	0.3	1.3	1.7
Earmarked taxes	15,583	2.2	10.5	13.6
Transportation tax[2]	10,000	1.4	6.8	8.7
Education tax[2]	3,651	0.5	2.5	3.2
Special tax for rural Development[2]	1,932	0.3	1.3	1.7
Customs duties[1]	6,847	1.0	4.6	6.0
Local taxes	**33,133**	**4.6**	**22.4**	**100.0**
Property-related taxes	18,851	2.6	12.8	56.9
Acquisition and registration taxes	13,053	1.8	8.8	39.4
Taxes on property holding[4]	4,019	0.6	2.7	12.1
Automobile tax	1,778	0.2	1.2	5.4
Resident tax[5]	4,558	0.6	3.1	13.8
Tobacco consumption tax[1]	2,384	0.3	1.6	7.2
Local education tax[2]	4,009	0.6	2.7	12.1
Other[6]	3,331	0.5	2.3	10.1
Social security contributions[2]	**35,870**	**4.9**	–	–
Total revenue	**183,667**	**25.3**	–	–

Source: National Tax Service (2004), *Statistical Yearbook of National Tax;* Bureau of Local Finance and Economy, Ministry of Government Administration and Home Affairs (2004), *Financial Yearbook of Local Government*; and author's calculations.

1. Partially earmarked to specific uses; see Table 7.A.1 in Appendix for details.
2. Fully earmarked to specific uses; see Table 7.A.1 in Appendix for details.
3. The stamp tax, excess profit tax, carryover from the previous year.
4. The property tax, tax on aggregate landholdings, urban planning tax, community facilities tax, and businessplace tax on property.
5. Imposed as a surtax; see Table 7.A.1 in Appendix for details.
6. The license tax, motor fuel tax, agricultural income tax, butchery tax, leisure tax, businessplace tax on income, regional development tax, and carryover from the previous year.

The marginal tax rates for the personal and corporate income taxes are moderate by international standards. As shown in Table 7.4, the personal statutory tax rates and the number of brackets have been reduced during the past couple of decades, in a pattern similar to those seen in developed countries. However, the personal income tax base has not been broadened enough to make a significant revenue impact.[17] The narrow base of the personal income tax is attributable in part to generous allowances and

Table 7.4 Statutory Tax Rates of the Personal Income Tax (%)

Year of Change	Number of Brackets	Bottom Rate	Top Rate	Top Rate Inclusive of Surcharges[1]
1980	17	6	62	79.05
1982	17	6	60	76.50
1983	16	5	55	70.13
1989	8	5	50	63.75
1991	5	5	50	53.75
1993	6	5	50	53.75
1994	6	5	45	48.38
1996	4	10	40	44.00
2002	4	9	36	39.60
2005	4	8	35	38.50

Source: Ministry of Finance and Economy.

1. Currently, a 10 percent resident tax is levied on personal income taxes payable.

credits and in part to the low effective taxation of the self-employed and of capital income, which in turn reflects various enforcement problems. Tax subsidies to wage and salary workers include an initial wage deduction, a special wage credit, basic and extra exemptions for family members, and standard or itemized deductions.[18] These tax breaks have been provided partly as a savings incentive and partly as a means of maintaining horizontal equity between employees and the self-employed, the compliance of the self-employed being very low.

The corporate income tax has two brackets, and the tax rates have been steadily reduced, as shown in Table 7.5. At 27.5 percent (inclusive of the local resident tax), the top corporate rate is close to the OECD average.[19]

Table 7.5 Statutory Tax Rates of the Corporate Income Tax (%)

Year of Change	Bottom Rate	Top Rate	Top Rate Inclusive of Surcharges[1]
1981	25	40	53.00
1982	22	38	50.35
1983	20	30	39.75
1991	20	34	36.55
1994	18	32	36.40
1995	18	30	34.25
1996	16	28	30.80
2002	15	27	29.70
2005	13	25	27.50

Source: Ministry of Finance and Economy.

1. Currently, a 10 percent resident tax is levied on corporate income taxes payable.

The bottom rate is applied to small corporations with taxable incomes below 100 million won.[20] A wide range of incentives are available in the corporate tax system, including exemptions, deductions, accelerated depreciation, investment tax credits, and tax-free reserves for bad debts and R&D. Losses can be carried forward for five years, but not backward. A partial credit for corporate taxes paid is available for dividend payments. Investment incentives are currently focused on small and medium-sized enterprises, R&D, and foreign direct investment. There is a minimum tax that partially offsets the effects of these incentives.

Since its introduction in 1977, the VAT has retained most of its statutory features: the tax is charged at a single rate of 10 percent on a broad range of goods and services, with a zero rate applied to exports and to certain selected goods and services.[21] There are a variety of exempted supplies, including unprocessed foodstuffs, agricultural products, and finance and insurance services, among others.[22] In addition, a simplified scheme is applied to businesses with annual turnover between 24 and 48 million won, with those having turnover of less than 24 million won being exempt. In this simplified scheme, the tax is levied by applying a prescribed value-added ratio, which varies across industries,[23] to the turnover of a business.

The excise tax system is very complex and includes a variety of earmarked surcharges. The special consumption tax, introduced to alleviate the distributional consequences of the VAT, is levied on some luxury goods and consumer durables, including automobiles. Financial transactions are subject to various excises. The securities transaction tax and the special tax for rural development are levied at 0.15 percent each on the value of stock transactions on the Korea Stock Exchange.[24] The education tax is imposed on the gross receipts of financial institutions, at 0.5 percent.

Earmarking is important in Korea. The three national earmarked taxes alone provided 10.6 percent of total and 13.6 percent of national taxes. In addition, the revenues from the special excise tax on automobile sales and the liquor tax are also earmarked to finance certain specific expenditure needs.[25] At the local level, the revenues from the local education tax and about half of revenues from the tobacco tax are earmarked to finance local education. Bird and Jun (2005) estimated the total revenue from earmarked taxes to be 3.5 percent of GDP, or 17.2 percent of total taxes collected, or about as much as the corporate income tax. In addition to these earmarked taxes, a fixed proportion of internal tax revenue is earmarked

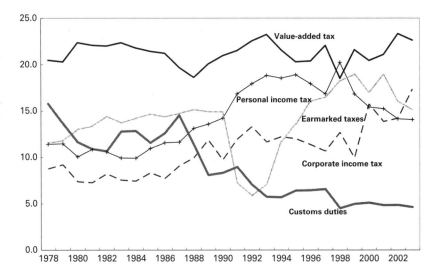

Figure 7.1   Trends in Major Taxes, 1978–2003 (as a Percentage of Total Tax Revenue).

Source: National Tax Service.

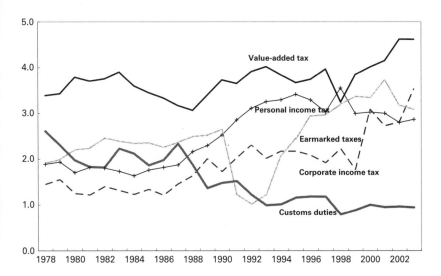

Figure 7.2   Trends in Major Taxes, 1978–2003 (as a Percentage of GDP).

Source: National Tax Service.

for central government grants.[26] If these grants are taken into account, almost 35 percent of total tax revenue was earmarked in 2003.[27]

Figures 7.1 and 7.2 show the trends of major Korean taxes as a percentage of total revenue and GDP, respectively. The VAT has been the most important source of revenue since its introduction in 1977. Its revenue as a share of total taxes is comparable to the cases in other OECD countries at 22.6 percent in 2003, but as a percentage of GDP it is relatively low at 4.6 percent. The personal income tax and the corporate income tax had both increased steadily in importance up until the time of the financial crisis in 1997. Interestingly, the revenue share for the personal income tax has since declined, while that for the corporate income tax has sharply increased. As discussed later in this chapter, changes in economic structure and government policy in the wake of the crisis appear to be the cause behind these contrasting trends. Tariffs were a more important source of revenue than either the personal or the corporate income tax until the late 1980s. However, their share has since fallen sharply in accordance with the acceleration of free trade arrangements during the 1990s. The figures also show that with the exception of a few years in the early 1990s, earmarked taxes have been an important source of revenue throughout the period shown.[28]

GROWTH OBJECTIVES AND TAX ENFORCEMENT

In the setting of tax policy objectives in Korea, growth has come before redistribution. Generous savings and investment incentives were provided to promote domestic capital formation. Raising revenue to finance public infrastructure and education was another central concern of tax policy. In contrast, the fiscal system has played a very limited role in income redistribution. As shown in Table 7.6, the effects of the tax-transfer system on income distribution are weak in Korea; its implementation reduced the Gini coefficient only moderately, which is in sharp contrast to the experiences in the other countries shown. The redistributive role of the transfer scheme is especially weak in Korea, reflecting the lack of a strong safety net that is observed in rich countries. Table 7.6 also shows that income inequality before taxes and transfers is very low in Korea relative to other countries in the sample, although it has increased significantly since the financial crisis.[29]

The weak redistributive role of taxation in Korea is largely a reflection of the small scope of the personal income tax as well as the low overall tax burden. Raising revenue of less than 3 percent of GDP, the personal

Table 7.6 Redistribution in Korea and Selected Developed Countries

Country	Gini Coefficients			Reduction in Gini (in percent)	
	Market Income (A)	After Transfers (B)	After Taxes and Transfers (C)	Overall (C–A)/(A)	From Transfers Alone (B–A)/(A)
Korea					
1995	0.244	0.242	0.233	4.5	0.4
1998	0.314	0.311	0.303	3.5	0.8
2003	0.282	0.277	0.266	5.7	1.5
United States, 1999	0.513	0.457	0.433	15.6	10.9
United Kingdom, 2001–2002	0.530	0.390	0.360	32.1	26.4
Japan, 1996	0.441	0.372	0.361	18.4	15.7
Canada, 2001	0.431	0.359	0.320	25.8	16.7

Source: Sung, Mung-Jae, Park, and Jun (2004).

income tax is unlikely to have a meaningful effect on income distribution, even though its progressivity appears to be in line with the situations in developed countries. The distributional consequences of consumption taxes are probably more important than those of the personal income tax in Korea. Charged at a single 10 percent rate, the VAT might have negative distributional implications. In an attempt to enhance vertical equity, the government has introduced special consumption taxes on luxury goods and applies progressive rate structures to taxation of real property holdings and capital gains. These efforts do not seem to have had a serious impact on distribution, however.[30]

With regard to the growth objectives of Korean tax policy, the effectiveness of savings and investment incentives has been a source of controversy. As shown in Table 7.7, the ratio of total tax expenditures to actual tax payments in 2003 was 16.3 percent for the tax items shown.[31] About 70 percent of total tax expenditures were accounted for by the personal and corporate income taxes, which is a disproportionately high level compared to their revenue share. For these two taxes, tax expenditures amount to 30.9 and 22.9 percent of tax actually paid, respectively.[32] A significant portion of the allowances and credits available under the personal and corporate tax systems represents savings and investment incentives, as discussed in the previous section. The question is then whether these incentives have enough impact on domestic capital formation and technology development to justify their associated revenue and efficiency costs. While evidence on the benefits of these incentives is very sparse and, if anything,

Table 7.7   Tax Expenditure by Type of Tax, 2003

	Taxes Paid (billions of won) (A)	(%) (B)	Tax Expenditures (billions of won) (C)	(%) (D)	(C)/(A)
Direct taxes	**47,735**	**44.4**	**12,331**	**70.4**	**25.8**
Personal income tax	20,787	19.3	6,429	36.7	30.9
Corporate income tax	25,633	23.8	5,870	33.5	22.9
Inheritance and gift taxes	1,315	1.2	32	0.2	2.4
Indirect taxes	**52,978**	**49.3**	**5,056**	**28.9**	**9.5**
Value-added tax	33,447	31.1	3,263	18.6	9.8
Special excise tax	4,733	4.4	268	1.5	5.7
Liquor tax	2,726	2.5	44	0.3	1.6
Transportation tax	10,000	9.3	1,032	5.9	10.3
Security transaction tax	1,606	1.5	403	2.3	25.1
Stamp tax	457	0.4	47	0.3	10.2
Telephone tax	8	0.0	0.0	0.0	0.0
Customs duties	**6,847**	**6.4**	**121**	**0.7**	**1.8**
Total	**107,560**	**100.0**	**17,508**	**100.0**	**16.3**

Source: Ministry of Finance and Economy.

unfavorable,[33] their efficiency costs are estimated to be very high, due to distorting behavior and creating arbitrage opportunities.[34]

TAX BASE PROTECTION

If tax allowances and credits do not sufficiently encourage savings and investment behavior, why then would the government keep these incentives in place despite their implied revenue and efficiency costs? One thought is that some of these tax breaks might have been intended, from the beginning, to have inframarginal impacts for equity purposes. Yet another possible explanation is that, in the face of enormous evasion pressures, the government might be using these incentives, along with certain nontax benefits, as a means of preventing erosion of the tax base into the informal sector. The government might well perceive these base protection effects to be large enough to justify the associated costs. As a clue, some tax incentives in the personal income tax and the VAT system have been intended to facilitate enforcement itself,[35] raising the possibility of a similar line of policy intention prevailing through the whole tax system.

From the early stages of economic development, raising sufficient revenue to finance public infrastructure has been a primary concern of tax policy in Korea. The government's ability to collect taxes, however, depends on the extent of information available to it on the earnings of firms and individuals. It is very unlikely for the government to know exactly the taxable sales and incomes of businesses operating in the informal sector or the cash economy. Tax enforcement hinges critically on use of the financial sector by firms, since cash-only transactions leave no paper trail necessary for the collection and checking of relevant information. The design of a country's tax system is then likely to be influenced by the size of its cash economy, since unobservable transactions are not taxable. Gordon and Li (2005) explore various policy choices for protecting the government's tax base, given monitoring difficulties with firms operating in the informal sector.[36]

The size of the informal sector in Korea is nonnegligible by international standards. According to Schneider (2005), the estimate for Korea for 2002–2003 was 28.8 percent of GDP, a much higher level than in developed countries.[37] In particular, informal financial markets (curb markets) have played an important role in investment financing for small businesses, while the state-controlled banks have been more focused on large manufacturing corporations. Figure 7.3 shows the trends in Korea in

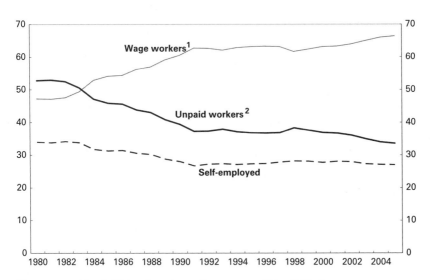

Figure 7.3   The Self-Employed as a Percentage of Total Workers.

Source: Korea National Statistical Office.

1. Wage workers include regular, temporary, and daily workers.

2. Unpaid workers include the self-employed and their unpaid family workers.

nonwage workers and the self-employed (including their family workers), as a percentage of total civilian workers.[38] This ratio is also very high compared to other countries. At 34 percent in 2004, the self-employment ratio in Korea is the fourth largest among the OECD countries.[39] Note that more than half of civilian workers in Korea were self-employed in the early 1980s. The share of self-employment declined significantly during the 1980s and has remained stable since then.

Smaller businesses tend to rely more on cash transactions. While evidence on such informal transactions is hard to obtain, Figure 7.4 reveals that smaller firms tend to hold greater amounts of cash relative to their assets.[40] As a percentage of total assets, the cash holdings of small and medium-sized firms have exceeded those of large firms by about 5 percentage points in recent years, with the ratios for the *chaebols* (large business groups in Korea) being even lower. Interestingly, the cash-holding ratios for smaller firms have shown a declining trend in recent years.[41]

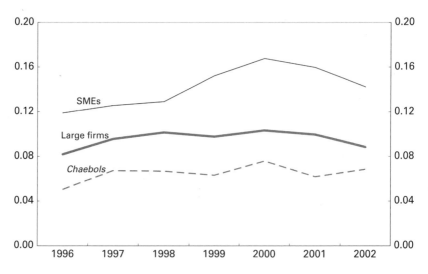

Figure 7.4   Cash Holdings, by Firm Size (as a Percentage of Total Assets).

Source: Author's calculations using KIS-VALUE firm database.

Notes: Cash, cash equivalents, and short-term financial instruments are included.

The sample consists of firms registered with the Financial Supervisory Service. An SME is defined as a company with 300 or fewer employees. A *Chaebol* is a large business group whose combined assets exceed a certain limit. The Korea Fair Trade Commission announces the list of *chaebols* each year. Large firms include *chaebol firms*.

In summary, the size of the informal sector and the share of self-employment in Korea are quite high by international standards, and the tendency to hold cash appears to be higher for smaller firms. Therefore, the narrow bases for the personal income tax, the VAT, and the corporate income tax are likely to reflect enforcement problems of the Korean tax system. As noted in the preceding section, generous tax breaks in the personal income tax system are often justified by a need to subsidize wage and salary workers vis-à-vis the self-employed and the owners of financial capital who are taxed relatively lightly. The low effective taxation of the self-employed and capital income in large part reflects enforcement difficulties.

PERSONAL INCOME TAX

The business incomes of the self-employed do not receive preferential treatment as do wages and salaries, but statutory loopholes and a weak bookkeeping culture, along with a limited auditing capacity, lead to a very low level of compliance. To alleviate the burdens of bookkeeping for small businesses, the government allows those within certain turnover limits to use an estimation method for their tax calculation, which typically reduces their effective tax burdens. Accordingly, the self-employed have a very strong incentive to underreport their turnover, which also leads to underreporting of taxable income at the personal level.

The moderate taxation of financial income also reflects difficulties in gathering information for tax enforcement. Before the introduction of the real name system for ownership of financial assets in 1993, it was practically impossible to subject financial income to global taxation. Interest, dividends, and capital gains were either exempt or subject to final withholding taxes at varying rates. Since 1997, individual interest and dividends combining to exceed 40 million won have been taxable under the global income tax system.[42] Nonetheless, the withholding nature of capital income taxation is very much alive, as the first 40 million won of dividends and interest is still subject to a final withholding rate.[43] In addition, capital gains on securities and real property are subject to separate scheduler taxation.[44]

Table 7.8 shows the mix of the personal income tax revenue in 2003. Taxes on wage and salary income are mostly withheld at their sources and account for about 40 percent of total personal taxes.[45] The revenue share for taxable dividends and interest income that are subject to final

Table 7.8   Personal Income Tax, 2003

	Trillions of Won	% of GDP	% of PIT
Personal income tax	**20.8**	**2.9**	**100.0**
Wage and salary income (withholding)	8.4	1.2	40.2
Global income (tax returns)	4.2	0.6	20.4
Dividend and interest income (withholding)	3.4	0.5	16.2
Capital gains (tax returns)[1]	2.9	0.4	13.9
Other income[2]	1.9	0.3	9.2

Source: Ministry of Finance and Economy.

1. Gains on real property were 2.5 trillion won (0.34 percent of GDP). The rest is gains from share transactions.
2. Withheld parts of business and retirement income, timber income, etc.

withholding is 16.2 percent, bringing the proportion of personal income tax payment through withholding to 56.4 percent. Capital gains on securities and real property, which are either exempt or subject to separate scheduler taxation, account for another 14 percent of personal income taxes.[46] Personal income that is not subject to scheduler taxation is to be taxed under the global taxation scheme.[47] Since the amount of dividends and interest that are taxed as global income is estimated to be small, the main component of "global income" is the taxes paid on self-employed income.

The narrow base of the personal income tax is shown in the distribution of tax payments across taxpayer groups. As Table 7.9 indicates, 45.8 percent of wage and salary earners did not pay taxes at all in 2003, owing mainly to the generous allowances and credits available under the system.[48] Among actual taxpayers, the upper 10 percent account for about half of total taxes paid. With the next decile group added, about three-quarters of taxes on wages and salaries are paid by the richest 20 percent of taxpayers. As for the global income tax, which requires filing a tax return, about half of eligible taxpayers are under the threshold point. Among those who owe taxes on their business income, about one-half use the estimation method instead of accounting to derive their taxable income. As noted earlier, this method is very likely to lead to underestimations of true tax liability. By deciles, the highest 10 percent of taxpayers account for 78 percent (the top 20 percent almost 90 percent) of global income taxes. This is a higher degree of concentration than for employees and means that the tax base is narrower for business income than for wage income.

Table 7.9   Distribution of Personal Income Tax by Taxpayer Type, 2003

	Taxpayers		Taxes Paid
	(thousands)	(%)	(%)
Wages and salaries tax (withholding)	**11,547**	**100.0**	
Under-threshold	5,289	45.8	
Paying taxes	6,258	54.2	100.0
Top 10%			56.6
Next 10%			17.9
Global income taxes (tax returns)	**4,227**	**100.0**	
Under-threshold[1]	2,112	50.0	
Paying taxes	2,115	50.0	100.0
Bookkeeping	1,018	24.1	69.8
Income estimation	1,096	25.9	30.2
	2,115	100.0	100.0
Top 10%			78.3
Next 10%			10.6

Source: National Tax Service (2004), *Statistical Yearbook of National Tax,* and author's calculations.

1. Also includes those who do not file tax returns, the number of which is estimated by the National Tax Service using business-registration information.

VALUE-ADDED TAX

With regard to the VAT, special arrangements for small businesses as well as generous exemptions and a zero-rating policy have been major causes of base erosion. Small businesses in the simplified scheme receive tax subsidies in two forms. First, the value-added ratios prescribed in the law have typically been lower than the actual values (Table 7.10), implying tax benefits. Second, these small firms are allowed to claim a partial input tax credit[49] while paying taxes on value added, not turnover.[50]

In addition, the simplified scheme provides opportunities to evade taxes. Since there is no invoicing obligation, firms in this scheme can easily underreport their turnovers. Even general taxpayers will have opportunities to evade taxes on the parts of their turnovers supplied to firms in the simplified scheme. In the presence of generous tax benefits, firms that are not eligible for this scheme may also have strong incentives to push their reported turnovers under the threshold. Moreover, this base erosion of the VAT can also lead to personal tax evasion, since turnover reporting is closely linked to income reporting by the self-employed.

Table 7.10   The Value-Added Ratio for the Simplified Scheme,[1] 2004

	Prescribed Ratios for the Simplified Scheme[3] (A)	Actual Ratios for General Taxpayers[2] (B)	(A)–(B)
Agriculture, hunting, forestry, and fishing	30	34.9	–4.9
Manufacturing	20	23.6	–3.6
Electricity, gas, and water	20	18.5	1.5
Retail sales	20	19.3	0.7
Construction	30	29.7	0.3
Restaurants	40	50.6	–10.6
Hotels	40	30.8	9.2
Transportation, storage, and communication	40	54.2	–14.2
Agent, intermediary, and contract	30	43.0	–13.0
Other services	30	38.1	–8.1
Total	–	**24.7**	–

Source: National Tax Service (2005), *Statistical Yearbook of National Tax;* Ministry of Finance and Economy; and author's calculations.

1. Value-added ratio = (turnover-inputs)/turnover * 100.
2. These ratios are for the first half of 2004.
3. Businesses in mining, wholesale, and real estate dealing are not eligible for participation in the simplified scheme.

Table 7.11 shows that the current VAT system collects very little from those businesses in the simplified scheme (0.3 percent in 2003), while the number of taxpayers who use this scheme or are exempt approaches half of the total. Among general taxpayers, the share for corporations is more than four times that for the self-employed. According to a more detailed breakdown not shown here,[51] the top 10 percent of firms subject to the general scheme account for about 80 percent of total taxes paid for this group.

Although the simplified scheme does not contribute much to tax revenue, tax relief implicit in the system might reflect a fine balance the government

Table 7.11   Value-Added Tax by Taxpayer Type, 2003

	Taxpayers (thousands)	(%)	Taxes Paid (billions of won)	(%)
General	**2,221**	**55.6**	**33,246**	**99.7**
Corporations	359	9.0	27,303	81.9
Individuals	1,862	46.6	5,943	17.8
Simplified + Exemptions	**1,774**	**44.4**	**103**	**0.3**
Total	**3,995**	**100.0**	**33,349**	**100.0**

Source: National Tax Service (2004), *Statistical Yearbook of National Tax.*

must maintain between the need to bring as many small businesses as possible into the formal sector and the ease with which these firms can disguise their turnover in the prevalent culture of cash transactions and weak bookkeeping. Since the extent of cash transactions is large for small businesses, it is difficult to gather adequate information about their true tax liabilities. A strong enforcement effort in this case would push these businesses further into the informal sector, aggravating the information problem.

CORPORATE INCOME TAX

The importance of the corporate income tax has been increasing steadily in Korea, and it has brought in more revenue than the personal income tax in recent years. Its revenue as a fraction of GDP is around 4 percent, an impressive level considering the moderate marginal tax rates and widespread allowances and credits. The relatively high compliance among large conglomerates might be a reason why there is less base erosion here than is the case with the personal income tax. As shown in Table 7.12, a surprisingly small number of firms at the top pay the majority of corporate taxes. Only 185 firms, or 0.06 percent of the total, account for 60.8 percent of all corporate taxes. An additional 14 percent of revenue comes from the next 650 firms, so that about three-quarters of corporate tax revenues are accounted for by 835 firms, or 0.27 percent of the total. On the other hand, a tiny portion of corporate taxes comes from the corporations in the lower bracket.

Table 7.12 Distribution of Corporate Income Tax by Tax Base Size, 2003

Tax Base (millions of won)	Taxpayers (number of firms)	(%)	Taxes Paid[1] (billions of won)	(%)
Low bracket (15%)	**259,079**	**85.37**	**514**	**2.30**
Deficit	102,387	33.74	4	0.02
0–10	70,913	23.37	29	0.13
10–100	85,779	28.27	481	2.15
High bracket (27%)	**44,383**	**14.63**	**21,832**	**97.70**
100–1000	37,927	12.50	1,796	8.04
1000–10,000	5,621	1.85	3,323	14.87
10,000–50,000	650	0.21	3,126	13.99
50,000+	185	0.06	13,587	60.80
Total	**303,462**	**100.00**	**22,346**	**100.00**

Source: National Tax Service (2004), *Statistical Yearbook of National Tax.*

1. These figures are based on tax returns and therefore differ slightly from final payment, as reported in Table 7.3.

This high concentration of corporate taxable income among a small number of large firms may be a combined effect of high concentration of economic activities among these firms and their relatively high compliance. Unlike small businesses, large firms find it very difficult to bypass the services of financial institutions. As shown in Figure 7.4, larger firms in Korea tend to hold less cash relative to their assets than do smaller firms in Korea. To the extent that larger firms are more dependent on the financial sector, their profits are more likely to be exposed to tax authorities through financial transaction records. To the extent that the benefit from use of the financial sector is greater than the resulting tax liabilities, the firm will stay in the formal taxed sector. This implies higher effective tax rates for large and capital-intensive firms, which presumably receive greater benefits from financial transactions.[52]

As shown in Figure 7.5, the effective corporate tax burden is greater for large firms than for small and medium-sized companies in Korea, a result predicted in the above discussion.[53] Surprisingly, the effective tax rates for large conglomerates classified as *chaebols* are lower than those for other large firms. Since economic activities are highly concentrated among these top manufacturing firms, however, their revenue shares could still be high, as suggested in Table 7.12. Their relatively low effective tax rates

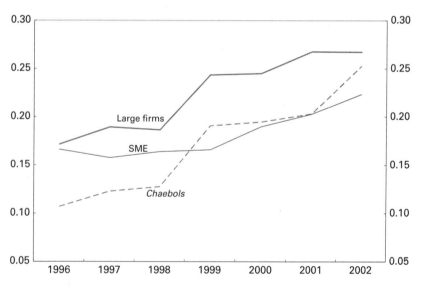

Figure 7.5   Corporate Tax Paid (as a Percentage of Operating Surplus).

Source: Author's calculations using KIS-VALUE firm database.

are likely due to the following factors. First, these firms are highly capital-intensive and export-oriented, so they usually benefit more from generous investment incentives as well as export subsidies.[54] Second, they are typically more leveraged than other large firms and thus reap more tax benefits from interest deductions. This is because directed loans from state-owned or controlled banks with explicit and implicit loan guarantees,[55] as well as the practice of cross-guaranteeing loans among *chaebol* affiliates, have made bankruptcy risks associated with debt financing very low.

These tax and nontax benefits from the government and the state-controlled banks seem to have played a critical role in protecting the corporate tax base, since firms have had to remain in the formal sector and use banks to receive such benefits. While these subsidies lead to some revenue and efficiency costs, the government also gains in part from the extra revenue on new investment induced by investment incentives or subsidized loans and in part by keeping marginal firms from disappearing into the informal sector. This prediction appears to fit well with the experience in Korea.

The Korean government has not been as enthusiastic in inviting multi-nationals into the country as have other developing countries. As shown in Figure 7.6, foreign direct investment as a percentage of GDP has been much lower in Korea than in most other countries. Foreign capital has

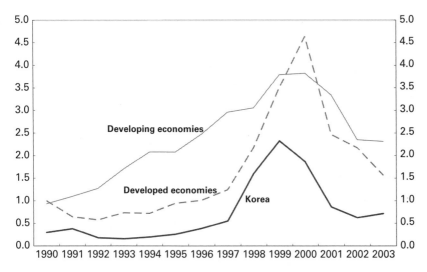

Figure 7.6   FDI Inflows, 1990–2003 (as a Percentage of GDP).

Source: UN, Comtrade Database.

instead been typically imported in the form of loans, which were in the past redirected through state-controlled banks to domestic firms. What triggered this avoidance of direct foreign ownership of local firms is not clear, but it might have helped to protect tax revenue, since multinationals typically pay a lower effective tax rate through income-shifting activities across borders.

Actual corporate taxes paid by large manufacturing firms might not fully reflect the benefit of protecting these firms. There are two additional aspects in which protection of the corporate tax base might have contributed to the total tax receipts. First, there are a wide variety of so-called quasi-taxes consisting of fees, charges, and contributions, most of which are imposed on corporations. The revenues from these highly discretionary sources, estimated at 1.3 percent of GDP (Son et al., 2004), are used mainly to finance off-budget expenditures. Second, quite a significant amount of taxes is collected from the financial sector (Table 7.13), which could be an implicit burden on firms using bank services. The corporate tax share for financial firms reaches almost half of that for manufacturing firms, and taxes on financial services are nonnegligible. These taxes could be shifted in the form of higher financial charges. Since major Korean manufacturing firms used to rely heavily on bank loans for capital financing, they might have paid higher charges in reflection of the taxes on banks.

Table 7.13   Taxation of the Financial Sector, 2003

	Financial (A)	Manufacturing (B)	(A) + (B)	All Industries
Corporate income tax				
Billions of won	4,228	8,669	12,897	22,346
% of corporate income tax	18.9	38.8	57.7	100.0
% of GDP	0.6	1.2	1.8	3.1
Taxes on financial services	Billions of won			% of GDP
Education tax	515			0.07
Security transaction tax	1,607			0.22
Special tax for rural development	708			0.10
Total	2,830			0.39

Source: National Tax Service (2004), *Statistical Yearbook of National Tax*; OECD (2005), *Revenue Statistics 1965–2004*; and author's calculations.

Notes: The education tax is levied on financial institutions at 0.5 percent of gross receipts. The securities transaction tax (0.15 percent and up) and a special tax for rural development (0.15 percent) are levied on the value of securities transactions.

CHANGES AFTER THE FINANCIAL CRISIS

After the outbreak of the financial crisis, the most immediate concern of tax policy was to alleviate the adverse effects of the crisis and to promote structural adjustments. The government introduced various tax measures to boost economic activity, mitigate adverse distributional consequences, facilitate restructuring of the corporate and financial sectors, and encourage foreign direct investment and capital inflows.

Wage and salary earners received tax relief in the form of increased deductions and a cut in the marginal tax rates.[56] The tax burden on the self-employed was reduced by introducing a tax credit for formal bookkeeping and expanding the allowances for credit card sales. Global taxation of capital income was suspended in 1999 and 2000 to prevent negative impacts on the financial markets,[57] and the personal capital gains tax rate was reduced to boost the real estate market. To encourage private consumption, special consumption taxes were reduced or eliminated.[58] To stimulate investment, tax incentives were provided to small and medium-sized enterprises, including tax exemptions on capital gains and stock options in venture capital businesses. Temporary investment tax credits were reinstated, and eligibility for them was expanded. In an effort to promote inflows of foreign investment, tax preferences were introduced and expanded.[59] With regard to restructuring, the focus of changes in the tax code was on reducing the costs of asset and equity transactions and debt payments.[60] Tax relief was also provided for financial sector restructuring.[61]

While these tax changes focused on short-term policy objectives, changes in the economic structure triggered longer-run and probably much more important impacts of the crisis on the level and structure of tax revenue. There are three particular cases in point. First, the capital structures for most Korean firms changed dramatically in a few years after the crisis, with the debt-equity ratios of large manufacturing corporations dropping from around 500 percent before the crisis to below 200 percent in the early 2000s. This change had an immediate impact on the effective tax rates as depicted in Figure 7.5,[62] leading to a sharp increase in revenue from the corporate income tax after the crisis (Figures 7.1 and 7.2). The long-run implications for tax revenue of this change in the corporate capital structure are unclear, however. The elimination of preferential treatment for debt-financing means such as cross-guaranteeing and directed loans will possibly have negative consequences on corporate tax revenue, since new investment and production could be curtailed unless firms can obtain adequate equity financing.

Second, financial sector restructuring can have strong implications for the scope of the informal sector by facilitating the use of banks among small businesses. As the function of the financial sector improves, the benefits that firms receive from using this sector will increase. Indeed, the financial sector in Korea has undergone drastic structural changes, resulting in more market-based operations and a sharp increase in foreign ownership. In particular, competition and advanced techniques from foreign-owned banks will not only increase the overall profitability of the Korean financial sector, but also provide more value-added to businesses. To the extent that these changes improve financial intermediation among existing users of the financial sector and pull businesses that used to rely on cash transactions or the curb markets into the formal sector, the government can collect more revenue.

Lastly, restrictions on the inflow of foreign capital were substantially reduced, making Korean markets more open. The revenue implications of increased foreign ownership of local assets and firms are unclear. A more open economy will expand business opportunities and taxable profits accordingly. At the same time, however, the scope for tax evasion and avoidance will increase, since transactions through foreign financial intermediaries are not easily observable. In addition, multinationals can shift profits among their affiliates by manipulating transfer pricing and thus report smaller domestic taxable incomes.

These changes in the Korean economic structure have conflicting implications for tax enforcement, and their long-run revenue impacts are uncertain. A better-functioning financial sector will likely lead to a reduction in size of the informal sector, whereas a more open economy will lead to increased opportunities for tax avoidance. Nonetheless, these structural changes have had a clear impact on the focus of tax enforcement and the structure of tax revenue. In the aftermath of the crisis, the government implemented several measures to enhance tax compliance, with particular attention given to the self-employed sector.

In 1999, an incentive for use of credit cards was introduced, under which taxpayers became able to deduct parts of their credit card usage in excess of a threshold, up to a certain limit.[63] A similar incentive was available for sales by the self-employed paid by credit cards.[64] These incentives for credit card usage appear to have had an important role in increasing the fraction of consumption expenditures paid for by credit cards, as shown in Table 7.14. Between 1999 and 2002, this ratio increased about three times. Boosted by this success, the government introduced a similar incentive for cash transactions based on receipts in 2005.[65] Apart from such incentive measures, the government also reduced the scope of the simplified scheme under the VAT in 2000 by lowering the turnover limit from 150 to 48 million won.[66] In addition, a number of administrative changes were made in an effort to improve taxpayer service and the function of the National Tax Service.[67]

The effectiveness of these policy changes in broadening the tax base is very likely to be linked to the quality of tax information, which appears to have improved significantly as a result of the structural changes discussed above. The credit card incentives were unlikely to be effective unless retailers and buyers found the benefits of using credit cards per se to be small. More usage of credit cards could lead to better-termed bank loans, for example.[68] The scaling back of the simplified scheme for the self-employed and small firms could have pushed some taxpayers into the informal sector, rather than increasing their taxable income. While the administrative changes were desirable steps in reducing administrative and compliance costs, a more fundamental issue regarding enforcement is the availability of information, as stressed in this chapter. The self-assessment scheme, for example, will be of little value unless adequate taxpayer information is available.

The suggestion that the financial sector improvement may have led to a reduction in informal activity is speculative at this point. Nonetheless, there are some descriptive pieces of evidence in favor of such an argument. Figure 7.7 shows that the number of self-employed people filing tax returns, those paying taxes, and those doing bookkeeping have all increased relative to their respective populations since the financial crisis. We also noted in Figure 7.4 that the ratios of cash-holding to assets for smaller firms have

Table 7.14 Private Consumption Expenditures Attributable to Credit Card Usage *(trillions of won, %)*

	Credit Card Usage (A)	Private Consumption Expenditures (B)	(A)/(B)
1990	5.3	93.5	5.7
1994	18.9	176.0	10.7
1998	30.8	250.3	12.3
1999	42.6	274.9	15.5
2000	79.5	312.3	25.5
2001	135.3	343.4	39.4
2002	174.0	381.1	45.6
2003	170.5	389.1	43.8
2004	167.0	401.5	41.6

Source: National Tax Service.

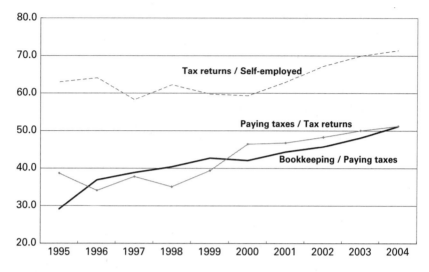

Figure 7.7   Changes in Tax Compliance for the Self-Employed.

Source: National Tax Service; Korea National Statistical Office.

Note: The terms used here are explained in Table 7.9.

been declining in recent years. A more rigorous statistical investigation will be a necessary next step.

In summary, the increase in the level of tax revenue as a percentage of GDP (Table 7.1) and the sharp change in revenue structure since the financial crisis (Figures 7.1 and 7.2) reflect changes in both the tax rates and bases. Structural changes in the corporate and financial sectors appear to have had base-broadening effects by reducing interest deduction for most corporations and encouraging use of the financial sector instead of cash transactions for the self-employed and small firms. As shown in Figure 7.8, the ratio of the VAT base to private consumption and the ratio of the corporate tax base to GDP have both increased sharply since the financial crisis. The improvement of financial services may also have increased the effectiveness of policy measures aimed at enhancing compliance, such as the deduction for credit card usage, by making more businesses sensitive to marginal incentives available in the financial sector.

CONCLUSION

Over the past several decades, Korea's tax policy has focused on protecting the revenue base to finance economic growth, in the face of significant

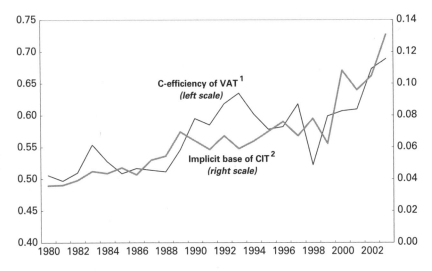

Figure 7.8   Efficiency Ratios, Korea, 1980–2003.

Source: The Bank of Korea, *National Accounts*; National Tax Service, *Statistical Yearbook of National Tax*; and author's calculations.

1. VAT revenue / (tax rate * private consumption).

2. Corporate tax revenue / (top marginal tax rate * GDP).

enforcement problems. With a nonnegligible size of the informal sector and a weak bookkeeping culture, the government had to focus on a small number of large corporations in collecting revenue. A wide range of tax and nontax subsidies were provided to protect businesses from disappearing into the informal sector. Many of the tax incentives in place might have been more effective in mitigating enforcement problems than in promoting the targeted activities.

To the extent that this base-protection effect has been significant, the revenue and efficiency costs associated with these tax preferences in most tax debates appear to be overstated. Statutory loopholes and lenient enforcement, which have been criticized as sources of inefficiency and tax evasion, often reflect a rational response by the government caught between evasion pressures and base-broadening needs. The proportional taxation of capital income and the simplified scheme for taxation of the self-employed are representative cases in point. The government has also had to adopt some unconventional means of raising revenue, such as earmarked taxes and surcharges.

All of these factors have made the tax revenue structure in Korea quite different from what is observed in developed countries. The personal income tax is of relatively minor importance in Korea, and the bases for the corporate and VAT are quite narrow. Earmarked taxes and property transaction taxes both account for significant shares of total tax revenue. Unless these underlying factors change greatly, a drastic reshaping of the tax structure is unlikely to be either feasible or desirable. A shift to the more conventional tax policies observed among developed countries could possibly generate more revenue and efficiency costs than theories suggest.

The financial crisis in Korea provides an interesting case study of how tax design can be affected by a change in the economic structure. In the aftermath of the crisis, the Korean corporate and financial sectors underwent drastic restructuring, and the economy was made more open. These structural changes led to a lower-leveraged capital structure for most corporations and a more open and better-functioning financial sector. To the extent that businesses come to receive more benefits from using the financial sector, the relative size of the informal sector will shrink. Indeed, the base for the VAT, the most important source of revenue, appears to have been improving in the years since the crisis. The long-run revenue implications of these changes are inconclusive, however. A reduction in debt financing may lead to declines in new investment and production. In addition, an increase in capital mobility will lead to more opportunities for tax avoidance.

Considering the potential costs of reunification and the soaring welfare expenditures stemming from the rapid aging of the Korean population and the maturing of public pensions, the top priority for taxation is to expand the revenue base in an efficient and equitable manner. For base-broadening purposes, conventional prescriptions include the elimination of "unnecessary" deductions and exemptions in the personal income, corporate income, and VAT systems.[69] Reducing the scope of earmarked and transaction taxes is also a favorite menu item, with various inefficiencies associated with these taxes being cited. As emphasized in this chapter, however, some of these instruments play a role in protecting the tax base from erosion into the informal sector, and this offsets their revenue and efficiency costs. Probably a more useful and urgent task is to create an environment in which tax information is more readily available. Further reform of the financial sector as well as more efficient sharing of information among government agencies will be a step in the right direction. Financial incentives for compliance and administrative changes toward self-assessment will also likely be more effective when taxpayers find it useful to remain in the formal sector.

APPENDIX

Table 7.A.1   Tax Revenue by Type of Tax, 1980 and 2003

	1980			2003		
	Billions of Won	% of GDP	% of Total	Billions of Won	% of GDP	% of Total
Total tax revenue	**6,687**	**17.2**	**100.0**	**183,667**	**25.3**	**100.0**
Individual income	**766**	**2.0**	**11.5**	**23,245**	**3.2**	**12.7**
Personal income tax	661	1.7	9.9	20,787	2.9	11.3
Surtax on personal income tax[1]	105	0.3	1.6	2,457	0.3	1.3
Corporate income	**738**	**1.9**	**11.0**	**28,149**	**3.9**	**15.3**
Corporate income tax	485	1.3	7.3	25,633	3.5	14.0
Surtax on corporate income tax[1]	253	0.7	3.8	2,516	0.3	1.4
Consumption	**3,119**	**8.0**	**46.6**	**63,247**	**8.7**	**34.4**
Value-added tax	1,471	3.8	22.0	33,447	4.6	18.2
Excise tax	1,500	3.9	22.4	23,791	3.3	13.0
Special excise tax	583	1.5	8.7	4,733	0.7	2.6
Liquor tax[2]	298	0.8	4.5	2,734	0.4	1.5
Tobacco consumption tax (local)[3]	0.0	0.0	0.0	2,384	0.3	1.3
Leisure tax	0.0	0.0	0.0	896	0.1	0.5
Transportation tax[4]	0.0	0.0	0.0	10,001	1.4	5.4
Securities transaction tax	0.0	0.0	0.0	1,607	0.2	0.9
Special tax for rural development on security transactions[5]	0.0	0.0	0.0	708	0.1	0.4
Education tax for financial institutions[6]	0.0	0.0	0.0	515	0.1	0.3
Other[7]	619	1.6	9.3	1,109	0.2	0.6
Surtax on excise taxes[8]	148	0.4	2.2	213	0.0	0.1
Property	**594**	**1.5**	**8.9**	**23,443**	**3.2**	**12.8**
Taxes on transactions	295	0.8	4.4	14,368	2.0	7.8
Registration tax (local)	122	0.3	1.8	7,550	1.0	4.1
Acquisition tax (local)	163	0.4	2.4	5,503	0.8	3.0
Inheritance and gift taxes	10	0.0	0.1	1,315	0.2	0.7
Surtax on transaction taxes[9]	0	0.0	0.0	1,704	0.2	0.9
Taxes on wealth holding	296	0.8	4.4	6,255	0.9	3.4
Property tax (local)	119	0.3	1.8	903	0.1	0.5
Tax on aggregate landholdings (local)[10]	0.0	0.0	0.0	1,603	0.2	0.9
Automobile tax (local)	57	0.1	0.9	1,778	0.2	1.0

(*continued*)

Table 7.A.1 *(continued)*

Other[11]	120	0.3	1.8	1,971	0.3	1.1
Surtax on wealth taxes[12]	2	0.0	0.0	1,116	0.2	0.6
Customs duties	**1,014**	**2.6**	**15.2**	**7,174**	**1.0**	**3.9**
Customs duties	762	2.0	11.4	6,847	0.9	3.7
Other[13]	252	0.6	3.8	327	0.0	0.2
Social security and payroll	**107**	**0.3**	**1.6**	**36,291**	**5.0**	**19.8**
Social security contributions[14]	73	0.2	1.1	35,870	4.9	19.5
Taxes on payroll and workforce (local)[15]	34	0.1	0.5	421	0.1	0.2
Other[16]	**349**	**0.9**	**5.2**	**2,116**	**0.3**	**1.2**
Memorandum items						
Taxes on financial services	n/a	n/a	n/a	7,058	1.0	3.8
Surtax	873	2.3	13.1	14,157	2.0	7.7
Earmarked taxes	856	2.2	12.8	22,322	3.1	12.2
GDP	38,775			724,675		

Source: National Tax Service (1981, 2004), *Statistical Yearbook of National Tax*; OECD (2005), *Revenue Statistics 1965–2004*; and author's calculations.

1. Defense tax as a surcharge on income tax and the exemption of income tax (repealed in 1990); resident tax on income tax; special tax for rural development on the exemptions of income tax (since 1994).
2. Fully earmarked for local spending.
3. Forty-five percent of tax revenue earmarked for local education.
4. Earmarked: 85.8 percent for transportation facilities; 14.2 percent for local spending (environment from 2005).
5. In addition to securities transaction tax, special tax for rural development is levied on special excise tax, and as a surcharge on the exemptions of corporate income tax, personal income tax, customs duties.
6. 0.5 percent of gross receipts of financial institutions. Education tax is also levied as a surcharge on special excise tax, transportation tax, and liquor tax.
7. Monopoly profit (repealed in 1988), telephone tax (repealed in 2001; earmarked for local spending), defense tax, leisure tax, butchery tax, license tax, and regional development tax.
8. Defense tax, special tax for rural development, education tax, motor fuel tax as a surcharge on transportation tax, and local education tax as a surcharge on tobacco consumption tax and leisure tax (since 2001).
9. Special tax for rural development as a surcharge on acquisition tax and the exemption of registration tax and acquisition tax; local education tax as a surcharge on registration tax.
10. Replaced by comprehensive real estate holding tax since 2005.
11. Urban planning tax, community facilities tax, stamp tax, revaluation tax (repealed in 2000), and businessplace tax (since 1990).
12. Defense tax as a surcharge on inheritance and gift taxes; special tax for rural development as a surcharge on tax on aggregate landholdings; local education tax as a surcharge on tax on aggregate landholdings, property tax, and automobile tax.
13. Education tax as a surcharge on special excise tax on imported goods; special tax for rural development as a surcharge on the exemption of customs duties.
14. National welfare pension fund, unemployment insurance, health insurance, teachers' pensions, government employees' pensions (employees), military personal pensions (employees), and industry workers' insurance fund (employers).
15. Businessplace tax on income (0.5 percent of wages and salaries).
16. Taxes on previous year base.

NOTES

The author is grateful to Roger Gordon and Richard Bird for comments and to Young-Im Shin for research assistance.

1. The tax burden in Korea is close to that in the United States, much lower than that in Sweden, and higher than that in Mexico.

2. The respective ratios were 15.1 and 30.3 percent in 1975, when Korea's tax burden was much lower than even that of the United States.

3. The OECD average for personal income and corporate income tax shares are about 24.9 and 9.3 percent, respectively, according to the OECD Revenue Statistics Database. The corresponding figures for the United States are 35.3 and 8.1 percent.

4. The average share for property taxes in OECD is about 5.6 percent, and the share for the United States is about 12.1 percent.

5. This had been true at least until the late 1990s when the corporate sector restructuring took place in the wake of the financial crisis.

6. For most minority shareholders, capital gains from stock transactions are tax exempt.

7. In 1996, these two categories together accounted for 43.4 percent of the expenditures of the consolidated central government (26.2 and 17.2 percent, respectively). The shares for welfare and defense spending were 19.3 and 24.3 percent, respectively. The spending mix has not changed much since the financial crisis, while the share for welfare spending began to rise (20.2 percent in 2003).

8. These three major taxes together accounted for 11 percent of GDP, or 54 percent of total tax revenue, exclusive of social security contributions in 2003.

9. Since property transfer should be registered at the government authorities, its information is readily available for taxation purposes. The government may have preferred taxes on property transactions to those on holdings because the taxes on property transactions elicit less resistance from taxpayers. Transaction taxes on real estate, along with the capital gains tax, have also been partly motivated by the objective of curbing housing-price speculation, although possible lock-in effects may have led to opposite results by reducing transactions.

10. These include a resident tax levied on top of personal and corporate income taxes payable as well as several earmarked taxes (education taxes and special tax for rural development).

11. A detailed description of individual tax items is provided in Table 7.A.1 in the Appendix.

12. These are the transportation tax, the national education tax, and the special tax for rural development. While the transportation tax is imposed on the sales of petroleum products, the other taxes take the form of surcharges on other taxes as shown in Table 7.A.1 in the Appendix.

13. The tax share figures reported in Table 7.3 do not account for social security taxes.

14. In 2003, the share for local government spending was 53 percent.

15. Unlike the case in developed countries, local autonomy is very limited. By the constitution, the central government has the power to set the tax bases and rates. Local governments instead have some discretionary power to apply flexible rates on certain tax items such as the resident tax.

16. Taxes on transactions involving real estate and automobiles are a dominant type of property taxation, providing about 45 percent of total local tax revenues. The resident tax is levied on top of personal and corporate income taxes payable.

17. Tax brackets are not indexed for inflation, resulting in a downward base-broadening effect.

18. Additional exemptions are available for family members 65 years or older and 6 years old or younger, for handicapped, and for female heads of families with dependents. Itemized deductions are available for insurance premiums, medical expenses, educational expenses, interest and mortgage loans for housing, and charitable donations.

19. According to OECD revenue statistics, the unweighted average was 30.7 percent in 2003 when the Korean rate was 29.7 percent.

20. This low level of threshold allows only very small firms to be eligible for the lower rate.

21. Indirect exports: certain machinery and materials for agriculture, fishery, livestock, and forestry industries; services supplied by ships and aircraft in international traffic; and social infrastructure and building projects supplied to government authorities.

22. Basic necessities, social welfare services, certain goods and services of cultural content, personal services of specified categories, and others.

23. As of 2005, the ratios include 20 percent to manufacturing, utilities, and retail; 30 percent to agriculture, fisheries, construction, and real estate rental; and 40 percent to transportation, warehousing, communication, restaurants, and hotels.

24. The securities transactions tax rates are higher for securities listed on the KOSDAQ and for unlisted securities.

25. Revenue from the liquor tax is earmarked to finance local spending, while the proceeds from the special excise taxes on automobile sales are split into transportation facilities, local spending, and local education.

26. Fifteen percent for local expenditures and 13 percent for local education in 2003; these ratios were increased to 19.13 and 19.4 percent in 2005, respectively.

27. Customs duties imposed on railroad-related imports are also earmarked to an account for railroad facilities. In addition to taxes, numerous fees, charges, and levies are earmarked to various government activities, many of which are operated through on- or off-budget funds.

28. During the 1980s, the defense tax, imposed as a surcharge on a wide range of income and consumption taxes, was the most significant example of earmarking, deriving revenues of up to about 2 percent of GDP. When this tax was repealed in 1991, the government initially struggled to make up the lost revenue. It did so essentially by introducing new earmarked taxes such as the transportation tax and the special tax for rural development. Revenue from earmarked sources has reached about 3 percent of GDP in recent years.

29. Comparison of the Gini coefficient across countries is tricky because the definition of income used often differs. The Korean measures are based on the income of urban working households and thus do not include self-employed and capital income, which are likely to be more unequal than wage income.

30. Property transactions are taxed more heavily than property holdings. Taxes on real property gains are nonnegligible at 0.3 percent of GDP, but their impact on distribution is limited.

31. Tax expenditures are defined in the Korean tax laws as revenue losses caused by the exclusion of some items from the tax base, and they take many forms: exclusions, exemptions, deductions, credits, a preferential rate of tax, or a deferral of liability. There were no tax expenditures for the education taxes and the special tax for rural development, which are mostly collected as surcharges.

32. The VAT is the next largest tax-expenditure item.

33. Since Korea is already a country with high savings, it is often argued that the impact of tax preferences might largely be inframarginal and not induce much new savings. According to unpublished government studies, the effects of most investment incentives are very limited. The World Bank (1993) reports a very modest contribution of tax policy to economic growth, that is, about 6 percent of total GDP growth for the period 1962–1982.

34. Domestic evidence on the efficiency costs is also very limited and unreliable. Considering empirical estimates from the United States (e.g., Feldstein and Feenberg, 1996), however, these costs could be very large since the tax bases are narrower in Korea than in the United States.

35. These incentives are discussed in a later section.

36. State-owned banks will allow the government easier access to information about firms. They also predict tariff protection and directed credits for the taxed sector as well as other instruments hindering activity in the untaxed sector.

37. The average for the OECD is 16.3 percent. The ratio for Mexico is 33.2, that for the United States 8.4, and for Sweden 18.3.

38. The broadly defined self-employed includes unpaid family workers.

39. According to the OECD (2006), Turkey, Greece, and Mexico are the top three. The OECD average is 17.4 percent.

40. These figures are calculated from the author's firm database, consisting of 2,340 firms which are either listed on a stock exchange or registered with the Financial Supervisory Service.

41. Of course, this is not direct evidence on the extent of cash transactions, since firms may hold cash for reasons other than transactions purposes.

42. Global taxation of capital income was suspended during 1998–2000 to prevent negative impacts on the financial markets.

43. It was 15 percent as of 2003 and had declined to 14 percent in 2005.

44. Final withholding rates depend on the sources of gains, characteristics of ownership, and holding periods, with share gains at 10 to 30 percent and real property gains at 9 to 70 percent of 2005. Gains from share transactions are tax exempt for most minority shareholders (having share ownerships less than 3 percent and share values less than 10 billion won).

45. Those who have only wages and salary income are not required to file tax returns for global taxation.

46. Out of 2.9 trillion won of capital gains taxes, 2.5 trillion won (86 percent) are accounted for by real property gains. The rest is for share gains.

47. The self-employed and salary and wage earners with other income sources are subject to global taxation.

48. Employees find it very difficult to evade taxes because their income is taxed on a withholding basis.

49. This amounts to the product of the prescribed value-added rate and input taxes paid.

50. In a normal case, input tax credits are available only for taxes due on total turnover.

51. Author's calculation based on data available from the National Tax Service.

52. See Gordon and Li (2005) for a formal model. Capital-intensive firms are presumed to be closely tied to the financial sector, for example, because their needs to raise capital make bank loans valuable.

53. The effective tax rates for small firms are not as low as institutions forecast before the financial crisis, possibly implying a tax shifting between personal and corporate income. Note that the relative tax burden on personal income dropped due to sharply increased personal allowances after the crisis, implying a reduced incentive to shift personal income into corporate income.

54. Export subsidies were repealed in 1999.

55. Korean banks were either state-owned or under strict government control before the financial crisis.

56. Deductions for earned income, educational expenses, and charitable contributions were raised, and deductions for pension income were introduced. The elderly and disabled received additional deductions and tax-exempt savings opportunities. Income tax rates were reduced by 10 percent across the board, from 10–40 percent to 9–36 percent, effective from 2002.

57. Instead, withholding taxes were imposed on all dividends and interest at the source.

58. In 1999, special excise taxes on electronic goods, food and beverages, and other necessities were eliminated.

59. Foreign investors and firms investing in high technology or investing more than $100 million in a Foreign Investment Zone were made exempt from personal and corporate income taxes for seven years and granted a 50 percent reduction for a further three years. Additional tax incentives for such investments were made available by local governments in the form of reduced property, acquisition, and registration taxes.

60. Taxes on revaluation profits following mergers and acquisitions have been deferred; taxes on capital gains on asset and equity transactions for restructuring were put off; acquisition, registration, and securities transaction taxes were exempted on transactions related to restructuring; and taxes on capital gains accruing to assets that were sold to repay debt were exempted.

61. To facilitate the closures of nonviable financial institutions, proceeds from their liquidations, mergers, or sales of assets were exempted from taxation.

62. The author's analysis of the sources of changes in the corporate effective burden for listed Korean companies confirmed that the changes in the debt ratio were the dominating factor raising corporate tax burn after the crisis (see Jun, 2004). A follow-up, ongoing study using an expanded sample shows similar results.

63. As of 2005, a taxpayer can deduct 20 percent of credit card consumption in excess of 15 percent of income, up to 5 million won. For a rough illustration, a person who earns 50 million won a year and exhausts the deduction limit can reduce the effective tax rate by 10 percent of the marginal tax rate. This appears to be a strong incentive. The size of this incentive was increased further in the years following its adoption and has begun to be scaled down recently.

64. A tax credit for credit card sales has been available since 1994. In 2000, the government increased the credit rate from 1 to 2 percent and the maximum credit from 3 to 5 million won. In 2004, the credit rate was reduced back to 1 percent.

65. Like the case with credit card incentives, the purpose of this scheme is to create an audit trail of retail transactions. When a merchant issues a cash receipt, the transaction is electronically reported to the tax authorities.

66. In addition, the government introduced a penalty (a 10 percent surcharge) for underreporting of taxable income, and an incentive (a 10 percent tax credit, up to 1 million won) for bookkeeping by those operating under the simplified scheme.

67. These include adoption of a self-assessment system and a Charter of Taxpayers' Rights, overhaul of the organizational structure of the National Tax Service, and use of information technology in tax processing and in maintaining a taxpayer database.

68. Most Korean banks provide preferred rate loans to those customers with high levels of credit card usage.

69. See Dalsgaard (2000) and Ministry of Finance and Economy (2005), for example.

REFERENCES

Bird, R. M., and Jun, J. (2005). "Earmarking in Theory and Korean Practice." Paper presented to Asian Excise Tax Conference, Singapore.

Bureau of Local Finance and Economy Ministry of Government Administration and Home Affairs. Various years. *Financial Yearbook of Local Government.* Seoul: Bureau of Local Finance and Economy Ministry of Government Administration and Home Affairs.

Dalsgaard, T. (2000). "The Tax System in Korea: More Fairness and Less Complexity Required." *OECD Economics Department Working Papers No. 271.* Paris: Organisation for Economic Co-operation and Development (OECD).

Feldstein, M., and Feenberg, D. (1996). "The Effect of Increased Tax Rates on Taxable Income and Economic Efficiency: A Preliminary Analysis of the 1993 Tax Rate Increase." In *Tax Policy and the Economy,* J. Poterba, ed. Cambridge, MA: MIT Press.

Gordon, R., and Li, W. (2005). "Tax Structure in Developing Countries: Many Puzzles and a Possible Explanation." *NBER Working Paper No. 11267.* Paris: National Bureau of Economic Research (NBER).

Jun, J. (2004, May). "Firm Characteristics and Tax Burden: Alternative Measures of Effective Corporate Tax Rates." *Korean Journal of Public Economics,* 9(1). The Korean Association of Public Finance (in Korean).

Ministry of Finance and Economy (2005, September). "Directions of Tax Reform." Unpublished Mimeo. Seoul: Ministry of Finance and Economy..

————. Various years. "Korean Taxation." Seoul: Ministry of Finance and Economy.

National Statistical Office. (2006). *Economically Active Population Survey.* Seoul: Korea National Statistical Office.

National Tax Service. *Statistical Yearbook of National Tax.* Various years. Seoul: National Tax Service.

OECD. (2005). *Revenue Statistics 1965–2004.* Paris: OECD.

————. (2006). *Fact Book 2006.* Paris: OECD

Schneider, F. (2005). "Shadow Economies of 145 Countries All Over the World: Estimation Results Over the Period 1999 to 2003." Discussion Paper. University of Linz, Department of Economics, Linz, Austria.

Son, W., Jung, J., Kim, H. J., and Kim, S. H. (2004). "Quasi-taxes on Businesses and Their Policy Implications." Korea Institute of Public Finance (in Korean). Seoul: Korea Institute of Public Finance.

Sung, Mung-Jae, Park, H. S., and Jun, B. M. (2004). "The Effects of Tax Policy on Income Distribution and Resource Allocation." Korea Institute of Public Finance (in Korean). Seoul: Korea Institute of Public Finance.

World Bank. (1993). *The East-Asian Miracle: Economic Growth and Public Policy.* New York: Oxford University Press.

CHAPTER 8

Tax Structure and Tax Burden in Brazil: 1980–2004

José Teófilo Oliveira and Ana Carolina Giuberti

This chapter describes and illustrates the main features of the Brazilian tax system from 1980 to 2004. During this period, the Brazilian economy experienced a faulty economic growth process in the presence of very high rates of inflation, and a significant upward movement of the total tax revenue collected by the central, state, and local governments from a level of 25 percent of GDP to an all-time high of 32.8 percent in 2004. This effort to raise additional revenue occurred in the 1990s and is primarily explained by social security expenditures and by interest payments on public debt.

The data collected also indicate that the tax system is dominated by indirect forms of taxation. The use of taxes on goods and services represented nearly 50 percent of the total tax revenue for most of the period.

The chapter also identifies the key changes in the tax laws in the period and the current problems of design and administration of the tax system.

Finally, the macroeconomic context is presented, and an attempt is made to relate the ups and down in the rates of economic activity and inflation to tax revenues and internal and external debt.

TAX STRUCTURE

The 25-year period 1980–2004 was characterized by significant changes in the Brazilian tax structure and in the amount of money that the three levels of government diverted from private use through taxation.

The tax system that had been in place in the early 1980s was designed as part of a tax reform program implemented from 1965 to 1967.[1] This reform promoted major changes, the most important being the introduction of value-added taxation. This new mode of taxation came to replace two cumulative taxes: the tax on sales and consignments (IVC), which was the backbone of the states' revenue, and the misnamed federal "consumption" tax, which in reality taxed all sales within the industrial sector and imports in general. In addition, the 1965–1967 tax reform revitalized, or perhaps more appropriately, truly instituted income taxation in Brazil with the implementation of modern tax administration procedures.[2]

During the late 1960s, the Brazilian public sector raised revenues equivalent to 25 percent of GDP with the use of a dozen taxes and three contributions.[3] This picture changed as time progressed, however. The tax system of the 1980s had essentially remained unchanged from the system implemented in the late 1960s. New demands for expenditures, mainly in the social area, however, led to a new federal contribution, FINSOCIAL, in 1982. In addition, a new state tax (IPVA) was created in 1986, based on ownership of automobiles and other means of transportation.[4]

In 1988, the picture shifted even further, as Brazil enacted a new constitution. Even though the constitution was successful in terms of the construction of democratic values and institutions, it failed to develop an effective tax system. It should be recognized, however, that the constitution improved the taxation of goods and services by eliminating federal excises on fuel, electricity, minerals, communications, and interstate transportation, and by incorporating the corresponding tax bases in the Tax on the Circulation of Goods and Services (ICMS) (a VAT that is the main source of revenue of the states).

To summarize briefly, the new constitution reinstated the tax structure that existed in 1988[5] and added four new taxes and contributions: a local tax on the retail sale of fuels, a state personal income tax, a federal wealth tax, and a federal social contribution on net profits (CSLL). With the exception of CSLL, the other new taxes were abandoned in a few years for a variety of reasons.

In 1994 the federal government introduced a (provisional) bank debit tax with the purpose of raising some extra revenue for that particular fiscal year. This revenue source reemerged in 1996 as a contribution (Provisional Contribution on Financial Transactions—CPMF) to finance health care. In 2002, the Brazilian government implemented a federal fuel tax (a contribution earmarked for road maintenance and construction).

Given these changes the main taxes and contributions collected in 2004 by the federal government, states, and municipalities are shown in Table 8.1.

The data reveal that the federal government raised 69.72 percent of Brazil's total revenue, while the states collected 26.06 percent and the municipalities raised the smallest fraction, 4.22 percent.

Table 8.1   Main Taxes and Contributions in Brazil, 2004

Level of Government and Taxes	R$ million	% GDP	% Total
Federal Government	**442,280**	**22.78**	**69.72**
Fiscal Budget	**155,855**	**8.03**	**24.57**
Income Tax	110,308	5.68	17.39
IPI (VAT Industry)	22,538	1.16	3.55
Import Tax	9,181	0.47	1.45
IOF (Loans, foreign exchange, and insurance tax)	5,209	0.27	0.82
ITR (Rural Property)	245	0.01	0.04
CIDE (Fuel Tax)	7,816	0.40	1.23
Others	558	0.03	0.09
Social Security Budget	**246,466**	**12.69**	**38.85**
Social Security Contribution	93,765	4.83	14.78
COFINS (VAT)	77,593	4.00	12.23
PIS/PASEP (VAT)	19,417	1.00	3.06
CPMF (Financial Transactions)	26,340	1.36	4.15
CSLL (Contribution on Net Profits)	19,575	1.01	3.09
Others	9,776	0.50	1.54
Nonclassified	**39,959**	**2.06**	**6.30**
FGTS (Workers' Retirement Fund) payroll	28,269	1.46	4.46
Others	11,690	0.60	1.84
State Governments	**165,324**	**8.52**	**26.06**
ICMS (VAT)	138,275	7.12	21.80
IPVA (Vehicles)	8,910	0.46	1.40
ITCD (Inheritance Tax)	710	0.04	0.11
Others	17,429	0.90	2.75
Municipal Governments	**26,786**	**1.38**	**4.22**
ISS (Services)	9,682	0.50	1.53
IPTU (Urban Property)	8,965	0.46	1.41
ITBI (Property Transfer)	1,851	0.10	0.29
Others	6,288	0.32	0.99
Total	**634,390**	**32.77**	**100.00**

Source: IBGE/FRS.

Note: GDP (2004): R$ 1.9 trillion = US$ 663.6 billion.

Taxes and contributions collected by the federal government are divided to finance two independent budgets: the fiscal and the social security budgets.[6] The fiscal budget's main source of revenue is the income tax (personal and business). Other major sources of revenue include IPI, a value-added tax centered in the industrial sectors, an import tax, IOF (a tax on loans, the purchase of foreign exchange, and insurance premiums), and CIDE (a recently created federal fuel contribution tied to road repair and construction).

The social security budget[7] is fed by five contributions: (1) contributions of employees and employers, a 30 percent rate on payroll (20 percent paid by employers and 10 percent by employees); (2) COFINS—Contribution to Finance Social Security—a turnover tax created in 1982 that was converted to a VAT in 2004; (3) PIS, a contribution on turnover created in 1970 that was converted to a VAT in 2002; (4) CPMF, a contribution created in 1996 to finance health care (its rate of 0.38 percent to be applied to bank debit entries of current and savings accounts and other similar transactions); and (5) CSLL (contribution on net profits).

This brief description reveals that Brazil has not one, but four VATs. The states have one VAT, and the federal government has three. All considered, this mode of taxation raised 13.3 percent of GDP in 2004.

The primary source of revenue for the states is the ICMS—a broad-based consumption-type VAT that produced revenue of 7.81 percent of GDP in 2004 and is the most important tax collected in the country.

The states also raise revenues with two other levies: a tax on ownership of vehicles (IPVA) and an inheritance and donation tax (ITCD). The municipalities tax certain services (ISS) and urban property (IPTU).

The FGTS contribution (workers' retirement fund) is not an item of revenue of the federal treasury. It was created in 1996 to reduce labor market rigidities, and its proceeds are deposited in individuals' accounts. Sums can be withdrawn in the case of unmotivated dismissal, retirement, or death of the beneficiary.

Box 8.1 Tax Bases and Tax Rates

FEDERAL TAXES AND CONTRIBUTIONS
PERSONAL INCOME TAX
    Annual Taxable Income
    Under R$ 12,696—exempted
    From R$ 12,696 to R$ 25,380—rate of 15.0 percent (–) R$ 1,904
    Above R$ 25,380—rate of 27.5 percent (–) R$ 5,076

BUSINESS INCOME TAX
    Annual Taxable Income (profits)
    Basic rate: 15 percent
    Additional rate (annual profits above R$ 240,000): 10 percent

IPI—Tax on industrialized products
A value-added tax with differentiated rates in the industrial sector, wholesale and imports. Fifty-four percent of the tax revenue is derived from the sales of liquor and beverages, automobiles, tobacco, and imports by industry.

SOCIAL SECURITY CONTRIBUTIONS
(a levy based on payroll)
Employees pay a 10 percent rate
Employers pay a 20 percent rate

SOCIAL CONTRIBUTION ON PROFITS
The tax base is the same as the one used in the business income taxes. The rate is 9 percent.

PIS AND COFINS
PIS and COFINS are earmarked taxes and have the same tax base. For small firms the common base is gross revenue, and the rates are 0.65 percent and 3.0 percent, respectively. For large firms the common base is value-added (computed using the subtraction method) with rates of 1.65 percent and 7.6 percent, respectively.

CPMF. Taxes debit entries of current and savings accounts at a rate of 0.38 percent.

FGTS. The tax base is payroll, and the tax rate is 8 percent.

CIDE is a specific tax on fuel.

STATE TAXES
ICMS
Rates on value-added, computed using the tax-credit method:
Internal rates (within the state): 17 percent – 18 percent – 25 percent
Interstate commerce: 7 percent – 12 percent
Exports: Nontaxable (zero debit rate and creditation in full).

IPVA. Taxes the market value of vehicles at a rate of 2 percent to 4 percent depending on the state.

ITBI. An inheritance tax based on the value of bequest at a rate of (frequently) 4 percent.

(continued)

MUNICIPALITIES

TAX ON SERVICES. A tax based on the value of a well-defined (nationally) list of services with a flat tax rate of 2 percent and a maximum rate of 5 percent.

URBAN PROPERTY TAX. Modal rates are: 0.25 percent on buildings and 2 percent on bare land.

THE EVOLUTION OF THE TAX BURDEN (CENTRAL GOVERNMENT, STATES, AND MUNICIPALITIES)

In 1947, when the first national account statistics were published in Brazil, the overall tax burden corresponded to 13.8 percent of GDP. In the late 1960s, the ratio was pushed to 25 percent, as a result of a comprehensive tax reform. The 25 percent ratio, with some fluctuations, prevailed through the 1970s and even until 1989, as shown in Figure 8.1. In the troubled years of 1990 to 1993, however, the ratio reached a record level of 29.6 percent in the presence of very high rates of inflation and a stagnant economy. The ratio was subsequently restored to its historical level of 25 percent in the following years.

A new benchmark was established in 1994 when the tax burden corresponded to 27.9 percent of GDP. In that year, inflation was brought down to manageable levels as a result of a successful set of policies known as the

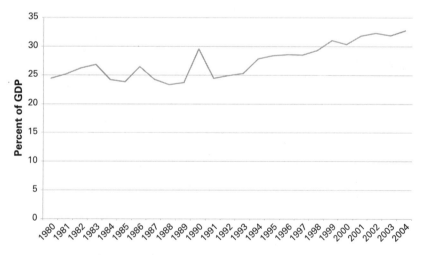

Figure 8.1   Total Tax Revenue.

Source: IBGE. Data available at IpeaData, elaborated by the authors.

Real Plan. (For a discussion of the Real Plan, see the Appendix to this chapter.)

Remarkably, in the period from 1993 to 2004, the ratio increased eight percentage points, moving from a 25 percent ratio in 1993 to its present level of 33 percent.

At this juncture, it is natural to ask why such an effort was made and how it was made. The short answer to the first question is that additional revenue was needed to sustain social expenditures (primarily pensions and health care), as determined by the new constitution, and to bring the public deficit under control. The mechanisms used were the traditional ones: rate increases and new taxes.

DIRECT AND INDIRECT TAXES

Table 8.A.1, which can be found in the Appendix to this chapter, shows the several levies collected under the usual titles of direct and indirect taxes; Table 8.A.2 exhibits some of the results.

For most of the 1980s, an almost fifty-fifty partition prevailed between direct and indirect taxes.[8] In the 1990s, indirect modes of taxation dominated, owing to the creation and rate increases of social contributions (FINSOCIAL, PIS, and CPMF). More recently, since 1997, the old parity has been restored, with the direct taxes prevailing.

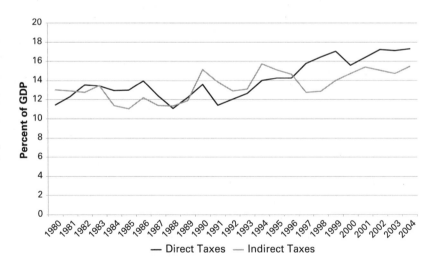

Figure 8.2   Direct and Indirect Taxes, 1980–2004.

Source: IBGE and Varsano et al. (1998), elaborated by the authors.

To shed further light on the evolution of the tax system in Brazil, we can break down the tax burden into five categories, as presented in Table 8.A.3 of the Appendix. The categories are: taxes on foreign trade, goods and services, property, income, and payroll. As shown in Figure 8.3, taxes on goods and services dominate the picture. Contributions based on payroll occupied a distant second place throughout the period, though income taxes have closed in on this category recently.

As shown above, property and import taxes have not been important in the formation of total revenue of the public sector in Brazil. More specifically, import taxes, which raised 50 percent of the federal government's revenue in the 1920s, have lost ground since the 1940s and continue to decline.

From 1980 to 2004, the total tax burden in proportion to GDP grew eight percentage points. Of this increase, almost five percentage points were the result of increases in taxes on goods and services—mostly contributions to finance social security. The remaining increase of three percentage points was due to an increase in income taxation.

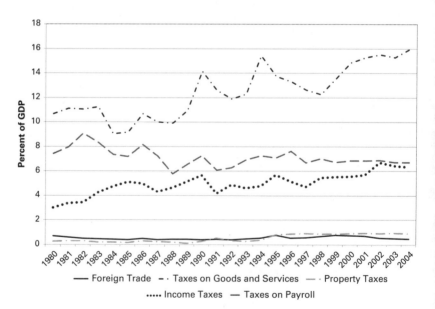

Figure 8.3   Tax Categories, 1980–2004.

Source: IBGE and Varsano et al. (1998), elaborated by the authors.

Table 8.2   Hiring Costs: Social Security and Other Costs (Selected Countries) *(as a percentage of total payroll)*

Brazil	103.46
France	79.70
Argentina	70.27
Germany	60.00
England	58.30
Italy	51.30
Netherlands	51.00
Uruguay	48.06
Belgium	45.40
Paraguay	41.00
Japan	11.80
Denmark	11.60
Asian Tigers (average)	11.50
United States	9.03

Source: Pastore (2005), p. 49.

The data reveal how social security expenditures have increased in the last 15 years. In 1989, the revenues that sustained the fiscal and social budgets as a percentage of GDP were 7.4 percent and 5.2 percent, respectively. In 2004, the proportions changed significantly—12.7 percent of GDP was allocated to social security versus 8.0 percent to the fiscal budget.

Contributions on payroll listed in Table 8.A.3 do not represent the only economic impact resulting from governmental intervention in labor markets in Brazil. Other legal provisions, associated with the hiring (and firing) of workers, are also relevant for economic analysis. In fact, payroll taxes represent only 35 percent of the total burden imposed by legal obligation on hiring workers. The wedge that exists between take-home pay and the wage paid by employers is around 100 percent. It seems that Brazil is, by far, the country that imposes the heaviest load on hiring workers in the world (Table 8.2). Most analysts agree that this fact has contributed to an increase in informal labor relations and unemployment.

TAXATION OF MINERAL RESOURCES

Brazil is a country rich in natural resources; it is a big exporter of iron ore and aluminum, and a self-sufficient producer of petroleum. The mineral industry is exempted from the federal tax on industrialized products (IPI) and is taxed by the states' VAT (ICMS). In addition, it pays a financial compensation (royalties) to the federal government and to the state and municipality where the extraction process takes place.

By far, financial compensations for oil production are more significant compared to those for other minerals. On this account, in 2004, oil producers paid R$ 11.1 billion (0.63 percent of GDP) to the federal government, states, and municipalities.[9] In the same year, non-oil mineral producers paid financial compensation amounting to R$ 326 million.

INTERNATIONAL COMPARISONS

Table 8.3, based on the work of Tanzi and Zee (2000), indicates that Brazil has a tax revenue to GDP ratio equivalent to that of a developed country and a tax structure that combines elements found in the tax structures of both developing and developed countries.

We can conclude from Table 8.3 that Brazil has the biggest tax burden among developing countries (the block "Other Countries" in the lower right-hand side in the table). The data seem to indicate that tax revenue in OECD countries rests on three pillars of almost equal size: income (14.2 percent), consumption (11.4 percent), and social security (9.5 percent). The proportion of income to consumption taxes in OECD countries is close to 1.2, while in Brazil, the ratio is about 0.6. With respect to social security taxes, Brazil exhibits a GDP ratio very similar to the ratio of OECD countries and well above that of other developing countries.

REVENUE SHARING

To understand how revenue sharing is carried out in Brazil, one must consider the country's institutional organization. Brazil is composed of 26 states, 1 federal district, and nearly 5,600 municipalities. Together, these entities collect 35 percent of total revenue and incur a similar percentage of public sector expenditures. The regional governments have an equal legal footing with the central government, and they form a decentralized federation.[10] From the early days of the republic (1889) and more intensively since the 1930s, there have been increased calls for the decentralization of expenditure capacity through mandated revenue-sharing mechanisms.

The constitution determines that 21.5 percent of the revenue of IPI and income tax (personal and business) must be distributed in favor of the states and 22.5 percent of the same sources in favor of local governments. Another proviso states that an additional 3 percent of those taxes must be reserved for regional development programs. This implies that almost half (47 percent) of the total revenue of IPI and income tax are allocated to

Table 8.3 Composition of Tax Revenue by Regions, 1985–1997 (as a percentage of GDP)

	1985–1987								1995–1997							
	Income			Taxes on Consumption					Income			Taxes on Consumption				
		of which:			of which:					of which:			of which:			
	Total	Business	Personal	Total	General[3]	Selective	International Trade	Social Security	Total	Business	Personal	Total	General	Selective	International Trade	Social Security
OECD Countries[1]	13.9	2.8	11.3	11.3	6.0	3.8	0.7	8.8	14.2	3.1	10.8	11.4	6.6	3.6	0.3	9.5
America	14.0	2.5	11.4	7.6	3.4	2.2	0.6	5.8	15.4	3.0	12.3	7.0	3.7	2.0	0.3	6.1
Pacific	17.1	3.9	13.2	7.5	2.3	3.7	0.8	2.8	16.3	4.3	11.4	8.4	4.3	2.6	0.6	3.5
Europe	13.3	2.7	11.0	12.4	6.8	4.0	0.7	10.1	13.7	2.9	10.6	12.4	7.3	4.0	0.3	10.8
Other Countries[2]	4.9	2.8	1.7	10.3	2.3	2.6	4.2	1.2	5.2	2.6	2.2	10.5	3.6	2.4	3.5	1.3
Africa	6.3	2.9	3.1	11.7	3.2	2.3	5.7	0.4	6.9	2.4	3.9	11.6	3.8	2.3	5.1	0.5
Asia	5.7	3.6	2.1	9.5	1.9	2.5	3.6	0.1	6.2	3.0	3.0	9.7	3.1	2.2	2.7	0.3
Middle East	4.7	4.3	1.0	9.1	1.5	2.4	4.4	1.2	5.0	3.2	1.3	10.3	1.5	3.0	4.3	1.1
Western Countries	3.7	1.8	1.0	10.6	2.6	3.0	3.7	2.4	3.7	2.3	1.0	10.6	4.8	2.3	2.6	2.5
Brazil	**5.2**	**2.0**	**3.2**	**8.8**[3]	**7.4**	**0.9**	**0.5**	**8.3**	**5.2**	**2.2**	**3.0**	**9.4**	**8.1**	**0.7**	**0.6**	**9.2**

(continued)

Table 8.3 (continued)

	Income/Taxes on Consumption		Business Income/Personal Income		Fiscal Extraction—% of GDP	
	1985–1987	1995–1997	1985–1987	1995–1997	1985–1987	1995–1997
OECD Countries[1]	1.2	1.2	0.2	0.3	36.6	37.9
America	1.8	2.2	0.2	0.2	30.6	32.6
Pacific	2.3	1.9	0.3	0.4	30.7	31.6
Europe	1.1	1.1	0.2	0.3	38.2	39.4
Other Countries[2]	0.5	0.5	1.6	1.2	17.5	18.2
Africa	0.5	0.6	0.9	0.6	19.6	19.8
Asia	0.6	0.6	1.6	1	16.1	17.4
Middle East	0.5	0.5	4.3	2.5	16.5	18.1
Western Countries	0.4	0.4	1.8	2.3	17.6	18.0
Brazil	**0.6**	**0.6**	**0.6**	**0.7**	**23.45**	**29.03**

Source: Tanzi and Zee (2000).

1. Excluding Czech Republic, Hungary, Korea, Mexico, and Poland.
2. A sample of 8 African countries, 9 Asian countries, 7 of Middle Eastern countries, and 14 Western countries.
3. Considers only ICMS and IPI.

Table 8.4   Revenue by Level of Government: The Role of Revenue Sharing, 1980–2004

	% of GDP				% of Total			
	Federal	States	Local	Total	Federal	States	Local	Total
Revenue Raised								
1980	18.50	5.40	0.70	24.60	75.1	22.0	2.9	100.0
1988	15.81	5.94	0.65	22.40	70.6	26.5	2.9	100.0
2004	24.96	9.81	1.99	36.76	67.9	26.7	5.4	100.0
Disposable Revenue (after transfers)								
1980	17.00	5.50	2.10	24.60	69.2	22.2	8.6	100.0
1988	14.00	6.00	2.40	22.40	62.3	26.9	10.8	100.0
2004	21.56	9.03	6.05	36.64	58.9	24.6	16.5	100.0

Source: Khair et al. (2005).

regional governments. Constitutional rules also mandate that 25 percent of ICMS revenue, the states' VAT, and 50 percent of IPVA (vehicles tax) be given to their respective local governments.

Table 8.4 indicates that mandated revenue sharing has increased the states' and local governments' share of total disposable tax revenue since 1980, while the federal government has had its share reduced to 58.9 percent. In terms of revenue raised, the federal government has been losing ground—75.1 percent in 1980 compared with 67.9 percent in 2004.

EARMARKING AND OTHER BUDGETARY CONSTRAINTS

Brazil uses revenue earmarking extensively, particularly at the federal level. It has been estimated that about 80 percent of federal tax revenues were earmarked in 2003 against less than 60 percent in 1988.[11] This includes mandated revenue sharing in favor of states and municipalities, as well as special-purpose funds. Revenue sharing accounts for about 15 percent of federal tax revenues and is concentrated on the income tax and IPI, which are the federal government's most income-elastic taxes.

Efforts to increase federal revenue net of mandated transfers to the regional governments have resulted in greater reliance on contributions whose revenues are earmarked to social security but not shared with regional governments.

To mitigate this problem, a provisional arrangement to withhold federal earmarked revenues has been in place since 2000. A constitutional amendment now permits the federal government to hold back 20 percent of all federal revenues (net of intergovernmental transfers), thereby reducing the extent of de facto revenue earmarking at the federal level.

In addition, there are significant expenditure rigidities at the federal and regional government levels. The constitution requires all levels of government to earmark a share of their revenues (18 percent for the federal government and 25 percent for state and municipal governments) to finance education. Moreover, the states and municipalities are required to earmark 12 percent and 15 percent of their revenues, respectively, to finance health care.

KEY CHANGES IN THE TAX LAWS

OPENING UP TO INTERNATIONAL TRADE

Brazil has a long history of utilizing tariff and non-tariff barriers to promote its industrialization and growth. This policy can be considered successful, given the creation of a broad and diversified industrial sector in the second half of the twentieth century and the GDP growth rates observed for more than 50 years up to 1980.

Despite these results, based on short- and long-run considerations, in the late 1970s, the social costs of protection appeared excessive to analysts and government officials. Consequently, legal (nominal) and effective tariff rates have been substantially reduced since 1988. Average nominal tariff rates were brought down from 55 percent in 1987 to 13.4 percent in 1998. The same path was followed by the effective rate, which was reduced from 67.8 percent in 1987 to its present level of 15 percent (see Figure 8.4).

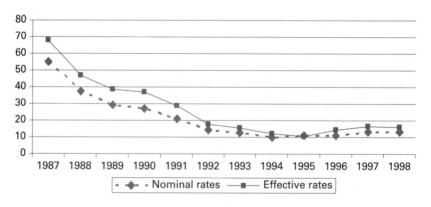

Figure 8.4   Nominal and Effective Tax Rates.

Source: Kume et al. (2003).

Note: Weighted by value added.

The process of eliminating trade barriers may be considered successful. The levels of imports and exports observed in 1987 (US $15 and US $26.2 billion, respectively) increased fourfold by 2004 (US $62.7 billion and US $96.4 billion), and there are strong indications that imports of capital goods contributed to the modernization and productivity gains in the economy as a whole.

Taxation of Small Businesses (SIMPLES)

In 1996, the federal government enacted a law to meet the recurring demands of small businesses for lower taxes, simplification, and reduced compliance costs.[12]

For this segment, tax rates on sales vary from 3 to 7 percent, progressively, and this payment substitutes for the payment of six federal taxes and contributions: the business income tax, social contribution on profits, PIS, COFINS, IPI, and the employer contribution to social security.

Taxation of Capital Goods under ICMS

Until 1996, capital goods were taxed under ICMS without the benefit of a tax credit. ICMS was then a gross-income VAT. With new national legislation (law 87/1996), however, a tax credit is permitted in 48 monthly installments, thus at least partially correcting an important distortion of the tax.

Taxation of Exports under IPI and ICMS

The rules and regulations of both IPI and ICMS distinguish two types of non-taxed products: the exempted or zero-rated and the immune ones. The former is a tax status that can be changed by ordinary legislation (laws and decrees), whereas the immune type is a constitutional provision.

Typically, for both taxes, the seller of an exempted or zero-rated product in the domestic market does not have the benefit of a tax credit. Of course this rule has negative consequences when the zero rate occurs in the intermediate stages of the productive process, in the form of cascading effects in the later stages of production and distribution.

The treatment of exports is a different matter. In the case of IPI, since its inception in 1967, sales abroad have a zero rate and producers can recoup the tax paid on raw materials, domestically produced or imported. The same rule applies to exports under ICMS after 1996. Before that date only industrial goods had the right to full tax credit while exports of agricultural products were taxed (at a 13 percent rate).

It was the law 87/1996 that corrected this problem by granting tax immunity to all exports and the benefit of full tax credit.

Transformation of Federal Turnover Taxes into Value-Added Taxes

Beginning in January 2002, the federal contribution known as PIS was tentatively converted into a VAT. As a turnover tax, it had a 0.36 percent rate and was replaced by a 1.65 percent VAT rate. Subsequently, in 2004, the federal government transformed COFINS, also a turnover tax, into a sort of VAT with a 7.6 percent rate.

PIS and COFINS are earmarked taxes (to social security) and have the same tax base. For small firms the common base is gross revenue, and the rates are 0.65 and 3.0 percent for PIS and COFINS, respectively. For large firms the common base is value-added (computed using the subtraction method) with rates of 1.65 and 7.6 percent respectively.

The conversion of PIS and COFINS into the VAT cannot be seen as a definite improvement in the direction of eliminating cascading effects. Indeed, the option of taxing value-added is only open to large firms (mainly exporters). These firms pay the tax, computing value-added by using the subtraction method (sales – value of inputs and materials used). Small and middle-size firms collect the tax based on their monthly turnover. On both counts, it can be said that the cumulative or cascading effects are still present.

The Creation of CPMF in 1994

CPMF (Provisional Contribution on Financial Transactions), a tax earmarked for health expenditures, is a tax on certain financial transactions levied on withdrawals from and other debits to bank accounts.

According to Coelho et al. (2001), a bank-debit tax was first introduced in Argentina in 1983 and was later implemented in Peru (1989), Brazil (1994), Venezuela (1994), Colombia (1998), Australia (1998), and Ecuador (1999). In all cases, the tax was introduced on a temporary basis, though in the case of Brazil, successive extensions have given it a permanent status. At present, only Brazil, Colombia, and Ecuador continue to enforce the tax, while the other countries have abandoned the experiment.

Overall, Coelho et al. (2001) considered CPMF to be the most successful example of this mode of taxation in Latin America. It has been generating revenue of 1.5 percent of GDP, a level that has been sustained for several years (see Table 8.A.2).

Coelho et al. (2001) point out that there is evidence that CPMF altered financial and investment behavior, especially in the wake of its reintroduction at the end of January 1997. In summarizing their analysis, the authors recommended that such taxes should be avoided; if they are to be used, they should only be levied at low rates, and the base should be defined so as to exclude, among other things, transactions in securities markets.

CURRENT PROBLEMS OF DESIGN AND ADMINISTRATION OF THE TAX SYSTEM

Construction of a better tax system in Brazil will require a profound revision of certain expenditure patterns that have developed during the last 15 years. Ultimately, it was this upward surge in public expenditures that created the demand for new resources.

Most analysts consider a 33 percent tax burden oppressive, and some even consider it abusive. Regardless of which description is more accurate, the percentage attained in 2004 is high for a developing country, according to international standards. Making matters worse is that this increase in the tax burden has been followed by a deterioration in public services at both federal and regional levels.

The underlying cause of deterioration in public services can be traced to the increase in current expenditures since the early 1990s. Such increases are due to social security concessions and to interest payments on public debt, which have increased twofold since 1994 (interest payments in 2004 represented 6.4 percent of GDP). In other words, the necessary fiscal adjustment has been accomplished primarily by increasing taxes and by compressing public investment. The greatest challenge now is to reconcile the need for continued fiscal consolidation with that of alleviating a high tax burden.

In the short run, progress can be made if interest rates can be reduced at a more rapid pace than that intended by the monetary authorities. In the long run, progress will demand more reforms of Brazil's public pension system. Currently, the public pension system costs 9 percent of GDP (above the OECD average); the system is unjust and expensive, and drains resources away from other strategic areas such as health, education, and infrastructure.

COMPLEXITY

The most common criticisms of the Brazilian tax system are that there are too many types of taxes and that the tax laws and regulations in effect are overly complex and difficult to control and comply with. Both criticisms are accurate.

Regressive Distribution of Tax Burden

A study by Vianna et al. (2000) reported incidence estimates for the Brazilian tax system. The results indicated that the tax system is highly regressive. Despite the fact that direct taxes are progressive, the final result is dominated by highly regressive indirect taxes.

Earmarking

A great amount of earmarking is embedded in the different taxes and contributions. In the case of the federal government, as noted earlier, earmarking is an especially serious problem. The obvious consequences of the phenomenon are the loss of budget flexibility, as well as the inefficient use of public money.

Tax on Payroll

Regulation of the labor market and taxation of payroll more than double the private cost of hiring labor. This fact seems to explain a significant part of the informal economy, which is a manifestation of disguised unemployment (see box).

THE MOVE TO REFORM ICMS

After an unsuccessful attempt to create a single VAT that would consolidate most of the indirect taxes in Brazil, the call for simplification of the tax system was directed toward creation of a single VAT legislation for all states. At present, Congress has set the basic rules of the VAT, and the states have a high degree of autonomy in setting internal rates. Congress also has been discussing new legislation with far-reaching implications, the most important being a provision that subtracts from the states the prerogative to legislate and regulate the tax.

Box 8.2 The Informal Economy in Brazil

The Brazilian Institute of Geography and Statistics (IBGE) conducted two surveys of the urban informal sector, known as ECINF 1997 and ECINF 2003. Based on the 2003 survey, IBGE reported that the informal sector in urban areas was comprised of 10.5 million small businesses, half of which had no legal registration.

According to the 2003 survey, the annual revenue of those firms was R$ 217.5 billion, which corresponded to 14 percent of GDP. The investments they made were R$ 7.2 billion, equivalent to 2.3 percent of total investment registered in the national accounts. The most common economic activities in the informal economy were retail trade and repair (33 percent), construction (17 percent), and manufacturing and extraction (16 percent). The survey also registered that 31 percent of the owners of informal firms declared that they opened the business because they could not find any job and 17.6 percent because they needed to improve their family's income.

IBGE has estimated that between 1997 and 2003, employment in the formal sector increased 4 percent while the urban informal sector increased by 8 percent (from 12.9 to 13.9 million workers). This last figure corresponded to 26 percent of the labor force, and, of the total employed, only 6 percent had social security registration.

Concern with the informal sector in Brazil is important because of job precariousness and its social consequences (e.g., lack of unemployment compensations, retirement income, access to financial services, etc.). A substantial share of Brazil's workers is without legal registration (60 percent), and approximately the same percentage (62 percent) of private sector workers have not been contributing to social security.

The figure below contains data collected by Cardoso Jr. and Fernandes (2000) in which occupied workers are classified according to legal status in the 1980s and 1990s.

The formal segment of the labor market is comprised of workers with legal registration in the private sector and public employees (civil and military). The second group is comprised of those workers without legal registration, the self-employed, and workers without pay.

The data indicate the dominance of informal labor relations in both periods. In addition, the data show an increase in informality in the 1990s, which seems to be independent of GDP cyclical behavior in contraposition to the (cyclical) behavior observed in the 1980s.

Barros et al. (1993) and Amadeo and Camargo (1996) provide empirical results supporting the hypothesis that labor market regulations and payroll taxes are the main factors behind the high degree of informality in the Brazilian labor market.

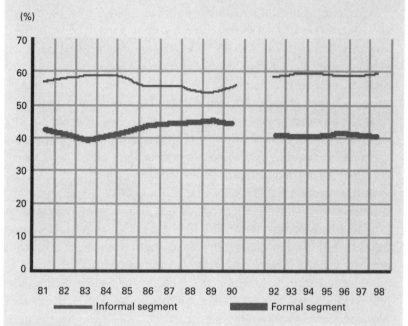

Occupied Workers According to Legal Status, 1981–1998.

Source: Cardoso Jr. and Fernandes (2000).

TAX ADMINISTRATION: METHODS AND EXPERIENCES

In the last decade Brazil has made significant progress in tax administration and in reducing tax evasion. These developments deserve additional attention and are presented below.

TECHNOLOGICAL ADVANCES

Most Brazilian taxes and contributions are self-assessed, with the exception of property taxes and CPMF (tax on financial transactions). For this reason, tax administrators in Brazil try to monitor physical transactions among taxpayers by tracking invoices and accounting books. Such activities are increasingly accomplished through the use of information technology.

INTERNET TAX FILINGS

According to Bill Gates,[13] several countries, including the United States and Australia, allow the electronic filing of taxes. Brazil, however, was the first country to enable large-scale tax filings electronically. This solution was implemented on March 30, 1997, and was made available to the public during the month of April, the last month required for an individual's income tax filing (business filings are due at the end of May). In 2002, 100 percent of businesses and 95 percent of individual taxpayers filed electronic returns in Brazil.

SISCOMEX

Another important development in tax administration was the creation of SISCOMEX in 1993. This system integrates the activities of registration, follow-up, and control of foreign trade in such a way that all federal agencies that play a role (including taxation) in the control of imports and exports operate exclusively using the data source provided by SISCOMEX. The benefits of such a system are represented by a paperless environment, the reduction of red tape, and the sharing of information among agencies and the private sector.

SINTEGRA

In the area of control, the creation of SINTEGRA in 2000 deserves attention. SINTEGRA is a system that allows for the electronic exchange of information of the states' VAT (ICMS), linking databases of the states as a mean of controlling interstate trade and standardizing procedures. The system also contains a portal where taxpayers can check data on suppliers, ensuring that they are active taxpayers in the registers of each state. This is important because the amount of ICMS due is the result of a debit/credit calculation on multiple stages of the economic chain. SINTEGRA is based on the experience of the European VIES–VAT information exchange system (see http://europa.eu.int/comm/taxation_customs/data bases/viesen.htm), and it has resulted in gains of scale due to the shared collection, treatment, and storage of information.

APPENDIX
THE MACROECONOMIC SETTING: 1980–2004

The story of the Brazilian economy during the last 25 years can be deduced from GDP growth rates, as exhibited in Figure 8.A.1. The fluctuation of these rates resembles that of a faulty engine. After 50 years of steady growth, averaging 6.5 percent per year, GDP growth in Brazil has almost ground to a halt, averaging only 2.4 percent a year from 1980 to 2004.

Brazil entered 1980 facing a macroeconomic situation that combined high inflation rates, high external debt, and a critical situation in its external accounts. In 1980 the inflow of external resources (US $9.6 billion) was insufficient to cover the current account deficit of US $12.7 billion. This figure was the result of the trade balance deficit (US $2.8 billion) and, more importantly, of resources sent abroad to service external debts.[14] In 1980, the country's gross external debt was US $64.3 billion (27 percent of GDP), and the annual inflation rate was 110.2 percent.

From 1981 to 1983, Brazil faced a period of contraction in its economy, with GDP growth dropping to an average rate of 2.16 percent per year. This situation was the result of a restrictive monetary policy (high real interest rates) aimed at two objectives: redirect internal production to exports

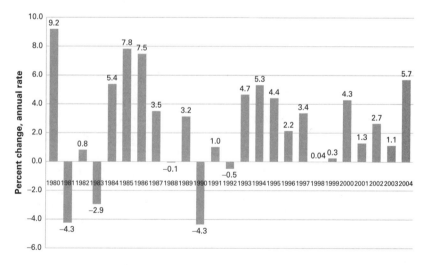

Figure 8.A.1   Real GDP Growth 1980–2004.

Source: IBGE. Data available at IpeaData, elaborated by the authors.

by reducing internal demand and attract foreign capital to overcome the balance-of-payments imbalance. The initial results of this policy came in the form of small trade surpluses in 1982 and 1983; however, these surpluses were not sufficient to cover the balance-of-payments deficit. In 1982, after a significant loss of international reserves, Brazil signed an agreement with the International Monetary Fund and raised US $4.2 billion in loans.[15] In 1983, the government promoted another 30 percent devaluation of the exchange rate and obtained good results. The restrictive monetary policy, assisted by the maturation of investments carried through the II National Development Plan,[16] resulted in an increase of the trade balance and a BP surplus in 1984. Also, in 1984, a promising recovery of economic activity was observed, with a real growth in GDP of 5.4 percent.

The adjustment of the external accounts was painful; the ratio of external debt to GDP increased in the early 1980s, reaching its highest level in 1984 and representing 54 percent of GDP (Figure 8.A.2). Brazil was confronted with the fact that the external debt was predominantly public but the commercial surplus was private.[17] This worsened the internal fiscal problem, resulting in a higher public deficit, since the government was unable to obtain sufficient tax revenues to pay the costs of this indebtedness. However, the public external debt was not only the result of budget deficits accumulated over the years, but also the outcome of a government process that converted a significant share of the external private debt into internal public debt.[18]

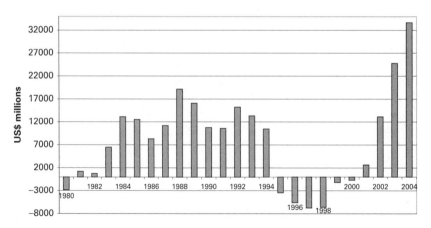

Figure 8.A.2   Trade Balance, 1980–2004.

Source: BCB, elaborated by the authors.

During the 1980s and the first half of the 1990s, the external debt played an important role in forming the net public debt.[19] With the renegotiation of external debt and the implementation of the Real Plan, internal debt took the dominant position (Figure 8.A.4). This development was related to monetary policy. High interest rates attracted foreign capital that was converted into domestic currency, expanding the monetary base. At the same time the government, concerned with inflation, issued public bonds to sterilize the monetary base increase.

The price level throughout the 1981–1984 period increased at an accelerated pace. In 1981, annual inflation was 95.2 percent, followed by 99.7 percent in 1982, 221 percent in 1983, and 223.8 percent in 1984 (Figure 8.A.5).

In 1985, democratic elections were restored after two decades of military dictatorship. At that time inflation—its causes and cures—was at the center of the national economic debate.[20]

In 1985, the inflation rate was 235.1 percent, and the trade balance registered a surplus (US $12.5 billion). However, this result, though aided by the inflow of foreign capital, was unable to cover the current account deficit. Interest payments alone represented a diversion of resources of US $11.6 billion. Remarkably, GDP grew 7.8 percent in 1985.

In 1986, the government implemented the first of five stabilization plans designed to bring inflation under control. The Cruzado (1986) along

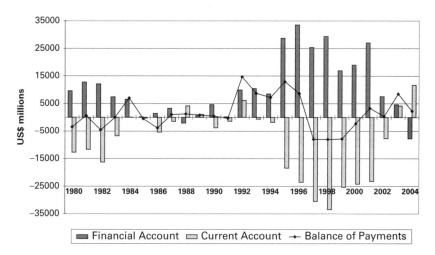

Figure 8.A.3   Balance of Payments, 1980–2004.

Source: BCB, elaborated by the authors.

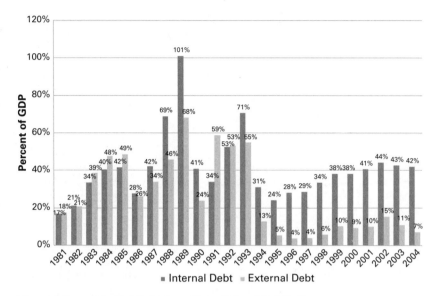

Figure 8.A.4   Net Public Debt—Consolidated Public Sector, 1981–2004.

Source: BCB. Data available at IpeaData, elaborated by the authors.

with other plans—Bresser (1987), Verão (1989), Collor I (1990), and Collor II (1991)—identified the generalized indexation of contracts—a process in which contracts are adjusted according to past inflation in an attempt to recover real income lost with the rise of the price level[21]—as the main cause of inflation. The principal instrument adopted to solve the inflationary problem was the use of price control mechanisms. In all cases, the results were very poor.

Table 8.A.1 indicates the period that price control lasted in each stabilization plan, as well as its results. Looking at Figure 8.A.5, we can observe that price controls generally were not effective. The only exception was the Collor I Plan, which managed to reduce inflation from a rate of 81.3 percent in March 1990 to levels around 20 percent per month until the adoption of the Collor II Plan (April 1991).

Under the Cruzado and Bresser plans, the economy continued to grow: 7.5 percent in 1986 and 3.5 percent in 1987. However, use of restrictive fiscal and monetary policies reduced GDP growth to −0.1 percent in 1987. In 1989, with the Verão (summer) Plan, the economy grew 3.2 percent, but in 1990, GDP contracted 4.3 percent. This was the result of a severe monetary base reduction promoted by the Collor I Plan, which seized, for a period, all financial funds over 50,000 Cruzados Novos (approximately US $1,310).

Table 8.A.1   Price Control Effectiveness

Stabilization Plan	Begin	End	Duration (in months)	Accumulated Inflation (%) Before	During	After
Cruzado	March 1986	November 1986	9	11.1	10.3	14.5
Bresser	June 1987	August 1987	3	15.4	21.6	16.5
Verão	January 1989	May 1989	5	27.3	100.8	37.6
Collor I	March 1990	June 1990	4	72.8	71.1	18.3
Collor II	January 1991	April 1991	4	18.3	41.1	21.1
Mean			**5**	**28.8**	**44.4**	**21.6**

Source: Franco (2005).

Note: "Before" refers to the last month before the price control was introduced. "After" means the sixth month after the end of price controls. The mean for "During" considers the duration of the price control.

The crawling-peg exchange rate system that had been in effect since 1968 was also affected by the stabilization plans.[22] The Cruzado Plan established a monetary reform that substituted the old currency Cruzeiro (Cr$) for the Cruzado (Cz$) at the rate of Cr$ 1,000.00 for Cz$ 1.00. The exchange rate was fixed at the value prevailing the day before the adoption of the plan, and the crawling-peg system was abandoned. However, new inflationary pressures provoked the overvaluation of the domestic currency and led the government to reinstitute the crawling-peg mechanism. In 1987, the Bresser Plan devaluated the domestic currency by 9.5 percent and kept the crawling-peg mechanism. In 1989, the Verão Plan also promoted an almost 18 percent devaluation of the exchange rate and a monetary reform that replaced the Cruzado with a new currency called the Cruzado Novo. The value of the Cruzado Novo was fixed against the dollar at the rate of one to one. In 1990, the Collor I Plan adopted a floating exchange rate regime following the opening up of the Brazilian economy to external competition. However, this was a "dirty" floating since the Central Bank frequently interfered to reduce exchange rate volatility.

The Cruzado Plan was also characterized by a default on foreign debt. In 1986, a BP deficit of US $3.8 billion and the low level of foreign reserves (US $6.7 billion) forced the government to suspend payment on external debts as of January 1987.[23] In January of the following year, this anomalous situation ceased, but the thorny issue was only solved in 1992 with the Brady Plan.[24]

The small GDP growth (1 percent) in 1991 was not even repeated in the next year. In 1992, Brazil suffered a political crisis that ended with the impeachment of President Fernando Collor. Although the balance of payments registered a surplus of US $14.7 billion, high interest rates and the political crisis led to a fall of 0.5 percent in GDP. The country's economy recovered only in 1993, when the GDP growth was 4.7 percent. Inflation accelerated again after the failure of the Collor I and II plans, reaching 480.2 percent in 1991, 1157.8 percent in 1992, and 2708.2 percent in 1993. Of course, this state of affairs was unsustainable and, at last, in 1994, the government implemented an extraordinary set of policies entitled the Real Plan.

This time, inflation was brought down rapidly and remained low. In contrast with previous plans, price controls were not applied. Inertial inflation was eliminated through the complete indexation of the economy, followed by a monetary reform that created a new currency—the Real. At first, the stabilized prices were guaranteed by a combination of an overvalued exchange rate and high interest rates. The overvalued exchange rate allowed the use of imported goods to prevent local producers from raising their prices, and the high interest rates attracted short-term resources to ensure a balanced BP.[25]

The results of those policies were immediately evident. Along with lower inflation rates, there was a reversal in the trade balance results (Figure 8.A.5). After successive surpluses from 1981 until 1994, the economy suffered consecutive deficits during the period when the exchange rates

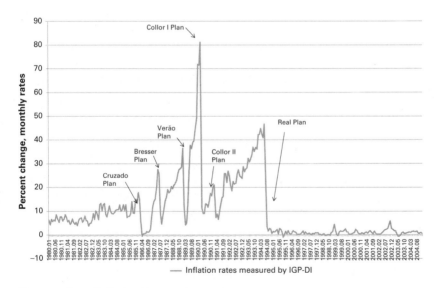

Figure 8.A.5 Inflation Rate, 1980–2004.

Source: FGV. Data available at IpeaData, elaborated by the authors.

Box 8.A.1 Seignorage

Given the very high rates of inflation observed in the 1980s and early 1990s, one should note the behavior of seignorage revenue[1] during this period. Following Rocha and Saldanha (1992), seignorage as a percentage of GDP was calculated, and the results are shown below.[2]

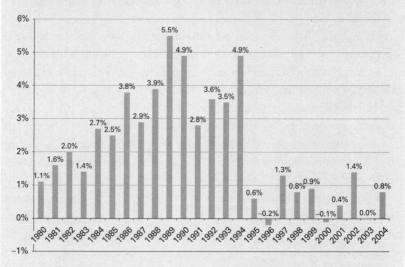

Seignorage Revenue as Percentage of GDP (1980–2004).

Source: Data available at IpeaData, elaborated by the authors.

As it should be expected, seignorage revenues were significant during the period 1988–1994 when annual inflation rates were above 1000 percent (in 1993 the rate reached 2708 percent). After the Real Plan (1994), when inflation was brought under control, seignorage as a percentage of GDP was reduced significantly.

---

1. The amount of real purchasing power that a government can extract from the public by printing money (Cukierman, 1992).
2. Seignorage as a percentage of GDP (S_t) was calculated using the following definition:

$$S_t = \frac{H_t - H_{t-1}}{Y_t} = \frac{\pi_t H_{t-1}}{Y_t} + \frac{H_t - (1 + \pi_t)H_{t-1}}{Y_t}$$

where:
H_t = monetary base at the end of t, π_t = rate of inflation between $t-1$, and t and Y_t = nominal GDP in t.

anchor was in effect. The deficit in the current account was compensated by the inflow of foreign capital, mainly short-term resources. In 1995, from the resulting US $28.7 billion in the financial account, US $9.2 billion were portfolio investments and US $8.2 billion were short-term commercial credits. In 1996, the amount of foreign capital used to buy stocks and bonds increased: with a US $33.5 billion financial account surplus, US $21.6 billion were portfolio investment, and only US $11.3 billion were represented by direct investment.

In the first three months of the Real Plan, the exchange rate followed a free floating system; however, negative results in the trade balance and the valuation of the exchange rate led the government to intervene. In March 1995, the government adopted a crawling band system, in which the Central Bank established a minimum and maximum value for flotation of the exchange rate. For the brief period between March and June of 1995, these limiting values remained fixed.

In the late 1990s, the Asian financial crisis and the Russian default caused a drop in the inflow of foreign resources to Brazil. This led to a deficit in the balance of payments (Figure 8.A.3) and difficulties in financing the successive current account deficits that reached US $33.4 billion in 1998. Thus, in January 1999, despite some desperate measures and a US $42 billion loan from the IMF, the Brazilian government was unable to defend the currency and a new devaluation took place. As a result, the

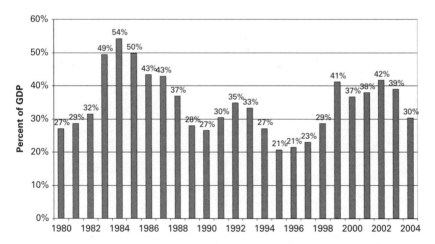

Figure 8.A.6   Gross External Debt, 1980–2004 (as a Percentage of GDP).

Source: BCB. Data available at IpeaData, elaborated by the authors.

Table 8.A.2 Direct and Indirect Taxes, 1980–2004 (% of GDP)

	1980	1981	1982	1983	1984	1985	1986	1987	1988	1989	1990	1991	1992	1993	1994	1995	1996	1997	1998	1999	2000	2001	2002	2003	2004
Total Tax Revenue	24.51	25.26	26.32	26.96	24.35	24.06	26.18	23.77	22.43	24.13	28.78	25.25	25	25.78	29.77	29.39	28.92	28.58	29.33	31.07	30.36	31.87	32.35	31.90	32.77
Direct Taxes	11.47	12.33	13.55	13.45	12.93	12.99	13.96	12.37	11.08	12.22	13.6	11.4	12.05	12.65	14	14.24	14.24	15.80	16.44	17.06	15.60	16.42	17.26	17.14	17.32
Income tax	3.01	3.37	3.46	4.24	4.76	5.13	5.01	4.31	4.67	4.94	5.13	3.9	4.18	3.85	3.83	4.78	4.3	3.89	4.68	4.84	4.78	4.98	5.81	5.47	5.30
ITR (Federal rural land tax)	0.02	0.03	0.03	0.01	0.01	0.01	0.01	0.01	0.01	–	0.02	0.02	–	0.01	–	0.02	0.03	0.03	0.02	0.03	0.02	0.02	0.02	0.02	0.02
Social Security Contribution	4.66	4.99	6.05	5.45	4.91	4.73	5.18	4.74	4.4	4.63	5.11	4.37	4.41	5.19	4.82	4.89	5.13	4.70	4.76	4.52	4.72	4.69	4.81	4.75	4.83
FGTS (Workers' retirement fund)	2.32	2.49	2.52	2.4	2.01	1.92	2.46	1.94	0.86	1.41	1.46	1.29	1.28	1.25	1.78	1.51	1.5	1.38	1.71	1.63	1.59	1.62	1.52	1.47	1.30
Contribution for education	0.22	0.26	0.25	0.22	0.2	0.26	0.23	0.24	0.22	0.21	0.32	0.08	0.26	0.15	0.27	0.36	0.38	0.32	0.27	0.24	0.21	0.24	0.24	0.22	0.19
IPVA (Vehicles tax)	–	–	–	–	–	–	0.14	0.1	0.06	0.05	0.09	0.15	0.13	0.11	0.18	0.37	0.4	0.48	0.45	0.42	0.45	0.48	0.47	0.46	0.46
IPTU (Urban property)	0.25	0.29	0.29	0.22	0.2	0.16	0.17	0.13	0.14	0.07	0.18	0.37	0.22	0.15	0.21	0.41	0.45	0.38	0.39	0.43	0.44	0.42	0.42	0.46	0.43
CPMF (Financial transactions)	–	–	–	–	–	–	–	–	–	–	–	–	–	0.07	1.06	–	–	0.74	0.83	0.75	1.23	1.32	1.38	1.36	1.36
Contribution on Net Profits	–	–	–	–	–	–	–	–	–	0.21	0.54	0.28	0.73	0.79	0.97	0.91	0.85	0.82	0.79	0.69	0.79	0.72	0.90	0.99	1.05

	1980	1981	1982	1983	1984	1985	1986	1987	1988	1989	1990	1991	1992	1993	1994	1995	1996	1997	1998	1999	2000	2001	2002	2003	2004
Others	0.99	0.90	0.95	0.91	0.84	0.78	0.76	0.9	0.72	0.7	0.77	0.94	0.84	1.08	0.88	0.99	1.2	3.07	2.54	3.52	1.36	1.93	1.69	1.96	2.38
Indirect Taxes	13.04	12.93	12.77	13.51	11.42	11.07	12.22	11.4	11.35	11.91	15.18	13.85	12.95	13.13	15.77	15.15	14.68	12.78	12.89	14.01	14.77	15.44	15.09	14.76	15.50
Import tax	0.7	0.59	0.49	0.45	0.41	0.4	0.48	0.4	0.43	0.43	0.39	0.42	0.4	0.45	0.52	0.76	0.54	0.55	0.67	0.74	0.72	0.70	0.54	0.48	0.47
IPI (VAT industry)	2.19	2.2	2.2	2.11	1.4	1.84	2.17	2.43	2.17	2.21	2.4	2.14	2.32	2.44	2.22	2.07	1.96	1.79	1.67	1.55	1.60	1.49	1.34	1.16	1.18
IOF (Loans tax)	0.94	1.16	1.14	0.72	0.86	0.55	0.67	0.57	0.35	0.16	1.3	0.59	0.62	0.8	0.69	0.5	0.37	0.40	0.36	0.46	0.27	0.28	0.27	0.26	0.27
Federal excise on fuel	2.12	2.16	1.87	2.11	0.29	0.16	0.14	0.31	0.31	0.04	0.02	0.02	–	–	–	–	–	–	–	–	–	–	–	–	–
Federal excise on energy	0.21	0.25	0.26	0.25	0.23	0.21	0.22	0.18	0.16	0.02	–	–	–	–	–	–	–	–	–	–	–	–	–	–	–
Federal excise on minerals	0.08	0.08	0.08	0.08	0.11	0.09	0.09	0.07	0.07	0.01	–	–	–	–	–	–	–	–	–	–	–	–	–	–	–
COFINS (VAT)	–	–	0.27	0.61	0.57	0.62	0.71	0.67	0.77	1.1	1.54	1.55	1	1.37	2.56	2.43	2.3	2.04	1.91	3.02	3.38	3.56	3.54	3.50	4.08
PIS (VAT)	–	–	–	–	–	–	–	–	0.4	0.64	1.14	1.05	1.08	1.16	1.07	0.91	0.95	0.81	0.77	0.92	0.85	0.88	0.87	1.02	1.03
Fed. contributions on maritime freight	0.14	0.16	0.13	0.17	0.24	0.19	0.19	0.17	–	0.10	0.14	–	–	–	–	–	0.06	–	–	–	–	–	–	–	–
ICMS (VAT)	4.87	4.95	5.08	5.03	5.29	5.44	6.35	5.49	5.34	6.41	7.24	6.76	6.42	6.04	7.33	7.3	7.15	6.35	6.22	6.37	6.98	7.24	7.13	7.02	7.10
ISS (Services)	0.26	0.32	0.14	0.36	0.29	0.28	0.32	0.31	0.33	0.33	0.43	0.44	0.41	0.35	0.43	0.51	0.56	0.51	0.50	0.47	0.53	0.50	0.54	0.54	0.54
IVVC (Retail sale of fuel)	–	–	–	–	–	–	–	–	–	0.03	0.06	0.06	0.06	0.06	0.07	0.03	–	–	–	–	–	–	–	–	–
CIDE (Federal fuel tax)	–	–	–	–	–	–	–	–	–	–	–	–	–	–	–	–	–	–	–	–	–	–	0.49	0.44	0.39
Others	1.53	1.06	1.11	1.62	1.73	1.29	0.88	0.8	1.02	0.43	0.52	0.82	0.64	0.46	0.88	0.64	0.79	0.33	0.78	0.47	0.44	0.77	0.41	0.34	0.44

Source: IBGE, elaborated by Varsano et al. (1998) from 1980–1996 and by the authors from 1997 to 2004.

Table 8.A.3 Tax Revenue by Category, 1980–2004 (as a percentage of GDP)

	1980	1981	1982	1983	1984	1985	1986	1987	1988	1989	1990	1991	1992	1993	1994	1995	1996	1997	1998	1999	2000	2001	2002	2003	2004
Total Tax Revenue	24.51	25.26	26.32	26.96	24.34	24.06	26.18	23.77	22.43	24.13	28.78	25.25	25	25.78	29.77	29.39	28.92	28.58	29.33	31.07	30.36	31.87	32.35	31.90	32.77
Foreign Trade	0.7	0.59	0.49	0.45	0.41	0.4	0.48	0.4	0.43	0.43	0.39	0.42	0.4	0.45	0.52	0.76	0.54	0.55	0.67	0.74	0.72	0.70	0.54	0.48	0.47
Import tax	0.7	0.59	0.49	0.45	0.41	0.4	0.48	0.4	0.43	0.43	0.39	0.42	0.4	0.45	0.52	0.76	0.54	0.55	0.67	0.74	0.72	0.70	0.54	0.48	0.47
Taxes on Goods and Services	10.67	11.12	11.04	11.27	9.04	9.19	10.67	10.03	9.9	10.95	14.13	12.61	11.91	12.29	15.43	13.75	13.29	12.64	12.26	13.54	14.84	15.30	15.52	15.30	15.96
ICMS (VAT)	4.87	4.95	5.08	5.03	5.29	5.44	6.35	5.49	5.34	6.41	7.24	6.76	6.42	6.04	7.33	7.3	7.15	6.35	6.22	6.37	6.98	7.24	7.13	7.02	7.10
IPI (VAT industry)	2.19	2.2	2.2	2.11	1.4	1.84	2.17	2.43	2.17	2.21	2.4	2.14	2.32	2.44	2.22	2.07	1.96	1.79	1.67	1.55	1.60	1.49	1.34	1.16	1.18
IOF (Loans tax)	0.94	1.16	1.14	0.72	0.86	0.55	0.67	0.57	0.35	0.16	1.3	0.59	0.62	0.8	0.69	0.5	0.37	0.40	0.36	0.46	0.27	0.28	0.27	0.26	0.27
COFINS (VAT)	–	–	0.27	0.61	0.57	0.62	0.71	0.67	0.77	1.1	1.54	1.55	1.0	1.37	2.56	2.43	2.3	2.04	1.91	3.02	3.38	3.56	3.54	3.50	4.08
PIS (VAT)	–	–	–	–	–	–	–	–	0.4	0.64	1.14	1.05	1.08	1.16	1.07	0.91	0.95	0.81	0.77	0.92	0.85	0.88	0.87	1.02	1.03
CPMF (Financial transactions)	–	–	–	–	–	–	–	–	–	–	–	–	–	0.07	1.06	–	–	0.74	0.83	0.75	1.23	1.32	1.38	1.36	1.36
ISS (Services)	0.26	0.32	0.14	0.36	0.29	0.28	0.32	0.31	0.33	0.33	0.43	0.44	0.41	0.35	0.43	0.51	0.56	0.51	0.50	0.47	0.53	0.53	0.50	0.54	0.54
IVVC (Retail sale of fuel)	–	–	–	–	–	–	–	–	–	0.03	0.06	0.06	0.06	0.06	0.07	0.03	–	–	–	–	–	–	–	–	–
Federal Excises[1]	2.41	2.49	2.21	2.44	0.63	0.46	0.45	0.56	0.54	0.07	0.02	0.02	–	–	–	–	–	–	–	–	–	–	–	–	–
CIDE (Fuel Tax)	–	–	–	–	–	–	–	–	–	–	–	–	–	–	–	–	–	–	–	–	–	–	0.49	0.44	0.39
Property Taxes	0.27	0.32	0.32	0.23	0.21	0.17	0.32	0.24	0.21	0.12	0.27	0.54	0.35	0.27	0.39	0.8	0.88	0.89	0.86	0.88	0.91	0.93	0.91	0.93	0.91
IPTU (Urban property)	0.25	0.29	0.29	0.22	0.2	0.16	0.17	0.13	0.14	0.07	0.18	0.37	0.22	0.15	0.21	0.41	0.45	0.38	0.39	0.43	0.44	0.42	0.42	0.46	0.43

IPVA (Vehicles tax)	–	–	–	–	–	–	0.14	0.1	0.06	0.05	0.09	0.15	0.13	0.11	0.18	0.37	0.4	0.48	0.45	0.42	0.45	0.48	0.47	0.46	0.46
ITR (Rural Land)	0.02	0.03	0.03	0.01	0.01	0.01	0.01	0.01	0.01	–	–	0.02	–	0.01	–	0.02	0.03	0.03	0.02	0.03	0.02	0.02	0.02	0.02	0.02
Income Taxes	3.01	3.37	3.46	4.24	4.76	5.13	5.01	4.31	4.67	5.15	5.67	4.18	4.91	4.64	4.8	5.69	5.15	4.71	5.47	5.52	5.57	5.70	6.71	6.46	6.36
Personal and Business	3.01	3.37	3.46	4.24	4.76	5.13	5.01	4.31	4.67	4.94	5.13	3.9	4.18	3.85	3.83	4.78	4.3	3.89	4.68	4.84	4.78	4.98	5.81	5.47	5.30
Contribution Net Profits	–	–	–	–	–	–	–	–	–	0.21	0.54	0.28	0.73	0.79	0.97	0.91	0.85	0.82	0.79	0.69	0.79	0.72	0.90	0.99	1.05
Taxes on Payroll	7.44	7.98	9.09	8.36	7.37	7.18	8.16	7.21	5.77	6.56	7.25	6.07	6.28	6.93	7.27	7.1	7.62	6.70	7.01	6.72	6.85	6.86	6.90	6.72	6.73
Social Security Contribution	4.66	4.99	6.05	5.45	4.91	4.73	5.18	4.74	4.4	4.63	5.11	4.37	4.41	5.19	4.82	4.89	5.13	4.70	4.76	4.52	4.72	4.69	4.81	4.75	4.83
FGTS (workers' retirement fund)	2.32	2.49	2.52	2.4	2.01	1.92	2.46	1.94	0.86	1.41	1.46	1.29	1.28	1.25	1.78	1.51	1.5	1.38	1.71	1.63	1.59	1.62	1.52	1.47	1.30
Contribution for education	0.22	0.26	0.25	0.22	0.2	0.26	0.23	0.24	0.22	0.21	0.32	0.08	0.26	0.15	0.27	0.36	0.38	0.32	0.27	0.24	0.21	0.24	0.24	0.22	0.19
Public servants	0.24	0.24	0.27	0.29	0.25	0.27	0.29	0.29	0.29	0.31	0.36	0.33	0.33	0.34	0.4	0.34	0.61	0.3	0.27	0.33	0.33	0.32	0.33	0.29	0.41
Others	2.43	1.87	1.89	2.39	2.55	1.98	1.52	1.59	1.46	0.93	1.02	1.43	1.14	1.18	1.31	1.22	1.38	3.4	3.3	4.0	1.8	2.7	2.1	2.3	2.8
Others direct	0.76	0.65	0.65	0.6	0.59	0.51	0.45	0.62	0.44	0.4	0.36	0.61	0.5	0.72	0.43	0.58	0.53	3.1	2.5	3.5	1.4	1.9	1.7	2.0	2.4
Others indirect	1.67	1.22	1.24	1.79	1.96	1.47	1.07	0.97	1.02	0.53	0.66	0.82	0.64	0.46	0.88	0.64	0.85	0.33	0.78	0.47	0.44	0.77	0.41	0.34	0.44

Source: IBGE and Varsano et al. (1998), elaborated by the authors.

Table 8.A.4 Tax Burden, 1980–2004 *(as a percentage of GDP)*

Year	Ratio (%)	Year	Ratio (%)
1980	24.45	1993	25.30
1981	25.18	1994	27.90
1982	26.24	1995	28.44
1983	26.84	1996	28.63
1984	24.19	1997	28.58
1985	23.83	1998	29.33
1986	26.50	1999	31.07
1987	24.25	2000	30.36
1988	23.36	2001	31.87
1989	23.74	2002	32.35
1990	29.60	2003	31.90
1991	24.43	2004	32.77
1992	24.96		

Source: IBGE. Data available at IpeaData, elaborated by the authors.

Table 8.A.5 Gross Domestic Product in Brazil, 1980–2004

Year	Real Billion	US$ Billion
1980	4.55E-09	237.3
1981	8.73E-09	257.9
1982	1.77E-08	271.2
1983	3.98E-08	189.6
1984	1.27E-07	188.2
1985	4.76E-07	210.9
1986	1.27E-06	256.5
1987	4.04E-06	283.0
1988	2.94E-05	307.9
1989	4.26E-04	413.0
1990	1.15E-02	465.0
1991	6.03E-02	407.7
1992	6.41E-01	390.6
1993	14.1	438.3
1994	349.2	546.2
1995	705.6	769.0
1996	844.0	839.7
1997	939.1	871.2
1998	979.3	843.8
1999	1065.0	586.9
2000	1179.5	644.5
2001	1302.1	554.0
2002	1477.8	505.9
2003	1699.9	552.2
2004	1941.5	663.6

Source: IBGE. Data available at IpeaData, elaborated by the authors.

government boldly reoriented its monetary policy through the adoption of inflation targeting and implemented a floating exchange rate regime.[26]

GDP behavior since the Real Plan has been frustrating. Initially, price stability enabled growth, due to gains in the real purchasing power of the poor. In 1994, GDP grew 5.3 percent and in 1995, 4.4 percent. However, the government's attempt to attract foreign capital through the adoption of high interest rates adversely affected GDP growth, which was 2.2 percent in 1996, 3.4 percent in 1997, and only 0.04 percent in 1998, a year in which the basic interest rate (Selic) reached 40 percent per year. Again, in 1999, high interest rates resulted in a GDP growth of only 0.3 percent. Despite the GDP growth of 4.3 percent in 2000, the next two years exhibited low rates of growth—1.3 percent in 2001 and 2.7 percent in 2002—due to conservative interest rate policies.

The year 2002 saw the election that brought a leftist party to the presidency. The fact that candidate Luiz Inácio Lula da Silva was leading in the polls caused instability in the financial markets, which provoked a new devaluation of the Real and entrance into a new agreement with the IMF. In 2002, the annual inflation rate reached 26.4 percent against 10.4 percent in 2001. To ensure the stability of the price level and to affirm to the financial markets a commitment to low inflation rates, the newly elected president tightened monetary and fiscal policies. The result was a small GDP growth of 1.1 percent in 2003 and an inflation rate of 7.7 percent.

One very important development in the Brazilian economy after the adoption of a flexible exchange regime in 1999 has been the continuous improvement in the trade balance and in the balance of payments.

In 2004, the excellent performance of the trade balance, due to a 32 percent growth in exports compared to 2003, surpassed the deficit in the financial account and guaranteed a BP surplus of US $2.2 billion. The expansion of the exporting sector stimulated GDP growth (5.7 percent), and the annual inflation rate was 12.1 percent.

Since 1980, Brazil has endured great economic difficulty. As a result, the country continues to search for a new paradigm that will enable a new path of sustained economic growth. The result of this search has been a transition from a model that relied heavily on public investments and initiatives favoring import substitution to a more liberal approach with less government intervention.

Economic liberalization began in 1990 with the Collor reduction of tariff and non-tariff barriers and the privatization of state-owned companies. The government of Fernando Henrique Cardoso continued this trend toward liberalization by eliminating the state monopoly in tele-communications and oil and by privatizing utilities and public service state-owned companies.[27] Most recently, it appears that the Lula admin-istration has kept things on track. Still, there continues to be intense debate on the best means of using newly conquered price stability and a comfortable position in Brazil's external accounts to achieve sustained economic growth.

NOTES

1. Detailed information regarding the 1965–1967 tax reform can be found in Giambiagi and Além (2000), pp. 242–246.

2. Income taxation was formally introduced in Brazil in 1923.

3. In the Brazilian tax system, contributions are a type of federal tax; the revenues raised from these contributions are earmarked to a specific destination.

4. The Brazilian constitution authorizes governments to impose three types of levies: taxes, contributions (social and others), and user charges. The legal distinction between a contribution and a tax is that the contribution is raised to finance a specific governmental activity (mostly social security), whereas the proceeds of taxes are used for general purposes.

5. The 1967 law that established the new tax system was modified over the subsequent years so that by 1988 the tax structure had changed.

6. Public budgets in Brazil are submitted to the legislature annually, in a single piece, containing all expenditures and sources of revenue. Budgets also contain the investment projects of state enterprises which need to be approved by the legislators.

7. Social security in Brazil encompasses pensions, health care, unemployment insurance, and social assistance. Private pension schemes are very limited, and the public sector is the main provider of pensions and of health care in the country.

8. In the table direct taxes are those based on income, property, payroll, and inheritance taxes, and indirect taxes are those based on transactions of goods and services.

9. Financial compensations in the oil industry have two main components: royalties—up to 10 percent of the gross value of production and an additional compensation—called special compensation—that is paid by good-quality, high-productivity oil wells as a percentage of net income (profits) with rates varying from 10 to 40 percent. Detailed information regarding financial compensation in the oil industry can be found at http://www.anp.gov.br.

10. Explanation and analysis of fiscal federalism in Brazil, see Afonso and Mello (2000), Serra and Afonso (1999), and Shah (1990; 1994).

11. Ministry of Planning and Budget (2003).

12. In 2004 "small" businesses were defined to be those businesses with annual sales up to R$ 1.2 million.

13. From the site http://www.microsoft.com/billgates/speedofthought/additional/brazil.asp.

14. The balance-of-payments data are from Banco Central do Brasil (Brazilian Central Bank), available at www.bcb.gov.br.

15. Hermann (2005), p. 110.

16. An analysis of the II PND's role in the 1983–1984 external adjustment can be found in Castro and Souza (1985).

17. Giambiagi and Além (2000), p. 136.

18. Ibid.

19. The concept of net public debt is the result of assets held by the public sector and the Central Bank minus their liabilities. In this concept the monetary base is included.

20. A characterization of the inflation debate can be found in Castro (2005).

21. For the theory of inertial inflation, see Lopes (1986).

22. A discussion of the crawling-peg exchange rate system can be found in Zini (1992).

23. Brazilian Central Bank. Available at www.bcb.gov.br.

24. A detailed analysis of the Brady Plan conditions for Brazil can be found in Portella (1994).

25. For a description of the Real Plan, see Castro (2005). An analysis of the origins of the Real Plan can be found in Franco (1995).

26. An analysis of the inflation-targeting system and its results can be found in Fachada (2001) and Fraga, Goldfajn, and Minella (2003).

27. For an analysis of the reform of the state and the privatization of state-owned companies, see Giambiagi and Além (2000).

REFERENCES

Afonso, J., and Mello, L. (2000). "Brazil: An Evolving Federation." Mimeo, Presented at the IMF/FAD Seminar on Decentralization in November 2000.

Afonso, J., and Ramundo, J. C (1995). "The Brazilian Federation: Main Features and Indicators." Mimeo.

Afonso, J., Ramundo, J. C., and Araujo, E. (1999). "Breves Notas sobre o Federalismo Fiscal no Brasil." Mimeo.

Afonso, J., Varsano, R., Ramundo, J. C, Araujo, E., Pessoa, E., and Silva, N. L. (1997). "Tributação no Brasil: Características Marcantes e Diretrizes para a Reforma." Mimeo.

Amadeo, E., and Camargo, J. M. (1996). "Instituições e o mercado de trabalho no Brasil." In *Flexibilidade no Mercado de Trabalho no Brasil*, J. M. Camargo, ed., cap. 2. Rio de Janeiro: Fundação Getúlio Vargas.

Araújo, C. H., and Siqueira Filho, G. B. (2002). "Mudanças de Regime no Câmbio Brasileiro." Banco Central do Brasil, Working Paper no. 41. Brasília: Banco Central do Brasil.

Arbache, J. S., and Corseuil, C. H. (2001). "Liberalização Comercial e Estruturas de Emprego e Salário." Texto para Discussão n. 801. Rio de Janeiro, Brasil: Instituto de Pesquisa Econômica Aplicada (IPEA).

Barros, R. P., Mello, R., and Pero, V. (1993). "Informal Labor Contracts: A Solution or a Problem?" Texto para Discussão n. 291. IPEA.

Cardoso Jr. J.C.P., and Fernandes, S. (2000). "A Informalidade Revisitada: A Evolução nos Últimos 20 anos e mais uma Hipótese para Pesquisa." Mercado de Trabalho: Conjuntura e Análise, 5(14), pp. 41–49.

Castro, A. B., and Souza, F.E.P. (1985). "A Economia Brasileira em Marcha Forçada." Rio de Janeiro, Brasil: Paz e Terra.

Castro, L. B. (2005a). "Esperança, Frustração e Aprendizado: As Histórias da Nova República." In Economia Brasileira Contemporânea (1945–2004), F. Giambiagi et al. eds. Rio de Janeiro, Brasil: Elsevier.

———. (2005b). "Privatização, Abertura e Desindexação: A Primeira Metade Dos Anos 90." In Economia Brasileira Contemporânea (1945–2004), F. Giambiagi et al., eds. Rio de Janeiro, Brasil: Elsevier.

Coelho, I., Ebrill, L., and Summers, V. (2001). "Bank Debit Taxes in Latin America: An Analysis of Recent Trends." IMF Working Paper 01/67. Washington, DC: International Monetary Fund (IMF).

Cukierman, A. (1992). "Central Bank Strategy, Credibility, and Independence: Theory and Evidence." Cambridge, MA: MIT Press.

Fachada, P. (2001). "Inflation Targeting in Brazil: Reviewing Two Years of Monetary Policy 1999–2000." Banco Central do Brasil, Working Paper no. 25. Brasília: Banco Central do Brasil.

Fraga, A., Goldfajn, I., and Minella, A. (2003). "Inflation Targeting in Emerging Market Economies." Banco Central do Brasil, Working Paper no. 76. Brasília: Banco Central do Brasil.

Franco, G. (1995). "O Plano Real e Outros Ensaios." Rio de Janeiro, Brasil: Francisco Alves.

———. (2005). "Auge e Declínio do Inflacionismo no Brasil." In Economia Brasileira Contemporânea (1945–2004), F. Giambiagi et al., (eds.). Rio de Janeiro, Brasil: Elsevier.

Giambiagi, F., and Além, A. C. (2000). "Finanças Públicas: Teoria e Prática no Brasil." 2nd ed. Rio de Janeiro: Campus.

Hermann, J. (2005). "Auge e declínio do Modelo de Crescimento com Endividamento: O II PND e a Crise da Dívida Externa." In Economia Brasileira Contemporânea (1945–2004), F. Giambiagi et al., eds. Rio de Janeiro: Elsevier.

Khair, A., Araujo, E., and Afonso, J. R. (2005, July). "Carga Tributária—Mensuração e Impacto sobre o Crescimento." Revista de Economia & Relação Internacionais, 4(7), pp. 27–42. São Paulo: FAAP.

———. (2005). "Quanto e Como Cresceu a Carga Tributária em 2004," Caderno n. 58, NEPP (Núcleo de Estudos de Políticas Públicas). São Paulo: UNICAMP.

Kume, H., Piani, G., and Souza, C. F. (2003). "A Política Brasileira de Importação no Período 1987–98: Descrição e Avaliação." In A Abertura Comercial nos Anos 1990: Impactos sobre e Emprego e Salário, C. H. Corseuil and H. Kume, eds. Rio, de Janeiro: MTE/IPEA.

Lemgruber-Viol, A. (2004). "A Guideline for Tax Administration Reform: Using Information Technology to Modernize the Traditional Way We Pay Taxes in Developing Countries." Mimeo.

Lopes, F. (1986). "O Choque Heterodoxo—Combate à Inflação e Reforma Monetária." Rio de Janeiro: Campus.

Mello, L. (2005). "Estimating a Fiscal Reaction Function: The Case of Debt Sustainability in Brazil." Economics Department, Working Paper no. 423. OECD, Paris.

Ministry of Planning and Budget. (2003). "Vinculações de Receitas dos Orçamentos Fiscal e da Seguridade Social e o Poder Discricionário de Alocação dos Recursos do Governo Federal." Brasília: Secretaria de Orçamento Federal.

Monteiro, J., and Assunção, J. "O Impacto da Lei do Simples sobre a Formalização das Firmas." Mimeo.

Neri, M. C. (2000). "Decent Work and the Informal Sector in Brazil." Mimeo.

Pastore, J. (1997). "Encargos Sociais: Para onde o Brasil quer ir?" 1st ed. São Paulo: LTR.

———. (2005). "A Modernização das Instituições do Trabalho." São Paulo: LTR.

Portella, F. P. (1994). "Plano Brady: Da Retórica à Realidade." Estudos Econômicos, 24(1), pp. 55–105. São Paulo.

Rocha, R. R., and Saldanha, F. (1992). "Fiscal and Quasi-Fiscal Deficits, Nominal and Real: Measurement and Policy Issues." WPS no. 919. Washington, DC: World Bank.

Serra, J., and Afonso, J. R. (1999). "O Federalismo Fiscal à Brasileira: Algumas Reflexões." Revista do BNDES, 6(12), pp. 3–30. Rio de Janeiro.

Shah, A. (1990). "The New Fiscal Federalism in Brazil." World Bank Discussions Papers no. 124. Washington, DC: World Bank.

———. (1994). "The Reform of Inter-governmental Fiscal Relations in Developing and Emerging Market Economies." World Bank Policy and Research Series Paper no. 23. Washington, DC: World Bank.

Soares, S., Servo, L. M., and Arbache, J. S. (2001). "O que (não) Sabemos sobre a Relação entre Abertura Comercial e Mercado de Trabalho no Brasil." Texto para Discussão no. 843. Rio de Janeiro: IPEA.

Tanzi, V., and Zee, H. H. (2000). "Tax Policy for Emerging Markets: Developing Countries." IMF Working Paper. Washington, DC: IMF.

Ulyssea, G. (2005). "Informalidade no Mercado de Trabalho Brasileiro: Uma Resenha da Literatura." Texto para Discussão no. 1070. Rio de Janeiro: IPEA.

Varsano, R. (1996). "A Evolução do Sistema Tributário Brasileiro ao Longo do Século: Anotações e Reflexões para Futuras Reformas." Texto para Discussão no. 405. Rio de Janeiro: IPEA.

Varsano, R., Pessoa, E., Silva, N., Araujo, E., and Ramundo, J. C. (1998). "Uma análise da Carga Tributária do Brasil." Texto para Discussão no. 583. Rio de Janeiro: IPEA.

Vianna, S., Magalhães, L.·C., Silveira, F., and Tomich, F. (2000). "Carga Tributária Direta e Indireta sobre as Unidades Familiares no Brasil: Avaliação de sua Incidência nas Grandes Regiões Urbanas em 1996." Texto para Discussão no. 757. Brasília: IPEA.

Zini, A. A. (1992). "Taxa de Câmbio e Política Cambial no Brasil." EDUSP/BM&F.

Oscar Cetrángolo is an economist in the field of public finance. He graduated from the University of Buenos Aires and the University of Sussex (Institute of Development Studies). He has been working at ECLAC (UN) since 2001 as an expert in public policy. He was Undersecretary at the Ministry of Economy between 1999 and 2001. He has published several works on public policy. He is Professor of Public Finance at the University of Buenos Aires.

Nada O. Eissa is Associate Professor of Public Policy and Economics at Georgetown University, and Research Associate at the National Bureau of Economic Research (NBER). From 2005–2007, she was Deputy Assistant Secretary of the Treasury for economic policy. Previously, she was on the economics faculty at the University of California at Berkeley, a National Fellow of the NBER, a visiting economist at the IMF and a visiting scholar at the American Enterprise Institute (AEI).

Ana Carolina Giuberti is Assistant Professor of Economics at the Federal University of Espírito Santo, Brazil. She received her BA and MS degree from the University of São Paulo, and is currently a PhD candidate there. She has papers published in the field of economics of the public sector applied to the Brazilian economy.

Roger Gordon is a professor of economics at the University of California, San Diego. He has also taught at the University of Michigan and Princeton University, was a member of the technical staff at Bell Laboratories, and a past editor of *Journal of Public Economics* and the *American Economic Review*. He is currently editor of the *Journal of Economic Literature*, as well as a research associate of the National Bureau of Economic Research and the Centre for Economic Policy Research, and a Fellow of the Econometric Society and the American Academy of Arts and Sciences. He received his PhD in economics from MIT and a Dr. oec. h.c. from the University of St. Gallen.

William Jack is an associate professor of economics at Georgetown University. He has held positions at the IMF, the Joint Committee on Taxation at the U.S. Congress, the Australian National University, and the University of Sydney. His research interests include micro development, public finance, applied microeconomic theory, and health economics. He holds a DPhil from Oxford University.

Joosung Jun is a Professor of Economics at Ewha Womans University, Korea. He is also a member of the Presidential Council on National Economy and a former president of the Korean Association of Public Finance. He was previously an Assistant Professor at Yale University and a Faculty Research Fellow at the National Bureau of Economic Research. Jun received his PhD in economics from Harvard University.

Sergei Koulayev is an economist at the Federal Reserve Bank of Boston, where he is working on problems of household finance. His other research interests include identification and estimation of the models of product search. His chapter in this book was written while he was a PhD student at Columbia University, New York. He received his MA in economics at New Economic School, Moscow, and his BA from Moscow State University.

José Teófilo Oliveira is presently Secretary of Finance in the state of Espírito Santo, Brazil. Mr. Oliveira has an MS and PhD degree from Purdue University (1972–1976) and was Assistant Professor at the Department of Economics, University of São Paulo, Brazil, from 1972 to 1999.

M. Govinda Rao is Director, National Institute of Public Finance and Policy. He is also a Member of the Economic Advisory Council to the Prime Minister of India. Prior to this, he was Director, Institute for Social and Economic Change, Bangalore (1998–2002) and Fellow, Research School of Pacific and Asian Studies, Australian National University. Dr. Rao's research interests include fiscal policy, tax policy and reforms, public expenditure efficiency and management, fiscal decentralization and federalism and state and local finances. He has authored 13 books and a number of articles in International Journals.

R. Kavita Rao is a professor at the National Institute of Public Finance and Policy, New Delhi. She heads the Tax Research Cell at the Institute. She has been actively involved in the debate on the design and revenue impact of VAT in India. Her research interests include tax policy and reforms, impact assessment of tax incentives, and growth and sectoral inter-linkages.

Juan Carlos Gómez Sabaini is an economist in the field of public finance. He graduated from the University of Buenos Aires, Williams College, and Columbia University. He is presently a consultant for ECLAC, IADB, and IMF. He was Undersecretary of Tax Policy for the Argentine government in 1970, 1985, and 1999. He has published several works on public policy, mainly taxation in Latin American countries. He is Professor of Public Finance at the University of Buenos Aires.

Joseph E. Stiglitz holds joint professorships at Columbia University's Economics Department, School of International and Public Affairs, and its Business School. From 1997–2000 he was the World Bank's Senior Vice President for Development Economics and Chief Economist. From 1995–1997 Dr. Stiglitz served as Chairman of the U.S. Council of Economic Advisers and as a member of President Clinton's cabinet. From 1993–1995 he was a member of the Council of Economic Advisers. Dr. Stiglitz was previously a Professor of Economics at Stanford, Princeton, Yale, and All Souls College, Oxford. As an academic, Dr. Stiglitz helped create a new branch of economics—"The Economics of Information"—which has received widespread application throughout economics. Dr. Stiglitz was awarded the Nobel Prize in economics in 2001.

INDEX

Note to readers: *Passim* indicates numerous mentions over the given range of pages.